Unwin Critical Library
GENERAL EDITOR: CLAUDE RAWSON

DON QUIXOTE

Unwin Critical Library
GENERAL EDITOR: CLAUDE RAWSON

Don Quixote

E. C. RILEY

Department of Hispanic Studies,
University of Edinburgh

London
ALLEN & UNWIN
Boston   Sydney

Allen & Unwin (Publishers) Ltd,
40 Museum Street, London WC1A 1LU, UK

Allen & Unwin (Publishers) Ltd,
Park Lane, Hemel Hempstead, Herts. HP2 4TE, UK

Allen & Unwin, Inc.,
8 Winchester Place, Winchester, Mass. 01890, USA

Allen & Unwin (Australia) Ltd,
8 Napier Street, North Sydney, NSW 2060, Australia

First published in 1986

British Library Cataloguing in Publication Data

Riley, E. C.
    Don Quixote. – (Unwin critical library)
1. Cervantes Saavedra, Miguel de. Don Quixote
I. Title
863'.3   PQ6352
ISBN 0-04-800009-4

Library of Congress Cataloging in Publication Data

Riley, E. C.
    Don Quixote.
(Unwin critical library)
Bibliography: p.
Includes index
1. Cervantes Saavedra, Miguel de, 1547–1616.
Don Quixote. I. Title. II. Series
PQ6352.R48 1985   863'.3   85-11179
ISBN 0-04-800009-4 (alk. paper)

199523

Set in 10 on 12 point Plantin by
Computape (Pickering) Ltd, Pickering, North Yorkshire
and printed in Great Britain by
Billings and Sons Ltd, London and Worcester

GENERAL EDITOR'S PREFACE

Each volume in this series is devoted to a single major text. It is intended for serious students and teachers of literature, and for knowledgeable non-academic readers. It aims to provide a scholarly introduction and a stimulus to critical thought and discussion.

Individual volumes will naturally differ from one another in arrangement and emphasis, but each will normally begin with information on a work's literary and intellectual background, and other guidance designed to help the reader to an informed understanding. This is followed by an extended critical discussion of the work itself, and each contributor in the series has been encouraged to present in these sections his own reading of the work, whether or not this is controversial, rather than to attempt a mere consensus. Some volumes, including those on *Paradise Lost* and *Ulysses*, vary somewhat from the more usual pattern by entering into substantive critical discussion at the outset, and allowing the necessary background material to emerge at the points where it is felt to arise from the argument in the most useful and relevant way. Each volume also contains a historical survey of the work's critical reputation, including an account of the principal lines of approach and areas of controversy, and a selective (but detailed) bibliography.

The hope is that the volumes in this series will be among those which a university teacher would normally recommend for any serious study of a particular text, and that they will also be among the essential secondary texts to be consulted in some scholarly investigations. But the experienced and informed non-academic reader has also been in our minds, and one of our aims has been to provide him with reliable and stimulating works of reference and guidance, embodying the present state of knowledge and opinion in a conveniently accessible form.

C.J.R
University of Warwick,
December 1979

CONTENTS

For Judy, Nicholas and Hannah

PREFATORY NOTE

A general study of a book as seminal and as regularly reinterpreted as *Don Quixote* is the most difficult sort of work to write. At least it is for me. Inevitably there will be simplification and much in this book which those who know Cervantes know already, although I hope it also contains a few things less familiar. I have avoided trying to dress my account of *Don Quixote* in the ready-made suiting of a particular theory, but have tried to keep the tailoring in line with a few consistent and serviceable norms.

My thanks to Professor C. J. Rawson and to a number of people who have answered my questions or helped me in other ways and have probably forgotten by now that they ever did so; to Professors A. A. Parker, Keith Whinnom, C. P. Brand, Robert Flores and Dorothy Severin; to Mr Daniel Rogers, Dr Jennifer Lowe, Dr Angus MacKay and Dr Edwin Williamson; and to Mrs Elaine Edgar for her fast and skilful typing.   E.C.R.

Works referred to in the text and in the notes by the author's name and a date may be identified in the Bibliography. The letter after the date indicates the section in which it will be found.

CHAPTER 1

The Man and the Moment

Miguel de Cervantes Saavedra says he has served Your Majesty many years in the campaigns on sea and land which have occurred in the past twenty-two years, especially in the Naval Battle [Lepanto], in which he received many wounds, including the loss of a hand from a harquebus ball. And the following year he was at Navarino and later in the action at Tunis and La Goleta. And en route to this Court with letters from my lord Don Juan [of Austria] and from the Duke of Sessa so that Your Majesty might show him favor he was captured in the galley *Sol*, he and his brother, who also served Your Majesty in the same campaigns, and they were taken to Algiers, where they spent such heritage as they had in ransoming themselves, along with their parents' whole estate and the dowries of two maiden sisters, who were impoverished through ransoming their brothers. And after their liberation they served Your Majesty in the Kingdom of Portugal and in the Terceiras (Azores) [Rodrigo, not Miguel] with the Marquis of Santa Cruz, and are even now serving Your Majesty, one of them as an *alférez* [subaltern] in Flanders and (the other) Miguel de Cervantes, was the one who brought the letters and information from the Mayor of Mostaganem and went to Oran on Your Majesty's orders; and since then he has served in Seville on business of the Armada, and under the orders of Antonio de Guevara, as stated in his records. And in all that time no favor whatsoever has been granted him. He requests and beseeches as humbly as he can that Your Majesty be pleased to favor him with *a post in the Indies*, one of these being the comptrollership of the new kingdom of Granada [Colombia], or the governorship of the province of Soconusco in Guatemala, or auditor of the galleys of Cartagena [Mexico], or corregidor of the city of La Paz; for he will fulfill any of those offices Your Majesty might grant him because he is an able and competent man and deserving of Your Majesty's favor and because his wish is to continue to serve Your Majesty always and to end his life in it as his forebears have, for in it he will receive great favor and reward.

(quoted in Byron, 1979B, pp. 347–8)

That was Cervantes in the bleak year of 1590 surveying his past career and petitioning the Council of the Indies for a crown appointment compatible with his previous loyal service to the king. As a curriculum vitae it is a little tinted, pardonably, but it serves to evoke something of the background of the author of *Don Quixote*. He did not get any of those appointments. Who knows whether *Don Quixote* would have been written if he had?

He had been born in 1547, probably on 29 September (the feast of San Miguel), the fourth of seven children of a surgeon whose family had seen better days. They moved from one city to another in Miguel's childhood. Nothing is known of his education until, as late as 1568, he appears as pupil at the Estudio de la Villa, a college in Madrid, run by an Erasmian teacher Juan López de Hoyos. The next year he went to Italy; possibly he was the 'student' of the same name wanted by the law for involvement in a wounding incident. He seems to have served for a short time in the household of Cardinal Acquaviva in Rome, but enlisted in 1570, thus beginning the years of military service and captivity. The petition quoted above does not refer to Cervantes's repeated and dangerous attempts to escape from Algerian slavery.

He was back in Spain in 1580, married Catalina de Palacios in 1584 and published *La Galatea* the year after. He was employed as commissary requisitioning provisions for the Armada and later (from 1594) in the no more congenial role of tax collector, mostly in Andalusia in both jobs. It was a life always on the move, haggling with municipal and church officials, arguing with auditors, rarely seeing his wife in Esquivias, excommunicated more than once, twice imprisoned. Indeed, most of the last thirty-five years of his life were as full of tedium, impecuniousness and petty annoyance as the previous ten had been of story-book adventure.

The years 1595 to 1602 are sparsely documented and culminate nearly in obscurity. But by the end of this period, perhaps in Esquivias, for certain in Valladolid, he was writing the book which brought him most fame, if not the favour he would have liked. He was close to his 57th birthday when the royal licence to publish *Don Quixote* was issued on 26 September 1604. It was a ripe age to be publishing a first great work, but effectively Cervantes's career as a published author was only just beginning. It would be crammed into less than a dozen years between that date and his death in 1616. He had a modest reputation as a playwright, but apart from a few poems, written mostly for other men's books, the pastoral romance *La Galatea* (1585) was his only printed work. Its success at home was limited, although it did rather better abroad. The only subsequent editions to appear in the author's lifetime were those of Lisbon (1590) and Paris (1611), both in Spanish.

The reputation of most writers depended much less on the publication of printed works than we have come to expect since then. Spain's forty-five most famous lyric poets between the year of the Armada (1588) and the death of Philip III (1621) could muster barely a dozen printed books of verse between them, excluding anthologies (Rodríguez-Moñino, 1968E, pp. 19–24). Dramatists, by the nature of their art, had even less immediate need of the printing press, though their plays did get printed, largely as a defence against piracy. But it was different with prose romances and novels. After the fifteenth century no writer of these could hope to make a real name for himself without such mass circulation as contemporary printing provided.

Cervantes had not yet proved himself as a novelist and there is little evidence that before *Don Quixote* he even saw it as his literary vocation. He seemed to be trying his hand at almost everything: verse, from popular *seguidillas* and *chaconas* to the most formal Italianate *canzone*; drama, from the farce of the short *entremeses* to the heroic tragedy of *La Numancia*; not to mention the broad range of his prose fiction. Epic poetry on the grand scale was the only major genre of imaginative literature which he left untried – and he might have retorted to this with the words of his Canon of Toledo, that 'the epic can be written in prose as well as in verse' (*Don Quixote*, I, 47; i, 567).[1] The known Complete Works are not all that voluminous even so: five works or collections of prose fiction (counting *Don Quixote*'s two parts separately), ten plays, eight dramatic interludes, one long poem, some miscellaneous verse. They fill about 1,700 double-column india-paper pages (with major attributions) in Valbuena Prat's single-volume Aguilar edition. The wonder is that before he left Andalusia for the last time, by 1603 at the latest, he found the leisure to write – and to read – as much as he did. And after that how he had the stamina.

His home life cannot have offered many consolations. There was, for example, the ugly and ridiculous affair in June 1605 when Cervantes and members of his family, trying to help one Gaspar de Ezpeleta who had been attacked in the street outside their house, found themselves under arrest. There were the sordid affairs of his natural daughter Isabel who lived with them. Later there was some spiritual solace perhaps. If his becoming a lay member of a fashionable religious order in 1609 was roughly the equivalent of joining a club, his becoming a Franciscan tertiary four years later argued a deeper commitment. In his final years there was at last some material solace, too, in the patronage of Sandoval y Rojas, Cardinal-Archbishop of Toledo, and of the Conde de Lemos.

Thanks largely to the massive if indigestible work of Luis Astrana Marín (1948–58B), modern biographical research has been able to fill in a lot of missing detail in what was previously known of Cervantes's life. We now know a good deal about the litigation surrounding him and his family, hard up as they usually were – the innumerable petitions, statements, warrants, depositions, even the exact figures of the accounts for which he was responsible when requisitioning provisions for the Armada and collecting tax arrears in the old kingdom of Granada (figures which a financial wizard could have got wrong in the circumstances). What is missing is what we should most of all like to have: really adequate materials for the personal history of Cervantes the novelist. Detailed first-hand evidence of opinions and feelings, motives and reactions is sparse. We lack personal letters of the kind that put colour into the pictures we preserve of Góngora, Lope de Vega and Quevedo. The second-hand testimony of those who knew him is too slight to help much, though he does come briefly to life through a contemporary document, the *Información de Argel*, and later Diego de Haedo's *Topografía e historia general de Argel* (1612), as the captive soldier, leader of daring escape attempts and rock of support for his fellow Christian slaves. But for the personal history of Cervantes the writer biographers have long had almost nothing more to rely on than his prefatory pages and that dangerous source, his fiction itself. With the partial exception of some autobiographical passages in the *Viaje del Parnaso*, the biographical dependability of his fiction is very uncertain. This has acted more as a stimulus than a deterrent, however, and there is a well-established tradition of fanciful intimate biographies.[2]

It is clear that Cervantes had very definite literary ambitions, and also that these were never quite satisfied by the recognition he did receive. Even after *Don Quixote*, Part I, we find him wanting his readers to *know* him. The prologue to the *Novelas ejemplares* (1613) contains that pen-picture of the author's appearance which is the only authentic portrait of him in any medium. Some evidence of continuing concern with how well known he and his works were is to be found in later prologues and dedications, but nowhere is this concern more pronounced than in the *Viaje del Parnaso (Journey to Parnassus)*.[3]

This allegorical fantasy in the fashionable mock-mythological vein, devoted to commemorating a host of contemporary writers and satirizing a few others, appeared in 1614. Considering that the *Novelas* had been published the year before, that he was deep in *Don Quixote*, Part II, and the *Persiles*, and had assembled certain plays and *entremeses* for publication, not to mention claims or hopes for several works which did not get as far as the printing press – his *Bernardo*, the *Semanas del Jardín* (*Weeks in the Garden*) and the sequel to the *Galatea* – we cannot but marvel at this last burst of creative energy. It was as if he now could not publish fast enough. With due allowance for the fact that the *Parnaso* was partly born out of a personal disappointment, the subjective part of the poem reveals some very mixed feelings.[4]

Cervantes wavers there between a frankly stated pride in his literary achievements and a sense of poetic insufficiency. He shows a certain general insecurity, and intermittently a more open dissatisfaction with his position *vis-à-vis* other writers and the wide public. He candidly wants recognition ('I was never content or satisfied with humbug affectations. I openly wanted praise for what I did well': *Parnaso*, IV, p. 114). Yet he is reconciled to not getting it ('I am content with a little, though I desire a lot': *Parnaso*, IV, p. 105). The role he gives himself in the action of his poem is symptomatic. It is both privileged and marginal. He is chosen as 'reporter' on the Parnassus expedition, and treated as an old and trusted friend by Apollo and Mercury, but he is unable to find a seat on Parnassus and to his irritation is left standing. Apollo tactlessly tells him to fold his cloak and sit on that. But Cervantes cannot afford a cloak and, unmollified by the genial deity's banal assurance that virtue is a cape which covers all, he remains, stiffly dignified, on foot (*Parnaso*, IV, pp. 105–6).

Although he names specific works of poetry (including dramas) among those works of which he speaks with pride, it is poetry that repeatedly provokes misgivings over his talent. In a much quoted tercet he speaks of having to watch and toil 'to have the appearance of that poetic grace which it did not please heaven to bestow on me' (*Parnaso*, I, p. 54). Perhaps, as Cernuda thought, he was too ready as a poet to take himself at other people's valuations (1964D, pp. 46 ff.); he refers rather often to the adverse opinions of others. However that may be, rightly or wrongly, he shows much more uncertainty over his poetry than he ever does over *Don Quixote*, for example.

There are undoubtedly a number of different reasons for Cervantes's ambivalent estimation of himself as a writer, but one of them must be that his greatest originality and gifts were exercised in a kind of literature which enjoyed little prestige. In the accepted hierarchy of genres, it was not so much that prose fiction came low through positive disesteem, as that critical authority was not sure what to do with new forms which had no clearly definable place in the traditional canon. As Cervantes said of the books of chivalry, they were works 'which Aristotle never thought of, of which St Basil had nothing to say, and of which Cicero had never heard' (*Don Quixote*, I, prol.; i, 56). Aristotle could therefore be used in arguments both to exclude and to admit them (see Weinberg, 1961E, II, 712). It was not that Cervantes's Spanish contemporaries were a race of dyed-in-the-wool classicists – far from it. Before the particular revaluation of literary genres which began in the eighteenth century it simply would not have occurred to them, on the basis of *Don Quixote*, to give Cervantes the place in the pantheon which posterity has done. He was plainly unsure himself just where he belonged.

There is much to suggest that he was near the edge rather than in the mainstream of the literary life of his time. But when we seek to account for it[5] we must not overlook either the doubtful status of prose fiction or how late in his life it was before real success came to him. He had had a hard life and a long wait before making any more than a modest name for himself. He had missed the bus with his drama, there was a gap of twenty years between his first two published works, and then the originality of his achievement with *Don Quixote*, in a genre generally regarded as inferior to poetry, was of an unfamiliar sort. His 'marginality', in the circumstances, is not surprising. One of the ironies surrounding his life and work was that the peak of his commercial success came posthumously, with the publication of *Persiles y Sigismunda* in 1617.

But behind the protective carapace of allegory, fantasy and irony in the *Viaje del Parnaso* we can see Cervantes coming to terms with ambition and disappointment. That characteristic humour, born of seeing things in their right relative proportions, asserts itself. The amused irony, which is never corrosive, settles like dew on everything and everyone, including himself. All the poets, even the good ones on the right side, look rather foolish *en masse*. The figure of Vainglory plays a prominent role in chapter VI. What absurd inflated vanity it is to care about literary reputation anyway.

There is no doubt about his devotion to the art of poetry, though. We can see clearly in the same book how exalted his ideal of Poetry was. In its prose appendix (*Adjunta*) his Apollo may poke fun at the whole breed of poets in general, but he decrees that the poet be ennobled by the art he practises.

Item, it is ordained that any poet, of whatsoever quality and condition, be ranked as a hidalgo by reason of the generous exercise in which he is engaged

(Item se ordena que todo poeta, de cualquier calidad y condición que sea, sea tenido y le tengan por hijodalgo, en razón del generoso ejercicio en que se ocupa: p. 189)

Twice more on the same page he declares that the name of poet is one to respect and be proud of.

What about the novelist, though? Cervantes has implicitly asked in the *Parnaso*. He surely belongs among them somewhere.

Whatever lingering uncertainties there may have been, a kind of serenity born of coming to accept things as they are breathes through the pages of Cervantes's last works, down to the dedication of the *Persiles* written three days before he died on 22 April 1616[6] – ready for death, yet still fired with the impossible hope of living on. Generations of readers have responded to it.

NOTES: CHAPTER 1

1   All references to *Don Quixote* are to the edition of Luis Murillo (1978A), normally cited by part, chapter; volume, page. Translations are my own throughout unless otherwise stated.
2   The latest in the series in English is William Byron's highly entertaining study (1979B). The most reliable and up-to-date biography is that by Melveena McKendrick (1980B), which is not at all fanciful.
3   Edited by Vicente Gaos (1973A). The best edition remains that of F. Rodríguez Marín (1935A). See Rivers (1973D), pp. 135 ff., and Canavaggio (1981[1]D).
4   Like Góngora, Cervantes had hoped to be chosen to fill a vacancy in the secretariat of his patron the Count of Lemos when the latter became Viceroy of Naples in 1610. Festivities there two years later helped to trigger off the work.
5   Américo Castro's questionable postulation of *converso* origins is one of the best-known theories (1966D, 1971D).
6   Probably not on 23 April, as used to be said. That was the day he was interred.

CHAPTER 2

Cervantes and Contemporary Prose Fiction

(i) ROMANCE

Cervantes wrote for a reading public which was very small by today's standards. The literate proportion of the population was perhaps 20 per cent. Nevertheless, it was not negligible, and was bigger than it had ever been before. With the expansion of education between 1500 and 1600, when the number of universities in the country rose from eleven to thirty-two, literacy had significantly increased. To more precise questions – just how large was this public? what was its composition? how did it develop? – only the most general answers can be given with any confidence. Detailed estimates are unreliable, interpretations are uncertain and sometimes confusing.[1] It must have consisted in the main of gentry, members of noble households, clergy, scholars and intelligentsia, and not all of these (Chevalier, 1976E, pp. 29–30). It seems safe to say that from the beginning of the seventeenth century the centre of this public had begun to shift to the small but growing urban middle class, that it was not confined only to the well-to-do, and that it included a fair proportion of women. It must also have been a good deal larger than the number of actual book-purchasers. Books could be hired for reading;[2] and, as Margit Frenk (1982E) has shown, the habit of reading aloud persisted to a degree which suggests that the transition to purely ocular reading was not yet complete. Readers must often have had an audience.

In basic ways the reading public was similar to the modern mass market. Most writers of the time were very conscious of its 'mass' aspect, known as the *vulgo*, and represented by sensitive authors as ignorant, malicious and blind to the finer points of art and morality. It was sharply distinguished from the 'discerning few', known as the *discretos*. Alemán addressed a prologue to readers in each category in *Guzmán de Alfarache*, Part I (1599). Writers might abuse the *vulgo*, but they knew it was a force to be respected, as did Cervantes when he called it 'that ancient legislator' (*Don Quixote*, I, prol.; i, 52). The power it exercised over the entrepreneurs of the publishing trade was increasingly evident to Spanish authors in the early seventeenth century (Cruickshank, 1978E, p. 817). Cervantes, Lope de Vega and most of their fellow novelists and dramatists were probably as conscious as most writers today of the need to know whom they were writing for, and to decide whether it was popular success they were seeking or the more enduring but less lucrative rewards of great art. Cervantes quite clearly aspired to both. *Don Quixote* should aim to satisfy the 'simple' as well as the 'discreto', the 'grave' and the 'prudente', the author's friend advises him in the first prologue (i, 58); and later the author was well pleased with its universal popularity.

Part I came on sale probably in January 1605. Far from being a rather splendidly isolated event, it appeared towards the end of a brief period of seven years (1599–1605) marked by a radically new development in the history of prose fiction. Within Spain these were also the peak years of a much longer literary period which was itself remarkable. For over a century the production of Spanish prose fiction had had no parallel in contemporary Europe in its quantity, variety, innovation and quality combined.

One may single out nine works published between 1492 and 1605 which were both influential in Europe and bestsellers at home. They are works of prose fiction or semi-fiction, designed primarily to entertain (whatever more serious purpose their authors may have also claimed). With one exception they figure in the top eight works of this sort listed by Keith Whinnom in an interesting and properly cautious study (1980E) of the problem of the bestseller in the Spanish Golden Age.[3] Though provisional, his findings serve our purposes perfectly well.

(1) (easily first) *La Celestina*, mostly by F. de Rojas. Dialogue fiction ('humanistic comedy').
(2) *Libro áureo de Marco Aurelio* (English title *The Dial of Princes*) by Antonio de Guevara. Educational, exemplary, anecdotic miscellany.
(3) *Guzmán de Alfarache* by Mateo Alemán. Picaresque novel.
(4) *Guerras civiles de Granada*, Part I, by Ginés Pérez de Hita. Moorish romance, posing as history.
(5) *La Diana*, by Jorge de Montemayor. Pastoral romance.
(6) *Don Quixote* by Cervantes.

(7) *Amadís de Gaula* (books I–IV). Chivalric romance reworked by Rodríguez de Montalvo.

(8) *Cárcel de amor* by Diego de San Pedro. Sentimental romance.

The exception referred to is *Lazarillo de Tormes*, in some respects the most revolutionary book of all, which comes lower down the list. It had had some trouble temporarily with the Inquisition. We shall return to it.

There are two points of interest about this list. One is the variety of works represented. No two are of exactly the same sort, and out of eight titles that is a little surprising. The Spanish fiction-reading public liked a varied diet. The second point is that, although no two works are of precisely the same type, four of the eight are different kinds (or subgenres) of romance – Moorish, pastoral, chivalric and sentimental. If we take these all together as varieties of basically idealistic romance fiction, we are looking at the most commercially successful kind of prose fiction in the Golden Age, despite competition from the *Celestina* and her progeny and from Guevara.

One type of romance, the romance of chivalry, as is well known, outstripped all the rest in terms of sheer mass-production before 1600, after which reading habits changed. Maxime Chevalier estimated forty-six new titles and some 251 known editions of chivalric romances between 1500 and 1605 (1968E, pp. 2–4).[4]

Although the last new romance of chivalry was published in 1602, idealistic romance as a whole at that date was far from dead or even moribund. The old favourites among the chivalric romances would continue to be published from time to time well into the later seventeenth century. The pastoral romances were flourishing and new ones were destined to go on appearing until the 1630s. Even the heroic romance, deriving from the ancient Greek romance in the manner of Heliodorus, was yet to enjoy a brief heyday in Spain in the second decade of the century, not to mention its more prolonged *succès fou* in France. Accustomed to viewing the scene with the later development of the mainstream realistic novel in mind, we generally dwell on the picaresque and *Don Quixote* at the expense of contemporary romance at this time, and thereby distort the picture.

The forms of art are always in a state of flux, and new genres grow out of old ones. Our period was one of vigorously interacting genres. Comedy is seen mixing with tragedy; *romanzo* flows into epic; aphorism, epistle and dialogue drift into essay; the subliterary form of the adage combines with the epigram to flower as the emblem, while the epigram puts new life into the sonnet.[5] There was also considerable awareness of genre among writers. The literary theory of the age, emanating from Italy, and especially the theory of J. C. Scaliger, was founded on it. One of the most momentous critical issues, the distinction between History and Poetry, was really a generic question: an attempt to map out some sort of coastline between the terra firma of History and the horizonless ocean of Poetry (which meant imaginative literature).

Contemporary critical theory took so little notice of prose fiction that one is not surprised that a much less developed sense of generic discrimination prevailed in that area of literature. This is immediately apparent in the vague and confused terminology applied to most kinds of prose fiction. There was no accepted word in Spanish for long prose-fiction works. *Libro* or *historia* usually had to do. *Novela* (from Italian *novella*) was just coming in (to oust other terms, like *patraña*) to signify 'short story'. That was perhaps a sign of growing sophistication in this area, however, and there were one or two others apparent from the early years of the seventeenth century on. Picaresque novèls were from the first associated with each other, and there was the exceptional case of Cervantes himself. He could not have written *Don Quixote* at all without a keen sense of the difference, and the relationship, between what we now think of as 'romance' and 'novel', although he did not know any such terms.

As there is still argument about genre, I had better state plainly that this book is based on the premiss that literary kinds or genres, and modes and subgenres, exist (although agreement on precise terminology is not to be expected). If not, it seems to me, one might as well dispute that people can be classed by blood group, psychological type, social class and so forth, just because everyone in the last analysis is a unique individual human being. It is useless to demand too much of the concept of genre – above all, to treat it as a system of precise and immutable categories. As Alastair Fowler makes very clear (1982E, p. 12), genres are unstable, as are the relationships between them and the subsidiary forms we discern within them; they change in time.[6]

To try to reduce a genre to the characteristics of a single model is futile; it is necessarily a collection of works. It is also a mistake to regard any one single trait as indispensable to a genre. The more stereotyped a work is, the easier it is to identify generically (which has led to the abuse of the word 'genre' in current film criticism). The more it departs from the average, the more uncertain its labelling will be. Some mixed works are easily recognizable as hybrids, others are more contentious. Just as there is general agreement about calling one area of the spectrum red and another one yellow, and one between these orange, further refinements soon lead to dispute. A genre, it seems to me, must be understood as capable of accommodating not only works that conform closely to type, but also those which exploit its possibilities, and even some which try to subvert it.[7] Genre theory is not an exact science but an ordering principle, a concept used by readers as much as by writers. There is much to suggest that generic pressures work powerfully at a level below that of fully conscious attention.

A particular literary genre or subgenre may come so to dominate the field that the criteria proper to it are applied to other distinct, though related, forms. This is notoriously the case where the modern realistic (or 'verisimilar') novel is concerned. We have been so conditioned by nineteenth- and twentieth-century novelistic realism that we still generally judge prose fiction by its norms, despite the prevalence nowadays of other sorts of modern novel. This has been particularly true in Hispanic literary criticism until very recently, and Cervantes criticism has certainly suffered from the widespread tendency to judge all his fiction by the same novelistic standards (see Deyermond, 1975E, and Sobejano, 1978D). Happily, things are starting to change there, and the autonomy of romance (to which English and American literary criticism is accustomed)[8] is becoming more readily recognized. So, indeed, it should in an age when science fiction and other sorts of fantasy have proliferated in all media – when the chivalric romance hero is reborn in James Bond, suitably accoutred for the later twentieth century with a degree of cynical materialism;[9] and reborn in purer form in the cosmic heroes of *Star Wars* and *Superman*.

I do not want to repeat here arguments which I have used elsewhere, but I am concerned to prevent misunderstanding, if possible.[10] Although one might use 'novel' as the comprehensive generic term and speak of 'idealistic' or 'fantastic' novels, I see no merit in discarding the useful and well-established English word 'romance'. I shall use it principally in contradistinction to 'modern realistic novel', despite its imprecision and the abuse to which the word, like so many other critical terms, is open. I use it to distinguish two different but related kinds in the family of prose fiction narrative. They are not antipathetic or incompatible with each other. If treated sometimes as a polarity, it must be understood that there is always free passage for movement between them; invariably there is an area of overlap.

Ortega y Gasset noted many years ago that the *Novelas ejemplares* of

Cervantes are basically of two distinct types (1957D, pp. 144–5). The distinction is between the predominantly realistic and the romance-based stories; none is *purely* one or the other, and two of them, *La ilustre fregona* and *La gitanilla*, are patently experimental hybrids. Ortega's shrewd suspicion that the works were generically different was not followed up in modern Cervantes criticism, however, and there used to be much head-shaking over inscrutable surrenders to modishly artificial tastes. How could the same man have written *Rinconete y Cortadillo* and *Las dos doncellas*, or, for that matter, *Persiles* and *Don Quixote*? The supposed incompatibility of such works pushed scholars into efforts to trace the chronological evolution of Cervantes's prose-writing along preconceived lines: from idealistic to realistic (thus González de Amezúa, 1956D, Vol. 1, pp. 482 ff.); and from realistic to idealistic (Ruth El Saffar, 1974D). The twin disadvantages of both theories are, first, that Cervantes's first and last published works are idealistic romances; and, second, that the theories have to rely, for many of the works, on dates of composition over which opinions differ and are often mere guesswork. Much more likely is the third theory, also commonly held, that Cervantes never moved definitively from one kind of narrative to the other, but was liable to write one or the other or in some combination of the two to the end of his days. The once perplexing problem of the difference between the *Quixote* and the *Persiles*, whose dates of composition in part overlapped, no longer looks problematical. Essentially, as Forcione suggested (1972D, pp. 150–1), the difference is one of genre.

Where the major kinds of romance are concerned, Cervantes notably cultivated two, the pastoral and the Greek romance. The most popular form of the age, the romance of chivalry, he simply used for his own well-known purposes. We are perhaps apt to exaggerate his preoccupation with the latter, given that it scarcely figures elsewhere in his writings. He spoofed material taken from Boiardo and Ariosto in his play *La casa de los celos* (see Canavaggio, 1977D, pp. 103 ff.); and he may have seen his *Persiles* as in part an updated chivalric romance, purged of unacceptable fantasy. The points of resemblance between the *Persiles* and the Canon of Toledo's outline of the qualities of the ideal romance of chivalry (*Don Quixote*, I, 47) strongly suggest this. But, apart from *Don Quixote* of course, that is all.

Cervantes served his prose-fiction apprenticeship in the pastoral romance.[11] The *Galatea* (1585), the fifth work of its kind to be published in Spain since Montemayor's *Diana* (1559), was evidently a labour of love from which the author must have learned a good deal about the craft of fiction. It shows typical features of his narrative method: the chance encounter which begins a story, narrated by the stranger, usually in instalments, often with more than one narrator, with suspenseful interruptions, the finale usually enacted on the main level of events. Notably, Gil Polo, author of the *Diana enamorada* (1564), had used this technique, derived from the Greek romance, in a similar way. Situations, character-types, themes, ideas, even turns of phrase in the *Galatea* turn up again in the author's later works. From the Timbrio–Silerio story both *El curioso impertinente* in *Don Quixote*, Part I, and *El celoso extremeño* in part derive. The basic situation of Daranio's wedding is elaborated in Camacho's wedding (*Don Quixote*, Part II) in an entirely different direction. Gelasia clearly anticipates the shepherdess Marcela who drives Grisóstomo to his death (Part I). Lesser incidents are likewise echoed. In a great writer self-repetition does not indicate poverty of imagination but the reverse. Intention, context, elaboration and tone can be decisively different. It is the novelist's sense of the infinite possible ramifications of events and the endless vagaries of human behaviour which make him return to a previously used situation or concept of character and develop it in a new way.

It is unjustifiable to dismiss pastoral as a defunct and inscrutable literary mode.[12] Arcadia is essentially a private world within the introverted mind of any lover, where only love and its attendant emotions matter, externalized by art into the stylized bucolic world. This world is neither wholly regulated by terrestrial norms of time and space nor yet quite free of them. It is not an exclusively emotional realm, however, and regularly provided a congenial setting for intellectual debates on the casuistry of love and the discussion or enactment of *cuestiones de amor*. It is, as C. S. Lewis so rightly said, 'a region in the mind, which does exist' (1965E, p. 352); 'something that carries us into a higher state of identity', as Northrop Frye has put it (1976E, p. 149). In Cervantes this private realm of courtly lovers dressed as shepherds, shepherdesses and nymphs is entered by figures who have been through harrowing experiences in the world outside, which they are ever ready to recount. But it is as lovers, past, present or potential, that they have access to Arcadia, usually at some moment of emotional crisis (cf. Marinelli, 1978E, pp. 57 ff.). They have left behind the material preoccupations of everyday social life (things which drop away from the thoughts of all distracted lovers) and wander distraught, or pursue or are pursued in the Arcadian countryside, which may abut on a semi-allegorical wilderness. They may be in blessed communion with, or conscious alienation from, the world of nature around them. Cervantes never ceased to write pastoral passages in his works after the *Galatea*, and his abiding affection for this kind of romance was never damaged by his capacity for seeing the funny side of it.

In his last work *Persiles y Sigismunda*, Cervantes consciously sought to renovate the romance of adventure by turning to the oldest known form of the genre. In the prologue to the *Novelas ejemplares* he described the work as one which 'makes bold to compete with Heliodorus', and he evidently also knew some version of Achilles Tatius' *Leucippe and Clitophon*.[13] Not only in the *Persiles*, but also in the *Galatea*, the *Novelas* and *Don Quixote*, much of the staple fare of romantic adventure derives directly or indirectly from the Greek romance. The central formula is very much that of the *Persiles*. A pair of noble young lovers, paragons of beauty and virtue, are separated, obliged to travel and to face all the tribulations that seafaring, tempest, shipwreck, piracy, captivity, torture threats, alien religious cults, greedy rapists, seductive voluptuaries and sheer mischance can supply. But they win through to a happy reunion and marriage, with virtue rewarded. Their love thrives on obstacles and in this respect is as romantic as that of Lancelot and Guinevere, but it is much more pure. Our common human prurience thrills to see their chastity put to the test, and when it comes through unsullied a no less basic human instinct is satisfied. Divine providence very much presides.

Lope had experimented with the modernizing of the Greek romance in his *El peregrino en su patria* (1604), a dozen years before, but Cervantes was still in the vanguard of literary fashion with the *Persiles*.[14] It is closer to its ancient model than the *Peregrino*, less miscellaneous in form, and more profound. Religious symbolism and mythic motifs are repeatedly visible beneath its torrent of episode. In no other work on this scale did Cervantes more manifestly aim to produce a palatable blend of edification and entertainment than in this romance.[15] Yet whereas the *Quixote* has not ceased to renew its relevance to life and art for readers across more than three and a half centuries the *Persiles*, like most old romances (though not romance in general), seems locked in its own era. *Don Quixote* has its starting-point in the person of its hero, and the implications of the work seem to radiate outwards endlessly. The *Persiles* seems enclosed in its absolutes. Nevertheless, the *Persiles* makes it abundantly clear what a long way the author of *Don Quixote* was from abjuring romance, whatever he thought about the chivalric sort.

(ii) THE PICARESQUE NOVEL

The modern novel certainly did not evolve simply as a mutation of
romance. It also inherited a good deal from a wide range of literature –
factual, speculative, prescriptive and the like, as well as fictional. If the
ancient romance derived its materials from the mystery religious cults,
drama, epic and history, the modern novel is, as Pío Baroja put it, 'a bag
that holds everything': letters, sermons, confessions, histories,
memoirs, travel accounts, dramatic pieces, poems, emblems, digests of
exotic information, collections of proverbs, aphorisms, jokes, anecdotes, tales – almost anything that circulated in print and oral tradition.[16] You can see the prose-fiction writers of the time utilizing them,
with varying degrees of organizational competence. The product sometimes differed only in degree from those miscellaneous compilations
which catered, in an embryonic way, for the taste which in a later age
would be satisfied by magazines.

Cervantes contributed, perhaps unwittingly, to one of these. The first
versions of *Rinconete y Cortadillo* and *El celoso extremeño* appeared in a
now lost *Compilación de curiosidades españolas*, consisting of tales, letters,
jokes, travel stories, grave and witty sayings, poetic tributes, put
together by Porras de la Cámara (*c.*1606), which, though unpublished,
was just such a miscellany. The revised versions, of course, appeared in
print in the *Novelas ejemplares.*[17]

The tendency of short stories to gather in clusters must stem mainly
from their oral origins. 'Tell us another one,' says the audience to the
storyteller. As soon as a few are put together on paper, if not before, a
problem of organization in some degree arises. This may resolve itself in
the finding of a common denominator or collective title ('Exemplary
Novels', 'Just-So Stories'), or in organization on some more holistic
principle. Whether a book consists of separate stories strung together
like beads on a string or of integrated parts of a solid narrative, there is –
particularly when storytellers are brought in as characters – no easily
measurable distinction apart from typographical convention between a
story, episode, instalment, chapter, incident and raw chunk of narrative
matter. The end-product may be like the Book of Genesis, Ovid's
Metamorphoses, the *Thousand and One Nights*, the *Decameron*, *Bleak
House* or *La Comédie humaine*.

It will be obvious to any reader of Cervantes that the short story was a
favourite unit of composition for him. The *Galatea* and *Persiles* are a
tissue of stories. Parts I and II of *Don Quixote* each contain half a dozen

'external episodes' which can be seen as basically independent stories. Cervantes never published any collection with a framework quite like that of the *Decameron*, although his fiction certainly has its worlds within worlds; but on three occasions he promised readers a book called *Semanas del jardín* (*Weeks in the Garden*), which sounds very much like a collection of *novelle* linked in the manner of Boccaccio. The last two of the *Novelas ejemplares* are linked by a framing device. All that unites the collection as a whole is the edifying claim in the title and a few statements of a similar nature in the prologue.

Spanish books of the period displayed in their preliminary matter a licence to publish, authorized by the Council of the Realm on behalf of the king, and usually one or more censorial *aprobaciones*. The vetting for the latter was delegated to ecclesiastics and to well-known writers. In three of those which preface the *Novelas ejemplares* the phrase 'de honestísimo entretenimiento' occurs four times right after the title, as though it belonged to it (i, 46, 49).[18] Descriptive titles of this particular sort had recently become associated with collections of *novelle* in Spanish. A Spanish version of Straparola's *Piacevoli Notti* appeared in 1580 under the pleasant and decorous title of *Primera parte del honesto y agradable entretenimiento de damas y galanes*. (There were a further five editions of Parts I and/or II by 1585, and two more in 1598 and 1612.) In 1589 a translation of fourteen tales by Bandello, based on the French version, was published and called, more severely, *Historias trágicas ejemplares* (republished 1596 and 1603). The year 1590 also saw the appearance of the *Hecatommithi* in a Spanish translation by Luis Gaitán de Vozmediano entitled *Primera parte de las cien novelas de M. Juan Bautista Giraldo Cinthio*. In his prologue Gaitán comments on the scarcity of translations of Italian and French *novelle* and the lack of native Spanish ones. He urges his countrymen to cultivate this genre, which, he believes, they would handle better than anyone else.[19] His plea was answered. Cervantes made the substantially justified claim to be the first to write original *novelas cortas* in Castilian (*Novelas ejemplares*, prol.; i, 52),[20] and throughout the reign of Philip IV (1621–65) this was the most flourishing form of prose fiction.

But, significant as is the wavelet of Italian *novella* translation and publication in the 1580s and 1590s, the really startling new development was of a different sort. This was the explosion of picaresque novel-writing which was triggered off by the publication in 1599 of Mateo Alemán's *Guzmán de Alfarache*, Part I. Between 1599 and 1605, in the

general category of Spanish prose fiction, five new works of four distinct
kinds were published: one romance of chivalry, one pastoral romance,
one romance of the old Greek type and two 'miscellaneous' works.[21] In
the same period four picaresque novels were published, and – which is
no less important – three more were composed. So, of course, was one
other realistic, non-picaresque novel: *Don Quixote*, Part I. The seven
picaresque works were:

1599	*Guzmán de Alfarache*, Part I, by Mateo Alemán
1602	Sequel to *Guzmán*, Part I, by Juan Martí
1604	*Guzmán de Alfarache*, Part II, by Mateo Alemán
1604	*El guitón Honofre* by Gregorio González (unpublished)[22]
c.1604	*Rinconete y Cortadillo* by Cervantes, the Porras version of the *novela corta*
c.1604	*El buscón*, probably first composed by Quevedo (published 1626)[23]
1605	*La pícara Justina* by López de Úbeda

Only two comparable 'moments' in the earlier history of prose fiction
come to mind. One was the decade of AD 160 in which *Leucippe and
Clitophon*, *The Golden Ass* and *Daphnis and Chloe* all appear to have been
composed. The other was 1215–40 when the great Vulgate cycle of
French Arthurian prose romances, from *L'Estoire del Graal* to *Le Roman
de Palamède*, were written. The difference was that none of these
Spanish works is a romance. However 'primitive' they may look when
set against works of Balzac, Dickens, Flaubert or Galdós, they share a
basically novelistic realism. The closest precedents in prose fiction
proper, if I am not mistaken, are to be found in the *Satyricon* of
Petronius, the *Golden Ass* of Lucius Apuleius and *Lazarillo de Tormes*.
The last of these was the most radical break with romance since
Apuleius' work in the second century, but it was not until the start of the
seventeenth century that the new genre of the picaresque came into
being.

That did not happen with the appearance of *Lazarillo*, because more
than one work is required to constitute a genre; but nor did it happen
without the vital participation of *Lazarillo*, either.[24] Published half a
century before its time, in 1554, *Lazarillo* had rather languished in the
later sixteenth century. Then, with the appearance of *Guzmán*, its
popularity suddenly boomed again. It was probably a shrewd book-
seller-publisher named Juan Berrillo who spotted the generic relation-

ship and cashed in on the success of *Guzmán* by reissuing *Lazarillo*, which promptly went through nine editions by 1603 (Guillén, 1971E, pp. 138 ff.; Moll, 1979E, pp. 99 ff.).

Few kinds of fiction look more obviously the product of their immediate environment than the picaresque. Yet when the social, economic and ideological circumstances of the time have been considered it is still not obvious – to me, at any rate – why the picaresque novel appeared when it did, and in Spain rather than elsewhere, despite the quantity of attention the question has received.[25]

The social and religious preoccupations of the greatest of the early Spanish picaresque novels are at heart inseparable. *Lazarillo* emerged out of the 'climate of social satire born of the urge to religious reform' (Parker, 1967E, p. 20) and had Erasmian affiliations. It is also difficult to divorce it from the Poor Law and the theologians' disputes on poverty and vagrancy which surrounded attempts to apply the law in the 1540s (Herrero, 1979E, p. 878). *Guzmán* and *El buscón* show a deep Counter-Reformation anxiety about evil and, when medicancy was again a major issue, Mateo Alemán certainly shared some of the concerns of *arbitristas* ('projectors') and social reformers like Miguel Giginta. His known personal connections with Cristóbal Pérez de Herrera, author of *Discursos del amparo de los legítimos pobres* (1598), guaranteed it.[26] On a less serious level, Spain did not have such a prolific rogue literature as Elizabethan England, though there were some memoirs by soldiers of fortune and one notable account of prison life, the *Relación de la Cárcel de Sevilla* (1596–9) by Cristóbal de Chaves.

But a topical interest in gaolbirds and beggars, phony or genuine, is not enough to account for the *pícaro* of Spanish fiction with his snakes-and-ladders life of social climb-and-fall. He must in some deeper sense be a product of the contemporaneous early growth of modern capitalist societies in Europe. Quevedo's Pablos, *el buscón*, is one of the clearest cases. Yet the picaresque novel emerged in a country which, though it moved rapidly away from feudalism, was one of the slowest to develop a capitalist economy.

In post-Armada Spain there was plenty to stimulate writers of a non-idealistic cast, especially – though not exclusively – those in socially marginal situations, like Alemán with his *converso* Jewish antecedents. National bankruptcy was declared in 1595, not for the first time. Inflation was, for those days, running riot. Harvests failed, famine followed, and in 1596 the plague arrived in northern Spain to sweep south in appalling epidemics which killed tens of thousands. There were military defeats for Spanish forces abroad. The early seventeenth century, says a historian, 'was not only a time of crisis, but a time of the awareness of crisis – of a bitter realization that things had gone wrong' (Elliott, 1963E, p. 294). At a less conscious level there was also the profoundly unsettling awareness, not confined to Spain, that the very model of the universe, which had been accepted for centuries, was beginning to fall apart. It was not yet 'all in pieces, all coherence gone', but it would be many years before Newton devised a new one. In 1605, Kepler completed his *Astronomia Nova* and Bacon published *The Advancement of Learning*.

Looking back from the 1980s at that epoch of apparent turmoil and decline, the emergence of some kind of literature of despair would not have seemed surprising. But that did not happen, though a mood of *desengaño* (disillusionment) is increasingly evident among writers. This was far from being universal, however. *Desengaño* scarcely typified the new drama. Even among the picaresque novels Alemán's guilt-racked *Guzmán* and the black satire of Quevedo's *Buscón* were not typical of the genre, whose range was wide. Social, economic and ideological circumstances alone do not account either for the picaresque novels or for *Don Quixote*. Each one was also the work of a complex individual, and part of a process of literary evolution, in which the relatively advanced state of Spanish prose fiction was a factor.

Each of the picaresque works which immediately followed Part I of *Guzmán de Alfarache* shows some sign of being a response or reaction to it of some sort. Juan Martí's sequel is, of course, about as close an imitation as anyone else could produce. Gregorio González is visibly indebted in his *Honofre* and acknowledges as much in a prefatory sonnet. On the other hand, far from brooding like Guzmán over sin and salvation, his *pícaro* is cheerfully irreverent. Cervantes, while utilizing certain basic structural components of the genre in *Rinconete y Cortadillo*, and even, in his ridiculing of the misdirected religious piety of Monipodio's gang, raising a serious religious problem worthy of Alemán, nevertheless reacts vigorously against his predecessor. So much so that many would consider this inconclusive short story, with a duplicated protagonist, told in the third person, in a light-hearted tone with little moralizing commentary, only marginally picaresque. Quevedo's *Buscón*, like *El guitón Honofre*, has some clear echoes of both *Guzmán* and *Lazarillo*, but a bias against the former is apparent from its almost total lack of moral comment. There is no breast-beating or tub-thumping, and the reader is left to draw his own conclusions from

Pablos' often grotesque and savage story. López de Úbeda's *Pícara Justina* is in some ways the most remarkable novel of them all. With its female rogue, casual virtuosity, non-stop garrulity and highlighted moral platitudes, it is generally accepted as being a 'send-up' of *Guzmán*, as well as having other more esoteric and virulent aims.[27]

Successive picaresque novelists down to 1605 thus exploit the possibilities of Mateo Alemán's successful formula and, often with a sharp eye also on *Lazarillo*, imitate, adapt, alter and even, on occasion, tacitly controvert it. They evidently and not surprisingly reacted most to Alemán's voluminous sermonizing commentary. González largely reduces his to proverbs and *sententiae*. Cervantes subsumes it almost entirely into the final reactions of one of his *picaro* protagonists, Quevedo eliminates it, López de Úbeda mockingly spells it out; but all of them capitalize on the witty and colloquial style, a blend of rhetoric and raciness, in which it is couched. Gregorio González opts for pithy sententiousness; López de Úbeda for a loquacious prattling which takes over much of the novel, making his female *picaro* narrator no mean ancestress of Tristram Shandy.[28] In *Rinconete*, Cervantes clearly intended linguistic entertainment to be derived from the dialogue. Quevedo, most spectacularly of all, did the same with the stylistic fireworks of *El buscón*. Much of the appeal of the picaresque novel lay in its familiar, chatty approach (a feature, too, of *Lazarillo*), as it still does.

The impact of *Guzmán de Alfarache* on the works of other kinds published between 1599 and 1605 is naturally less evident, but not wholly nonexistent. One of the miscellaneous works, *El viaje entretenido* (1603) by Agustín de Rojas, has clear picaresque affinities and indeed alludes to *Guzmán* and *Lazarillo* in one of the prologues (1972C, p. 66). Lope de Vega, starting *El peregrino en su patria* in 1600, cannot possibly have been unaware of the popular success of *Guzmán*. If there is any direct allusion to it in Lope's romance, it has escaped me, but the possible affinity and contrast between the Pilgrim and the Picaro has not escaped comment.[29] While it remains a matter of conjecture whether *El peregrino* is any kind of reaction to *Guzmán*, we cannot discount the possibility that it represents some sort of romance 'backlash'.

The picaresque novel is conventionally described, in generic terms, as a reaction against heroic and idealistic romance. 'The story of the hero produced the story of the rogue. Into the gap created by the recoil from the hero of fiction stepped the anti-hero of society – the Spanish picaro,' said F. W. Chandler in his classic study of 1899 (1961E, p. 14). Since then the picaresque has been generally seen as the countergenre or antitype of romance, and there is no compelling reason to quarrel with this.[30] From hero to antihero, from virtue to vice, from social heights to depths: the picaresque novel plainly does have characteristics diametrically opposed to those found in romance. Others it simply took over from romance with very little change: some basic features of narrative structure, for instance, such as beginning with the origins of the protagonist, his setting out to 'make his fortune', his travels, encounters and episodic adventures.[31] Some things were reversed or travestied, others stayed the same. Any new genre is bound to take over features from old ones, and is not necessarily thereby denatured.

The first picaresque novelists were undoubtedly reacting against romance fiction, yet surprisingly they did so almost without any open attack on the genre. Even signs of deliberate parody or travesty, as distinct from what is implicit and probably uncalculated in the notion of a countergenre, are scarcely demonstrable after *Lazarillo*.[32] And this was in spite of a famous precedent, known to all. I refer to *La Celestina*, which was certainly no picaresque novel, but which did, in Calisto, produce the parody of a courtly lover, thereby implicating the Spanish sentimental romance, most probably the *Cárcel de amor* and its hero.[33] But by and large the Spanish picaresque novelists did not advertise the opposition that existed between their works and the romances. The novels, as A. A. Parker observed, may historically be considered as reactions against the romances, 'but as alternatives and not as satires' of them. In this they differ significantly not only from *Don Quixote* but also from the 'anti-romance' works of Sorel and Scarron in seventeenth-century France.[34]

It appears not to have been easy for the picaresque novelists to break cleanly with romance. Even Mateo Alemán had not said goodbye to it when he included the basically idealistic, Moorish romance tale of Ozmín and Daraja in part I of his novel. Furthermore, romance was to reassert itself in a more subtle and lasting way within the very fabric of picaresque narrative. It was a compromise, to be sure, an infiltration of the picaresque by elements of romance which softened its harsher lines and lightened its tone. We even glimpse the finger of Providence again, on occasion, silver-lining the clouds and drawing them back for a happy ending. This process seems to have begun with Cervantes. It was continued in Vicente Espinel's *Marcos de Obregón* (1618) and certain novels of Salas Barbadillo and Castillo Solórzano. Only some, not all, of the Spanish picaresque novels were affected but, with the help of *Don*

Quixote, the effect was felt lastingly on the French and the English picaresque. A degree of accommodation between conventions of urban social realism and romantic idealism was similarly established in the so-called *novela cortesana* and in the cape-and-sword dramas of the seventeenth century.

The first suggestion of the moral upgrading of the *picaro* is to be found in *Rinconete y Cortadillo*, the text of which ends with the boys as yet not entirely absorbed in the criminal environment to which they are presented as ethically and intellectually rather superior. Cervantes very deliberately elevates the two male protagonists of his later story *La ilustre fregona* to a yet higher level. They are young gentlemen of whom the worst that can be said is that they are sowing a few wild oats, voluntary and self-made *picaros*. The most 'roguish' of the two is presented as almost a contradiction in terms: 'In short, the world discovered in Carriazo a virtuous *picaro*, clean, well brought up and of above-average discretion' (*Novelas ejemplares*, ii, 140). The kitchenmaid of the title, whom the other one eventually marries, of course turns out to be no such thing but a (rather passive) heroine of romance in every important respect.[35] Their union reflects a more calculated effort to marry the genres of romance and picaresque fiction than anyone had yet attempted. But Cervantes's most complete and complex riposte to Alemán is his magnificent *Coloquio de los perros* in the same collection. Anything but romantic, it goes to the heart of human beastliness, pits example against preaching and contains a commentary which undercuts commentary by exercising the 'reader's' (that is Cipión's, then Peralta's) right of reply. The *Coloquio* seems to me to be too far removed from the centre of the genre to belong to it properly speaking, but it is Cervantes's most acute comment on the picaresque.[36]

Like other Spanish writers in the first years of the seventeenth century, Cervantes evidently reacted to Alemán. He tried his hand at the new genre and reacted against Alemán's version of it. *Don Quixote*, too, contains reflections of *Guzmán de Alfarache*, but its fundamental inspiration and ethos are entirely different. In no important sense of the term is *Don Quixote* a variety of picaresque novel.

One key to the difference between them is found in their quite distinct relations to romance. With the probable but very partial exception of *Lazarillo de Tormes*, calculated parody of romance is not a characteristic of the Spanish picaresque. It is, on the other hand, absolutely basic to *Don Quixote*. The reaction of the picaresque novelists was a flight away from the romances. That of Cervantes was to engage it at close quarters in something between a grapple and an embrace. Parody implies a close relationship in which a critical attitude predominates, but which is not necessarily devoid of affection.[37] It is an altogether different attitude. If the picaresque novels are to be called 'anti-romances', then the term is not right for *Don Quixote*. Related though they are as early examples of modern novel (*La Celestina* may be regarded as another, hybridized), they are distinct.

NOTES: CHAPTER 2

1   See Whinnom (1980E); Cruickshank (1978E), pp. 810–11; Chevalier (1968E, 1976E); Eisenberg (1982E), pp. 89 ff.; Domínguez Ortiz (1971E), pp. 231 ff.
2   Mateo Alemán mentions women who would rather buy books than clothes and 'spend their money hiring books' (*Guzmán de Alfarache*, II, iii, 3; 1967C, p. 787).
3   Whinnom is careful to avoid any definitive claims about the works included or their precise ranking. He points out how fragile the bases of calculation are. There is very little to go on but the number of *known* editions. Non-fictional works of instruction, theory, edification and the like, translations and poetry are excluded from the list I have given. Then, as now, some of these were even more successful in publishing terms. My thanks are due to Professor Whinnom for further comments on his findings.
4   Riquer considers these figures an underestimate (1973D, pp. 284–5 n.).
5   Rosalie L. Colie (1973E), pp. 33 ff. See also C. Guillén (1971E), pp. 191, 385 ff.; and Alastair Fowler (1982E), pp. 149 ff.
6   Alastair Fowler (1982E) makes the most thorough, searching and sensible examination of the whole subject known to me. The doubts of, e.g., Eisenberg (1979E), Dunn (1979E, pp. 135 ff., 1982D, 1982E) and Reed (1981E), pp. 56 ff., over whether the picaresque has generic existence, seem to me to be entirely dispelled by Fowler's arguments (not that he refers to the above-named specifically). See also Rey Hazas (1982E).
7   'One motive for writing in a genre is the urge to question some of the underlying attitudes that shape that literary mode': Dubrow (1982E), p. 23.
8   See, in particular, Frye (1957E), pp. 303 ff., and (1976E); also Beer (1970E).
9   See Eco (1966E) and Dubrow (1982E), pp. 112–13, among others. The advertising of consumer products, the named brands of cigarettes, whisky, cars, marmalade, etc., in Fleming's novels is more significant than it looks. Ironically, the idealism of old romance has come to rest at the very heart of mass-consumer materialism: in advertising, especially the television commercial. Here all young women are lovely and desirable, all young men dashing and virile, children happy and smiling, mothers tirelessly caring, families harmonious and full of fun. A world of glamour and thrills is just around the corner for whoever has the price of a hair shampoo, chocolate bar, can of beer, motor car. Like the old romance-writers, the advertisers go to the secret heart of human desires.
10 See Riley (1981D). In the light of Fowler (1982E) I should now want to qualify and clarify some of the points made, but my main argument is unaffected. For the sake of clarity I reproduce here virtually the same list of what seem to me to be the principal characteristics of romance relevant to Cervantes and his period. Their incidence varies from one work to another; none is unique to the genre or indispensable.
    (1)   A romance is a story of adventure or love, and usually both.
    (2)   It normally comprises a journey, quest or ordeal.
    (3)   It is closer to myth than the novel is.

(4) There is no embargo on the supernatural.

(5) Time and place need not be subject to empirical norms.

(6) Heroes and heroines are more or less idealized in so far as they are blessed with exceptional beauty, youth, rank, wealth, virtue and intellect. Socially, they may be regarded as the flower of the aristocracy.

(7) Characters are psychologically simplified. They tend to work directly and strongly on the reader's emotions, to expand into psychological archetypes and to lend themselves to allegory and symbolism.

(8) Moral issues are simplified. Virtue may be expected to triumph, but a happy ending is not inevitable.

(9) Narrative action in full-length romances takes the form of a more or less prolific succession of incidents, sometimes comprising interlaced stories. These stories may be tightly plotted and form extractable *novelle*.

(10) The course and resolution of the action are much governed by reversals of fortune and chance encounters. To the modern reader accustomed to plots based on manifest causality, they look like crude manipulations of accident and coincidence. In ancient, medieval and Renaissance romance, however, they represent the intervention of divine Providence, which presides over human affairs and gives meaning to human existence.

(11) An approximation to dream, especially to dreams of wish-fulfilment, is often apparent.

(12) Descriptive detail may be profuse, sensuous and visually vivid.

(13) Verbal style is usually elevated above the mean and does not favour realistic dialogue.

(14) Romance is 'acutely fashionable, cast in the exact mould of an age's sensibility' (Beer, 1970E, p. 12). This explains why particular romances so quickly seem dated.

See Hume (1974E) for some other reflections on basic elements of romance.

11 Pastoral romance, on the whole, would have offered more to the budding *novelist* than would the romance of chivalry. Gil Polo's *Diana enamorada*, for instance, shows a clear movement towards novelistic treatment of character and motivation (see Solé-Leris, 1980E, pp. 54–5; Cozad, 1981E). Lope de Vega's *Arcadia* (1598) has certain other quasi-novelistic features (Osuna, 1972E, pp. 230, 243 ff.).

12 Thus Fitzmaurice-Kelly on the *Diana*: 'The truth of the matter is that the form pastoral is essentially artificial; the falsity of the *genre* was to the taste of the time and lent itself easily enough to Montemayor's alembicated talent which was alien from realism' (1926E, pp. 229–30).

13 Amyot's French translation of the *Ethiopic History* was rendered into Spanish in 1554, and Fernando de Mena's translation followed in 1587 (see Forcione, 1970D, pp. 56 ff.). A partial Italian version of Achilles Tatius' romance by Lodovico Dolce, the *Amorosi ragionamenti* (1546), inspired a loose partial imitation in Spanish, Nuñez de Reinoso's *Historia de los amores de Clareo y Florisea* (1552), which Cervantes probably read, though he may also have read Dolce's version or Angelo Coccio's complete version of 1551. (See Zimic, 1974–5D.) The first full Spanish version did not appear until 1617.

14 Spanish works of this kind appeared in translation at least five times in England between 1619, when the English version of *Persiles* appeared, and 1623 (Randall, 1963E, p. 124). There were twenty-four native French ones between 1620 and 1630, some of them huge multi-volume affairs. The vogue went on into the 1660s.

15 See especially Forcione (1972D) and Casalduero (1947D). Also Stegmann (1971D), Forcione (1970D), and Avalle-Arce's edition (1969A), introduction.

16 See Clements and Gibaldi (1977E), pp. 14–16. Also Márquez Villanueva (1973D), pp. 115 ff., on some of the proto-novelistic sources of Cervantes. Indeed, as Segre says (1974D, p. 192), the whole history of the novel can be seen as a succession of attempts to mix different types of novel.

17 The recent assiduous comparison by E. T. Aylward (1982D) of the two versions is to be welcomed. But it seems to me that his express *a priori* wish to demonstrate that the Porras versions are not by Cervantes undermines his reasoning, which is unlikely to change received opinion.

18 *Novelas ejemplares*, ed. J. Sieber (1980A). All references are to this edition.

19 On the evolution of the *novella* in Spain, see Pabst (1972E), Clements and Gibaldi (1977E), and Forcione (1982D), pp. 21 ff.

20 There are isolated exceptions like the Moorish story *El Abencerraje*.

21 Respectively these were: *Don Policisne de Boecia* (1602) by Juan de Silva, *El prado de Valencia* (1600) by Gaspar Mercader, *El peregrino en su patria* (1604) by Lope de Vega, *El viaje entretenido* (1603) by Agustín de Rojas and *Diálogos de apacible entretenimiento* (1605) by Gaspar Lucas Hidalgo. It is worth repeating that the picaresque 'explosion' did not spell the end of romance-publishing. At least nine older chivalric romances were reissued in this period. Lope's *Peregrino en su patria* appears in six different printings in 1604–5, and his pastoral *Arcadia* of 1598 goes through another seven editions by the end of 1605. On *Don Policisne*, see Russell (1982E).

22 That is, until edited by Hazel Généreux Carrasco (1973C).

23 This is the date accepted by Lázaro Carreter in his edition (1965C), pp. lii-lv, and most authorities, excepting Parker (1967E), p. 57.

24 See Guillén (1971E), pp. 135 ff.; Lázaro Carreter (1972E), pp. 195 ff.

25 See, more recently, Dunn (1979E), pp. 139 ff.; Michel Cavillac (1983E).

26 See Cavillac's edition (1975C), introduction, pp. cxxx ff. On *arbitristas*, see below, Ch. 10.

27 On the prominent part played by this work in the disturbance centring around *Guzmán*, see in particular Márquez Villanueva (1983E).

28 In an introductory chapter of more than forty pages in the edition by Antonio Rey Hazas (1977C), she addresses in turn a hair on the quill she is writing with, an inkstain, a mark on the paper, the book and the inkpot, before getting round to the event of her birth, where she briefly assumes the articulate persona of the vocal infant concerned.

29 See Avalle-Arce's edition (1973C), introduction, pp. 31 ff.

30 Thus, e.g., Guillén (1971E), p. 97; Wicks (1974E, 1978E); Scholes and Kellogg (1975E), p. 75; Bjornson (1977E), pp. 10, 153.

31 These are features of chivalric rather than pastoral romance, of course. Structural similarities with the latter can be found without difficulty in picaresque narrative. However, to regard *Rinconete* on that account as a type of pastoral, as has been done several times recently, strikes me as misleading.

32 The title, ironic first sentence of the prologue, and the opening of the story in this extraordinarily sophisticated little work do suggest parodic intent. The same might be true of parts of the *Guzmán*, but it is less obvious if so.

33 See June Hall Martin (1972E), Severin (1982E). I am indebted to Professor Severin for letting me see an advance copy of this essay, published in 1984.

34 There are rather more points of contact between the romances and the early picaresque novels than the above suggests, as I hope to show at a future date. For a different approach to the crucial relationship between *Don Quixote* and the picaresque, see Walter L. Reed (1981E).

35 The generic transformation is all the more startling in view of the ribald presentation of serving wenches at inns in contemporary folklore and the picaresque novel. See Joly (1983D).

36 See, pre-eminently, Forcione (1984D), pp. 15 and passim. Much has been written on Cervantes *vis-à-vis* Alemán and the picaresque. See especially: Blanco Aguinaga (1957D); Castro (1966D), pp. 42 ff.; Alfaro (1971D); Bataillon (1973D), pp. 226 ff.; Sobejano (1975D); Dunn (1979E), pp. 90 ff.; Dunn (1982E).

37 Harry Levin (1963E, pp. 43 ff., and 1973D, pp. 377 ff.) and Northrop Frye (1976E,
    p. 39) have rightly underlined the importance of parody as a link between romance
    and the modern realistic novel. It was not an indispensable bridge, however, as the
    Spanish picaresque novels show.

CHAPTER 3

Preliminaries

(i) THE PUBLICATION OF *DON QUIXOTE*, PART I

The remark at the beginning of the prologue to *Don Quixote*, Part I, where Cervantes likens the hero, or his story, to 'one engendered in a prison' (i, 50) has commonly been thought to mean that he conceived the idea of the book during one of his two spells in gaol, probably the one in Seville, 1597. The supposition is plausible, although the idea that he started writing there is less so.[1] The bulk of the novel was probably written between 1598 and 1604. One or two of the intercalated stories may have been composed earlier: 1589–90 has been proposed for the Captive's tale (I, 39; i, 473 n.).

It was in July or August 1604 that he sold the rights of *Don Quixote*, Part I, to the court publisher and bookseller Francisco de Robles, whose father had published the *Galatea* twenty years earlier. The sum Robles paid him is unknown, but it was probably more than the 1,330 *reales* paid for the *Galatea* and less than the 1,600 paid for the *Novelas ejemplares* in 1612. The royal licence to publish (the *privilegio*) was dated 26 September 1604. This protected the author's rights in Castile for ten years – in theory. There was no censorial *aprobación*. The dedication to the young Duke of Béjar was unusually brief and unoriginal, and the likelihood is that Cervantes entertained no very high hopes from his patronage.

Robles turned over the manuscript to the Madrid printer Juan de la Cuesta, who set and ran off the first printing of the work between September and December. The first edition was on sale by early 1605, probably January. Some scholars have thought there was a hurry to publish – a race with López de Úbeda's almost simultaneous *Pícara Justina* in Medina del Campo perhaps – although what the advantage of winning would be is not clear. Anyhow, success was immediate. Cuesta started printing a second edition at once and it was ready by May. Robles had procured a licence for Portugal and Aragon as well immediately after the first came out, but not soon enough to forestall the appearance of unauthorized editions in Lisbon and Valencia. By August the total was two Madrid editions, two published in Lisbon, and one in Valencia (or two in Valencia, if the slightly different printings are taken as distinct editions). There were to be four more (Brussels 1607, Madrid 1608, Milan 1610, Brussels 1611) before Part II came out in 1615. This was a handsome result in publishing terms, although not in the phenomenal class of the *Guzmán*.

Thanks to the ingenious and painstaking detective work of Robert Flores (1975D), some important facts about Cuesta's first two editions and their relation to Cervantes's long-vanished manuscript are now established. The compositors of the first edition worked directly from this manuscript, and the textual variants are due to them rather than to any copyists. The division of labour was highly irregular, and they subjected the orthography of Cervantes to a 'merciless defacing and mishandling' (p. 5). This goes a considerable way towards clearing Cervantes of the charges of sloppy spelling and careless style which so many editors and critics have laid against him.[2] At all events, we are not reading *Don Quixote* the way Cervantes wrote it. Nevertheless, deplorable though the state of the first edition of Madrid 1605 was, it is the only authoritative one we have, because the second edition was worse, and those which followed had nothing more to commend them.

Reprinting meant resetting, since used type was not kept, and changes proliferated in the second edition. Cuesta subcontracted the printing of five gatherings to another press, and the new compositors used their own methods, corrected old errors and made new ones. Cervantes himself had no more to do with the proof-reading or printing of the second edition than he had had with the previous one. It is therefore of very little use for correcting first-edition readings, as editors have habitually done. As Flores concludes with pardonable consternation (pp. 85–6), if the three compositors of Cuesta's second edition, working from a perfectly legible copy, made 3,925 changes, what are the four compositors of the first edition copying from Cervantes's manuscript likely to have done!

It was not only the spelling and punctuation. The printers were responsible for such things as omitting the heading of chapter 43 in the first edition and then inserting it in the wrong place in the second. Other faulty or misplaced headings, such as those of chapters 28, 29, 35 and 36, may be due to them or to Cervantes or both. The mistitling of chapter 10 evidently resulted from a change of plan on the author's part. The notorious muddle over Sancho's ass, which disappears and reappears inexplicably in the first edition, was purportedly rectified in the second. Unfortunately, the missing passages were inserted in chapters 23 and 30 instead of 25 and 42 (or a little before) to which they respectively corresponded. The author must have started the confusion with his change of plan, but the compositors probably compounded the error.[3] Cervantes is possibly acknowledging dual culpability in the discussion between Sancho and Sansón Carrasco when he makes Sancho say it must be either the author's or the printer's fault (II, 4).

It is clear that there was never an earlier edition, published in 1604, as a few authorities have thought. There is no reliable evidence for this theory at all. But there is, of course, nothing implausible in the notion of Cervantes reading, showing or talking about his work to others, and it is likely that it achieved some degree of renown in this way before it ever appeared in print.

In any case, Cervantes's heroes were famous almost as soon as the book was published. Quite apart from the reprintings, there is eloquent testimony to the way they caught the public imagination in the recorded presence of the figures of Don Quixote and Sancho at masquerades and carnivals. The first known instance was at the well-documented court festivities held in Valladolid in June 1605. By 1607 they had appeared as carnival figures in Peru, and in 1613 in Heidelberg. Don Quixote made at least ten such appearances by 1621. Copies of Cuesta's first or second editions apparently crossed the Atlantic in large numbers in 1605 (Leonard, 1949E, pp. 270 ff.). A copy is said to have turned up in Lima in December and more were reported in Cuzco, seat of the old empire of the Incas, in 1606.

(ii) THE FIRST PROLOGUE

The prologue to Don Quixote, Part I, presumably written in 1604, obliquely reflects something of the stir going on in the Spanish literary world in the first years of the new century.[4] Like none of the others Cervantes ever wrote, it engages with contemporary prose-fiction writing. This it does over one major issue. The immediate target was not Alemán and the picaresque but, to all appearances, Lope de Vega and the two romances he had published, one of them (*El peregrino en su patria*) probably only a few weeks earlier. Cervantes names no names, so we can never be certain, but these works of Lope fully answer to the description, although they do not preclude others, perhaps even a picaresque novel or two. One word would cover Cervantes's major criticisms. The word is *pretentiousness*. Literary pretentiousness can take many forms, of course, but what he expressly objects to is interference with the proper purpose of a work of fiction. It was not only the latter-day romances of chivalry which might be accused of extravagance, Cervantes evidently considered.

He affects concern to his 'friend' that his own book is going to be sadly deficient in footnote erudition, and quite undecorated with complimentary sonnets composed by 'dukes, marquesses, counts, bishops, ladies or celebrated poets' (I, prol.; i, 53). With a guffaw, the friend makes light of these difficulties, explaining how easy it is to get round them without being caught out and to win all the credit one would like. Most of the irony falls away as he reaches the climax of his argument:

> Moreover, if I understand you correctly, this book of yours needs none of the things you say it lacks, for the whole of it is an invective against the books of chivalry

> (Cuanto más que, si bien caigo en la cuenta, este vuestro libro no tiene necesidad de ninguna cosa de aquellas que vos decís que le falta, porque todo él es una invectiva contra los libros de caballerías: p. 57)

The positive message of the prologue under all the jocular irony is that what matters is the purpose of the work, not the trappings, and that this should govern its form. Three times it is said that the purpose is to discredit the romances of chivalry. For this, declares the friend, all that is needed is that you should write plainly and well, 'realising your intention as far as possible and to the fullest extent of your ability'. And aim to satisfy readers of every temperament and intellectual disposition, he goes on to advise (p. 58).

Lope de Vega is regularly taken to be the prime offender Cervantes had in mind. Their uneasy relationship had deteriorated sharply around this time. Lope's *Arcadia*, published in 1598 and never mentioned in *Don Quixote*, paraded quantities of gratuitous learning, mostly lifted from manuals and repertories, some of which have been identified. It advertised an index of historical and poetic names on the title page, and there are some 450 notes in addition to the information packed into the narrative. His *Peregrino en su patria*, whether or not Cervantes saw it just before writing his prologue, is hardly less ostentatious in its learning and name-dropping. Its prologue begins with a reference to Seneca, Epistle 31, and has four Latin quotations in the first ten sentences. Lope writing idealistic romance or heroic poetry could be very different from the dramatic author and apologist who extolled the claims of 'nature' over those of 'art' and giving the *vulgo* what it wanted. In fairness, we may give him some credit for seeking to dignify a genre not held in the highest esteem, rather than necessarily suppose he was only showing off, but we must admit that Cervantes was right to judge the means misguided. As for prefatory sonnets and other verses, the *Arcadia* has thirteen at the front, with the Valencia 1602 edition carrying two more at the end. The *Peregrino* has nine by quite celebrated persons, another poem with a reply by Lope after the prologue and three more at the end of the book. If some of Lope's admirers, like Avellaneda, thought that Cervantes was getting at him, he probably was.

But one does not have to look far to see how common these practices were even in works of fiction. The first picaresque novelists were less ostentatious about it, for the good reason that as a rule the *picaro* himself was supposedly relating the story. Even so, the author of *El guitón Honofre* cannot resist drawing his readers' attention to the praiseworthy sentences from Cicero, Demosthenes and others contained in his work, although he admits to a certain difficulty about working them into comic material. He had thought of putting references in the margins so that credit should be given where it was due, but decided that this was unnecessary (prol., p. 43). Was he being serious? one almost wonders.[5]

Mateo Alemán is known to have made use of exactly the kind of second-hand erudition ironically recommended by Cervantes's 'friend', available in the miscellanies and commonplace-books of the time (Cros, 1971E, p. 168), but his didacticism aims at moral impact rather than erudite ostentation. He does not seem to be Cervantes's main target. However, it is not unlikely that the author of *Don Quixote* found in Alemán's moralizing method another form of pretentiousness. Was the friend therefore thinking of *Guzmán* when he warned Cervantes off touting 'philosophers' maxims, counsels from Holy Writ, poetic fables, rhetorical speeches or saintly miracles'? Or when he said Cervantes's novel had no call 'to preach to anyone, mixing the human with the divine, which is a kind of motley, in which no Christian mind should clothe itself' (p. 57)? Whether or not he was, he did have a point. None of these types of pretentiousness did prose fiction, even in the age of the Counter-Reformation, any real good.[6]

A challenging, even provocative note chimes through the mock-modesty and the irony of the prologue, going beyond mere disclaimers of pedantry and pretentiousness. Cervantes dissociates himself from certain contemporary literary practices, unimportant in themselves, but indicative of a trend he might reasonably deplore both on aesthetic grounds and from the point of view of the writer mindful of his market. 'Snob appeal' was not what prose-fiction writers ought to cultivate. In his own novel Cervantes wants 'not to annoy the *simple* reader' ('que el simple no se enfade'), in addition to eliciting the admiration of the *discreto*, the approval of the *grave* and the praise of the *prudente* (p. 58). The tone may have been a little abrasive, but he shows more clear-headedness about the nature and functions of his own work than most contemporary prose-fiction writers showed about theirs. The note of self-sufficiency sounds loudly when he declares that he is too idle and sluggish to go seeking out authors to say what he knows very well how to say for himself (p. 53).

The slipperiness of Cervantine irony becomes apparent as we first recall that he is making this prologue largely out of the advice of a friend, and then we promptly suspect that this friend is imaginary. The self-sufficiency and the irony are present in the first paragraph, where he concedes to his reader what he claims for himself:

I do not want to follow the current of custom and beg you, almost with tears in my eyes, dearest reader, to pardon or conceal the faults you see in this child of mine [Don Quixote]. You are not a relative or friend of his, you have your own soul in your own body and your own free will, like the best of them, and you are master in your own house, as the king is over his taxes, and you know the popular saying: beneath my cloak I'll shoot down the king. All of which exempts you from all respect and obligation, and so you can say what you like about this story without fear of being abused for speaking ill or rewarded for speaking well of it.

(no quiero irme con la corriente del uso, ni suplicarte casi con las lágrimas en los ojos, como otros hacen, lector carísimo, que perdones o disimules las faltas que en este mi hijo vieres, y ni eres su pariente ni su amigo, y tienes tu alma en tu cuerpo y tu libre albedrío como el más pintado, y estás en tu casa, donde eres señor della, como el rey de sus alcabalas, y sabes lo que comúnmente se dice, que debajo de mi manto, al rey mato. Todo lo cual te esenta y hace libre de todo respeto y obligación, y así, puedes decir de la historia todo lo que te pareciere, sin temor que te calunien por el mal ni te premien por el bien que dijeres della: pp. 50–1.).

This prologue did ruffle some feathers. Avellaneda, in his own, described it as 'cocky and aggressive'. And if he is not reckoned a reliable witness Cervantes himself opened the prologue to the *Novelas ejemplares* with the remark that 'it did not go so well with the one I put in my *Don Quixote* that I should be anxious to follow up with this one' (i, 20). It looks as though he found the writing of neither prologue easy. Characteristically, however, he makes the prologue to *Don Quixote*, Part I, partly out of his very difficulties and critical preoccupations. They furnish the material for the dialogue with that no doubt imaginary friend. The point of departure for this conversation is that memorable sketch of himself – which gives place to a full-scale pen portrait in the prologue of the *Novelas* – sitting there, paper in front of him, pen on ear, elbow on desk, hand propping cheek, wondering what to say (pp. 51–2). This very self-conscious author absorbs criticism in creation and here, as so often, draws attention to the act of composing his work.

NOTES: CHAPTER 3

1   He distinguishes between conceiving and writing his *Novelas ejemplares* like this: 'my wit engendered them and my pen gave birth to them' (prol.; i, 23). But Avellaneda, author of the spurious sequel, took Cervantes to mean that he had written Part I in prison (Avellaneda, *Don Quixote*, prol. 1972C, i, 13: references are to this edition).

2   Rosenblat (1971D), pp. 243 ff., had already gone a long way in showing how groundless were many of the charges of linguistic impropriety in the novel.

3   Stagg (1959D), Flores (1980[1]D, 1980[2]D).

4   Though mainly devoted to other matters than those with which I am concerned here, the major critical works on the prologues of *Don Quixote* are by Castro (1967[2]D) and Socrate (1974D). See also Porqueras Mayo (1965E, 1968E) and Laurenti (1971E) for comparison with other prologues of the time.

5   In his prologue (i, 106) López de Úbeda attributes (Ovid's) *Metamorphoses* to the 'poet of the Odes' (Horace). With similar jocularity Cervantes ascribes lines from Aesop and Horace to Horace and Cato respectively (p. 55).

6   Yet another sort altogether is satirized in the verses attributed to Urganda the Unknown (p. 60), which mention the 'indiscreet hieroglyphics' on someone's trumped-up coat of arms. The perpetrator of this heraldic indiscretion was almost certainly either Lope de Vega or, as Marcel Bataillon cogently argued (1969E), López de Úbeda. Cervantes (like many others) was no friend of López de Úbeda, whom he satirizes in the *Viaje del Parnaso*, VII.

CHAPTER 4

Origins of the Work

(i) *DON QUIXOTE* AS PARODY

An elderly gentleman goes out of his wits through too much reading of romances of chivalry. He believes them to be factually true, and takes it into his head to become a knight errant himself and go out and redress wrongs and have adventures, as though the world were one of his story-books. It is hard to think of an idea for a story at once more out of the ordinary, more simple and yet more full of potential. How one would love to know what put it into Cervantes's head. Was it an anecdote about some sixteenth-century lunatic? A dotty relative? Simply reading *Orlando furioso* or one of the prose romances? The wish to amuse himself and others with a parody? An urge to test some critical theory, or even to root out a supposedly 'pernicious' literary form? Or was it the crystallization of some complex process of reflection on his own experience of life, split as it was between a past full of heroism and high adventure and the dreary grind of the present? It could have been almost any of these, or something else again. But the image of Don Quixote himself comes so immediately and overridingly to mind at the mention of the book that it is difficult to believe that any abstract considerations could have had priority, in any important sense, over the conception of the central figure.

At whatever stage the idea of a parody (or burlesque or travesty) came to him, it is basic to the novel. Cervantes is one of the world's great parodists, like Joyce. For contemporaries much of the delight of reading *Don Quixote* must have come from recognizing specific or typical incidents, situations and turns of phrase transplanted from their exotic habitat in the romances of chivalry and now blooming with pleasing oddity in its homely soil *Don Quixote* is built on intertextuality.

Romance seems to have a latent potential for parody and irony, waiting to be drawn upon by the writer and/or the reader, but not necessarily both. Hence in many original romances those moments or extended passages which cause some readers to suspect that the author

intended generic or self-parody or some sort of comic deflation – a
suspicion which may well never enter the heads of other readers. This is
particularly liable to happen to works now far removed in time.
Martorell's *Tirant lo Blanc*, for instance, has undoubtedly been read in
different ways by different people at different times.[1] At its best,
romance seems to demand a childlike simple-mindedness of both writer
and reader, which at one extreme can degenerate into plain silliness and
at the other into a cynical exploitation of generic convention. Writers of
some chivalric romances in Renaissance Spain could be disconcertingly
ambiguous about their own books (Riley, 1962D, pp. 166–8). In French
continuations of *Amadís de Gaula* the ridiculous side was sometimes
stressed almost to the point of anti-chivalric parody (O'Connor, 1970E,
pp. 103–5, 216–17). To tip chivalric romance over into comic parody
needed no great finesse. To use it with just the right blend of ridicule and
indulgence, as Chaucer and Ariosto did before Cervantes, required a
superior sensibility.

Don Quixote is a complex parody, only part of which is conventional.
For the most part it does not take the relatively straightforward form it
does in Pulci or Ariosto, for instance. The work is not a romance of
chivalry rendered comic by direct exaggeration, contretemps and incon-
gruities. The action is shifted into a different kind of work altogether
and thereby distanced from its original. The comedy of it arises from the
incompatibility of fantastic antiquated romance in a realistic modern
setting. The immediate agent of the parody is Don Quixote himself
rather than Cervantes.

Don Quixote's whole endeavour is to *be*, quite literally, a hero of
chivalric romance, which means that he is trying to turn his life into a
romance of chivalry. He even believes that his actions are being recorded
in a book (he is right in this, but the book is not what he thinks).
Inevitably he fails, because life cannot be treated that way. The result is
not a successful imitation of literature, but more like an inadvertent
comic parody of it. The effort is all the more absurd because the kind of
literature he chooses to imitate is not just fiction but peculiarly fabulous
fiction. The comic and ironic possibilities of this sort of parody were
endless.

Despite the extra remove, a few of the original situations are obvious
even to the modern reader: notably the retirement of the distraught
Amadis to Peña Pobre, avowedly imitated by the Knight in the Sierra
Morena (I, 25–6). Other incidents in *Don Quixote*, like the adventure of
the funeral party (I, 19), a quiet parody of an episode in *Palmerín de*

Inglaterra, are only known to most of us now through editorial foot-
notes.[2] The vigil and dedication of the hero's arms (I, 3), the fight with
the Basque squire (I, 8–9), the letter to Dulcinea (I, 25), the encounter
with the lion (II, 17), the Cave of Montesinos (II, 22–3), the boat on the
River Ebro (II, 29), the challenges, boasts and combats, and more
besides, would all have seemed divertingly familiar to Cervantes's early
readers. It is a tribute to the author's comic genius, however, that the
humour does not entirely depend on knowing the originals. If it did, his
novel would be hopelessly outdated.

For present purposes, it is not very important which were the books
Cervantes knew and used most. They certainly included Montalvo's
Amadís, probably *Don Belianís de Grecia*, the *Espejo de príncipes* and the
rest named in the scrutiny of Don Quixote's library (I, 6). The many
parodic reminiscences of *Amadís* may stand for all.[3]

Although not the first of the romances of chivalry printed in Spain as
the Priest claims (I, 6; i, 110), *Amadís de Gaula* started the Renaissance
wave of fascination with the genre in western Europe. The first printed
edition (Saragossa, 1508) is a reworking by Garci Rodríguez de Montalvo
of what was probably an early fourteenth-century original. There is a
Portuguese claim to authorship, but effectively the work is Spanish. A
fragment of a manuscript version dating from around 1420 exists. Montalvo claimed to have 'corrected' books 1 to 3 and 'translated and
amended' book 4, which probably means that he composed most of it. He
also wrote the first sequel, *Las sergas de Esplandián* (1510), the exploits of
the son of Amadis, book 5 in the series. Amadis of Gaul is in the Arthurian
tradition (see Williamson, 1984D, pp. 29 ff.) and achieved enormous
popularity. This is evident in the number of verifiable Spanish editions of
the first four books (twenty by 1600) and in the sequels and translations.
Continuations in Spanish bring the number of books up to twelve, Italian
ones raise the figure to eighteen, and French and German ones to a grand
total of twenty-four. Though *Amadís* came relatively late to England, this
supremely nostalgic literary vogue knew no frontiers.

There is some direct parody by Cervantes of the apparatus of chivalric
romance. A fleeting instance, surely based on Montalvo, is the alleged
discovery of the epitaphs and verses, at the end of Part I, on half-legible
parchments in a leaden box found in an old hermitage. In a very similar
way book 4 of *Amadís de Gaula*, with the *Sergas de Esplandián*, had

by good fortune appeared in a stone tomb which was found underground in a hermitage near Constantinople, and brought to these

parts of Spain by a Hungarian merchant, [written] in a script and on a parchment of such antiquity that it could only be read with great difficulty by those who knew the language (*Amadís de Gaula*, bk 1, prol.; 1959–60C, i, 9)

This was a well-worn fiction of medieval literature, parodied also by Rabelais at the beginning of his book of *Gargantua*. More important is the pretence that the manuscript of the bulk of *Don Quixote* was in Arabic, and most important of all the attribution of the 'history' to the Moorish chronicler, sage and magician, Cide Hamete Benengeli: both devices common to the romances of chivalry. (*Don Cirongilio de Tracia*, 1545, was represented as translated out of the Greek by the sage Novarco; and *Felixmarte de Yrcania*, 1556, as being out of an Italian version by Petrarch out of Plutarch's Latin rendering of a Greek original!) Whether or not the highly erratic chronology of the *Quixote* is also romance parody is less certain. But the best explanation of the wildly discontinuous time-sequence of Part II is certainly that Cervantes was parodying the mythic time-cycles favoured in the old romances (Murillo, 1975D).

The basic structural features of *Don Quixote* show only sporadic similarities with the average romance of chivalry, and I see no evidence of any attempt to model the book closely and consistently on this pattern. Some features correspond, others do not, or only in part. The chivalric romance normally begins at 'the beginning' with the parentage and birth of the hero. The *Quixote* opens with a hero who verges on 50, and we never learn more than a little of his 'prehistory'. On the other hand, the suspenseful interruptions are quite typical. The emphasis on the finality of Don Quixote's death in Part II (prol. and ch. 74) is certainly not parody in the first instance, but is designed to prevent his resurrection by any new Avellanedas. However, there was precedent in chivalric literature both for such an event as this and for attempts to forestall it. Feliciano de Silva revived Amadis of Gaul without more ado in the ninth book of the series, after the writer Juan Díaz had been so ill advised as to kill him off in the eighth. And the *Death of King Arthur* ended with the flat statement that Master Walter Map had now 'brought everything to a proper conclusion according to the way it happened; and he finishes his book so completely that no one can afterwards add anything to the story that is not complete falsehood' (1978C, p. 235). It is always difficult to dispatch the popular heroes of romance. Ian Fleming is dead, but James Bond lives on to have still more adventures.

Some of the parody of Cervantes is so delicate that excesses, or what now look like excesses, in the originals are actually toned down. The chivalric heroes were supermen of remarkable longevity as well as stamina. Amadís of Gaul was 80 years old in book 7; after resurrection in book 9, he carried on in his venerable prime, and a maiden could still fall in love with him in book 10. None of the major male characters in the full series died before book 21, and some of the warriors were well over 100 years old (O'Connor, 1970E, p. 124). This was simply in the Arthurian tradition. It is said of the combatants in the last great battle: 'they all knew Lancelot was the finest knight in the world and younger than Sir Gawain by about twenty-one years. At that time Sir Gawain must have been seventy-six years old and King Arthur ninety-two' (*Death of King Arthur*, 1978C, p. 186). By these standards Don Quixote, pushing 50, is almost a sibling. Much of the funniest humour in the novel stems precisely from the unsuitability of his years to the arduous exercise of knight errantry, but the fact remains that his prime models were still active as greybeards considerably older than he.

The subtlety of Cervantes's parody sometimes consists of a peculiarly refined exaggeration, however. In the best courtly-love tradition of *amor de lonh*, a hero like Esplandián could love Leonorina simply by repute (*de oídas*). This is essentially the situation of Don Quixote with Dulcinea; but he invents the repute as well, and everything else about the lady except her origin in Aldonza Lorenzo. What makes her Cervantes's supreme parody figure is that she is the courtly-platonic mistress *par excellence*, the ideally perfect dream-object of impossible amours.

On another level, words and phrases from *Amadís* can be found on many a page of the *Quixote*. If Dulcinea is 'peerless', so was Oriana. Marvels 'never before seen or heard of' in *Don Quixote* were so described in *Amadís* and elsewhere. Even such an inconspicuous sentence as 'had he dealt him a second blow there would have been no need of a surgeon to cure him' (I, 3; i, 91) appears in the same work (not to mention a close parallel in the *Death of King Arthur*).[4] Cervantes obviously relished the exquisite absurdity of phrases like the following, which readers of *Don Quixote* in Spanish will immediately recognize: 'quitar los tuertos y desaguisados de muchos que los reciben, especialmente de las dueñas y doncellas', and 'flor y espejo de toda caballería' (both from *Amadís*); 'la sobre todas espejo de la hermosura princesa Florisbella' (from *Don Belianís*). The letter Don Quixote entrusts to Sancho to bear to Dulcinea from the wilds of Sierra Morena could hardly fail to remind readers of the one which Oriana addressed to Amadis, causing him to retreat in despair to the island of Peña Pobre. It begins:

> He who is pierced by the spear point of absence and wounded in the strings of his heart, sweetest Dulcinea del Toboso, wishes you the health he does not have
>
> (El ferido de punta de ausencia y el llagado de las telas del corazón, dulcísima Dulcinea del Toboso, te envía la salud que el no tiene: I, 25; i, 315)

Oriana's letter is inscribed on the outside:

> I am the damsel pierced by the point of the sword through the heart and you are the one who wounded me
>
> (Yo soy la donzella herida de punta de espada por el coraçon, y vos soys el que me feristes: II, 44; ii, 371)

Perhaps above all Cervantes savoured some of the splendidly ludicrous names in the books of chivalry – names like Contumeliano de Fenicia, Ledardín de Fajarque, Angriote de Estravaus, Pintiquiniestra, Cataquefarás and Quirieleisón – and especially those of ogres like Mandansabul and Famongomadán of the Boiling Lake, and the giantesses Gromadaza and Andandona. Cervantes's own inventions, like the warriors Timonel de Carcajona, Espartafilardo del Bosque and Brandabarbarán de Boliche, the princesses Miulina, Micomicona and Antonomasia, the giant Caraculiambro and the unforgettable cross-eyed ogre Pandafilando de la Fosca Vista, are no more hilarious than their chivalresque prototypes. Giants tend to be a bit comic as well as terrifying.

There are also narrative passages of sustained parody. The more comic ones read like epitomes of some adventure in a book of chivalry and are usually invented by characters who have become embroiled in Don Quixote's affairs (Micomicona, I, 30, and Countess Trifaldi, II, 38–9, for instance). Those where the Knight himself indulges his fantasy are more restrained. Even the splendid description of the warrior nobles in battle array with their troops drawn from peoples of the Ancient World – all of them actually sheep – is in itself only comic in the choice of names and heraldic devices (I, 18). Although the physical reality of the combatants is so different, the reminiscence of countless romances and epics reaching back to the *Iliad* is obvious. The two chivalric episodes Don Quixote brilliantly extemporizes in Part I, chapter 21 (the Fortunate Knight), and chapter 50 (the Knight of the Boiling Lake), are even freer of crude burlesque. They are so faithful to their models, and their descriptive vividness and the pace with which they are told are such, that the pleasure they give comes from the perception of the imitation. Parody, after all, is not necessarily comic.

Nor is the parody confined to the chivalresque. The pastoral episodes in the book naturally evoke a style appropriate to their kind of fiction, and transitional styles may be used to bridge the gap with the more realistic world which Don Quixote and Sancho inhabit. Whether or not any of the four major pastoral episodes themselves (Grisóstomo and Marcela, and the fair Leandra in Part I; Camacho's wedding and the simulated Arcadia in Part II) can properly be described as parody with comic intent is debatable. I find it impossible to tell whether or when Cervantes's tongue has moved into his cheek. Perhaps, too, the second inn in Part I is a parody of Felicia's palace in Montemayor's *Diana*, and perhaps the rebuff of Rocinante's advances by the Galician mares (I, 15) is a pastoral spoof, as some critics hold, but I do not see how we shall ever know.

On quite a different scale, the decorative effulgence of a metaphorical sunrise which momentarily floods the main narrative between instalments of the Grisóstomo–Marcela story is another matter. The clause opening chapter 13, 'Scarcely had the day begun to show itself on the balconies of the Orient' (i, 167), becomes pastoral parody by virtue of its stylistic isolation in the immediate context and association with the pastoral episode in the preceding and the succeeding chapters.

Parody of the picaresque can be as hard to pinpoint with certainty as pastoral. But when the burliest and most villainous-looking member of the chain-gang, Ginés de Pasamonte, presents himself as writing his autobiography, which he is confident will outclass *Lazarillo* 'and all other works of that kind' (I, 22; i, 271), the explicit association with a fictional genre is a signal to alert the reader. It is certainly possible at this point to see Ginés, author and galley slave, as a parodic reminiscence of Guzmán. His later appearances, disguised first as a gypsy, and in Part II as Maese Pedro the puppet master, also suggest that protean ability of the *pícaro* to assume masks and efface himself in other personae. It is significant that the picaresque parody goes accompanied by some critical discussion of the literature which occasioned it, just as happens with the chivalric romance parody on a much greater scale.

The encounter with Ginés is not the first of its kind in the book, though. The innkeeper of Part I, chapters 2–3, is cast in the same mould. Not only is he the first of the many jokers who will play up to the deluded hidalgo and lead him on, but also he describes his life in terms which are a calculated picaresque travesty of the chivalresque. In his youth, he says, he had followed the same honourable profession as the Knight, in search of adventures (here he reels off a string of place-names notorious as the haunts of ruffians), 'doing many misdeeds, wooing many widows, undoing a few maidens and cheating a few school-children'. This inverts the Knight errant's formula, *deshacer tuertos*, *socorrer viudas*, etc., used in the previous chapter. Later he had retired to his 'castle' with his own and other people's property, ready to welcome all wandering knights and relieve them of their goods (I, 3; i, 88–9). There is something memorable in this encounter between the *picaro* has-been and the would-be chivalric hero. Though foreshadowed in *Baldo* (1542), the Spanish adaptation of Folengo's work, and for a fleeting moment visualized in *Guzmán*,[5] only now is there a full confrontation of the two generic kinds in a third kind of fiction big enough to hold both of them. It is hard to see how else this could happen except through the agency of parody.

(ii) THE QUESTION OF SOURCES

It used to be commonly supposed that there must have been a living model for Don Quixote. One of the most popular candidates for this honour, though in a rather different sense from the rest, was Cervantes himself. Even nowadays, adaptors of the book for stage, screen and radio seem to find the identification irresistible. There is something to be said for it, but it is doubtful that the Knight is much more essentially a projection of his creator than Sancho Panza is. Other contemporary figures have come under scrutiny because of their name or odd behaviour. A favourite is a relative of Doña Catalina's in Esquivias, apparently called Don Alonso Quijada. There has also been speculation about an eccentric conquistador, seeker of El Dorado and man of letters, named Gonzalo Jiménez de Quesada. Neither is compellingly probable.

Possible sources of basic inspiration, if not exactly models, have been discerned in various anecdotes and accounts of the time, some allegedly factual, of persons with obsessions or delusions or who reacted extravagantly to literary fiction. Cervantes could have read in Tommasso Garzoni of a man who took one of the windmills on the River Po for a giant. He could have heard of the quixotic Giulio Spiriti, obsessed with the idea of succouring others and liberating prisoners. But could he have known the story told by Sacchetti of the septuagenarian Agnolo di Ser Gherardo, who made a fool of himself by taking up the knightly sport of tilting and getting thrown from his bony old horse? *Il Trecentonovelle* of Sacchetti was not published until 1724. There were anecdotes about people whose reactions to fiction were extreme enough to be remembered, recorded and laughed at. In his *Suma de Filosofía* (1547), Alonso de Fuentes told of a man who went mad through reading too many fantastic tales. López Pinciano (1596) related how a wedding guest was found to have passed out with the shock of reading that Amadis of Gaul had died. There was the Milanese who burst into tears on hearing of the death of Orlando, went home and could hardly be induced to eat by his wife; the man who never left the house without taking *Palmerín de Oliva* with him; and the man ready to swear on the gospel that every word of *Amadís de Gaula* was true; and others. Or was Don Quixote suggested by the comic ugly knight Camilote in the romance of *Primaleón* and in Gil Vicente's dramatized version of this, *Don Duardos*? Or by Folengo's *Baldus* or the comic chivalric *romanzi* of Pulci, Boiardo or Ariosto?[6] Or even by some knight of chivalric literature before Orlando, who went off his head for a while – Lancelot, Tristan, Yvain?

A more immediate and much discussed possibility is the anonymous *Entremés de los romances*, a farce in which the chief character, Bartolo, loses his wits over the ballads which were so popular at the time and whose heroes he proceeds to imitate. There are detailed resemblances with chapter 5 of Part I. The trouble is that the work, although thought to have been composed between 1588 and 1591, did not appear in print until 1611 or 1612. Who imitated whom? The matter is not yet conclusively settled, but the most recent opinion holds that Cervantes was the originator.[7]

A major possibility of partial inspiration which has come under scrutiny derives from a comparison of Sancho Panza and Don Quixote with the traditional figures of Carnival and Lent respectively (Redondo, 1978D, 1980D). 'The chubby character with the corpulent stomach surrounded by rich and substantial eatables', and the tall emaciated Lenten figure, riding a scraggy horse (Redondo, 1978D, p. 42). The analogy is not fatally weakened by the fact that Lent was an old woman, but the connection with Sancho is the more striking of the two. His surname means 'stomach', he always enjoys his victuals and he is more than once accused of gluttony. In particular, the elaborate episode of his mock-governorship in the 'Isle' of Barataria (II, 42–53) is full of carnival reminiscences. Don Quixote is merely a frugal eater but, when mounted on Rocinante, there is an iconographic resemblance.

Precedent already existed in the distinctive shape of a pair of famous Italian comics, popular from 1574 on. These were Bottarga (a fat man) and Ganassa (thin), who seem to have had some association with the traditional figures of Carnival and Lent. Cervantes can hardly have failed to know of them at least, and it seems very plausible that, consciously or unconsciously, his creation of the figure of Don Quixote owes something to Ganassa.[8]

Apart from the festive humour, it is the iconographic aspect which is most important here. The folk-emblematic antecedents of Cervantes's two heroes can have contributed little or nothing to the subtleties of novelistic characterization, but they do much to explain their unusually powerful visual appeal. No two figures in Western literature are more immediately and universally recognizable, even to people who have never read the book. This effect is due not just to Cervantes's gift for vivid economical description, but also to something like an archetypal element in their recognizability.[9] A carnival ancestry also helps to explain why Cervantes's figures came so quickly to appear in festivities and processions worldwide.

All this said, it is prudent not to make too much of the importance of any of these precedents, historical, literary or even pictorial. Literary investigators, ever on the lookout for sources and affinities, are apt to underrate the imaginative originality of creative writers. Where live models are concerned, Cervantes may easily have felt as Graham Greene does:

I know very well from experience that it is only possible for me to base a very minor and transient character on a real person. A real person stands in the way of the imagination. (1980E, p. 298)

The same could well go for major literary 'models'.

NOTES: CHAPTER 4

1   By the author's contemporaries, by Cervantes and his, by nineteenth- and twentieth-century readers. See Terry (1982E), pp. 177 ff.; Yates (1980E), pp. 181 ff.; Riley (1962D), pp. 24–5. In the admittedly untypical early fourteenth-century romance of *El*

caballero Cifar the hero is briefly depicted at rest with his head in his wife's lap while she delouses him (1954C, ch. 39, p. 89). Deliberate comedy is almost certainly out of the question here.

2 Especially in the editions of Clemencín and Rodríguez Marín. See also Riquer (1961D; and 1967D, passim). And, on wider aspects of parody, Neuschäfer (1963D), Meyer (1968E), pp. 59 ff.

3 About sixty episodes from *Amadís de Gaula* are recalled in *Don Quixote* according to Gebhart (1911E, p. 220).

4 'Guerrehet fell from his horse to the ground in such a condition that he had no need of a doctor' (1978C, p. 122).

5 *Guzmán*, II, iii; 3, 788, where Guzmán briefly compares the damsels of chivalry and the books they figure in with himself and his novel. On the *Baldo*, see Blecua (1971–2E).

6 Maxime Chevalier (1966E) has shown that the detailed influence of *Orlando furioso* on *Don Quixote* is less than had been thought. Of course, Ariosto's poem remains a major link between the medieval romance and the *Quixote* in the history of fiction; the connection lies more in the sphere of narrative techniques than in types of character represented.

7 Murillo (1983D).

8 Joly (1976E); Redondo (1980D), pp. 40–4. A sixteenth-century engraving of Harlequin (possibly Ganassa), as a knight errant, wearing a tripod cooking-pot for a helmet, and riding a bony ass, looks remarkably like Don Quixote. It is reproduced in Oreglia (1968E), p. 13. I am grateful to Mr Daniel Rogers for drawing it to my attention. It also appears in Joly (1976E) and is discussed by her and Redondo, among others. On other emblematic aspects of Don Quixote, see Márquez Villanueva (1980D). Bakhtin (1968E, pp. 20–3) first saw the importance of the carnival precedent. On the carnivalesque aspects of Sancho's colloquy with Tomé Cecial and one or two other incidents, see Forcione (1984D), pp. 205–7.

9 In Calderón's *El alcalde de Zalamea* (*c*.1640), Don Mendo is thus described on first appearing:

> Un hombre
> que de un flaco Rocinante
> a la vuelta desa esquina
> se apeó, y en rostro y talle
> parece aquel don Quijote
> de quien Miguel de Cervantes
> escribió las aventuras.

(Act I, 11. 213–19)

CHAPTER 5

Don Quixote and Sancho in Part I

Generalizations about the character of Don Quixote are unavoidable; but they are often untrustworthy, for two main reasons. One is the built-in combination of madness and sanity, the other is the fact that the character markedly develops in the course of the novel. Yet again and again one finds the Quixote of the early chapters treated as definitive, as though the outlook and behaviour of the man who enters Barcelona were no different from when he defied windmills. However, it is no oversimplification to state that Don Quixote is central to the novel and that his madness is central to him. Almost everything relates back to him. Even the external episodes, the intercalated stories, can be justified by reference to him and Sancho.

Cervantes has a habit of blurring the distinction between the person of his hero and the written work in which he figures. At the start of the first prologue he refers to 'this book' as 'my brainchild', and then 'the story of a lean, shrivelled whimsical child' almost imperceptibly becomes Don Quixote himself, of whom, says the author, he is really the stepfather rather than the father. A moment later he is speaking of 'the defects you may see in this son of mine', meaning the book (i, 50–1). This, with other elaborated instances, suggests that for the author the central character was pre-eminent over all other aspects of the book.[1] He can hardly have thought of his *Galatea* in the same way.

While most heroes of romance are interchangeable, focus on individual character is probably the great distinguishing mark of the modern realistic novel. There is a difference between wanting to find out what will happen next to the hero and wondering what the hero will decide to do or how he will behave when something happens to him, as one does with Don Quixote. This is also how other characters in the book who know him or know about him tend to react. Américo Castro insisted in his later writings (1962D, 1966D, 1971D) that *Don Quixote* shows

character not as a fixed entity but as a self-defining existence and a con-
tinuous process of becoming. It was the genius of Cervantes, he said,
'to give expression to the way the invented figure finds itself existing in
what happens to it, rather than narrate or describe what happens to it'
(1971D, p. 25). In fact Cervantes does both, but Don Quixote and
Sancho are primarily defined by what they do and say, and Castro was
right to underline the originality and importance in a work of fiction of
showing a life directed from within.[2]

There was a kind of precedent in spiritual autobiographies like St
Theresa's. In prose fiction *La Celestina* probably came closest to convey-
ing the sense of inner lives geared to the physical existences which contained them. Something of the sort is also true of *Lazarillo*. However, as
Rosalie Colie has said, the typical *picaro* does not 'develop'; rather, 'his
sense of reality deepens with his serial experiences. His consciousness, if
not his literary personality, fills out and takes substance' (1973E, pp.
94–5). But it still tends to lack definition. Even Guzmán de Alfarache, in
his remarkable schizoid way, tends, like so many first-person narrators,
to dissolve into undefined if articulate consciousness.

Unlike the *picaros*, unlike even Emma Bovary, Don Quixote is depicted in his unique individuality rather than as a typical sort of person.
Who, after all, have you ever known or heard of who went off his head
through reading too much fiction? Yet we know almost at once that Don
Quixote, like Sancho, is one of us, as Dr Johnson noted. He is not a type
or an archetype and he is too complex to be a caricature. He is best
summed up, perhaps, as an extreme case, an extension of certain human
proclivities. That is one definition of madness, loosely speaking, and
that is what primarily marks out Quixote from the other characters and
from you and me.

Although his dissimilarity from others is obvious throughout the
book, in the famous opening passage he is first presented, surprisingly,
not in his uniqueness, but as one of a type or class, defined in terms of his
social and economic circumstances.

> In a village in La Mancha, whose name I do not wish to recall, there
> lived not long ago a gentleman, one of those with a lance in the rack,
> an ancient shield, a lean hack and a greyhound for coursing . . .

> (En un lugar de La Mancha, de cuyo nombre no quiero acordarme, no
> ha mucho tiempo que vivía un hidalgo de los de lanza en astillero,
> adarga antigua, rocín flaco y galgo corredor . . . : I, 1; i, 69)[3]

Hidalgos were members of the lesser gentry, the next in rank below *caballeros*. They might be of ancient lineage or newly arrived, rich or very poor. They sported coats of arms and enjoyed the coveted privilege of exemption from taxation. Don Quixote's financial circumstances appear to be a little below the mean, but he is certainly not impoverished like the Squire in *Lazarillo*.

The approach to the person of the hero is roundabout but swift. From his unnamed domicile we circle in via his social status, possessions, diet, clothing and household to his approximate age and appearance. At this point he almost fades into anonymity. There is a doubt about his surname – was it Quijada, Quesana, Quejana? This is not parody of chivalric romance, it is something altogether different.

Out of this socio-economic mediocrity and virtual anonymity is about to emerge the most individualistic of heroes. The figure best known for his ability to live untrammelled in the realm of his own imagination is first carefully situated in the confining context of his material circumstances. The whole of Don Quixote's story will rest on the conjunction, conflict and interplay of these two worlds, the material one in which he moves and the inner one within his mind.[4] The decisive dislocation between them comes within a page or so of the first sentence, when, following the description of his favourite reading, he goes mad. This is the most dynamic development of character conceivable. Mad he will remain in greater, then lesser degree until he recovers his sanity on his deathbed, 125 chapters later. The madness of Don Quixote is the point of departure for all that follows in the book and is absolutely basic. So it is important to be clear about it. Cervantes is quite unambiguous about its causes and the form it takes.

He gives slight but adequate indications of the grounds for this peculiar derangement in contemporary medical terms, which were based on the theory of the humours.[5] The energetic life of the middle-aged Alonso Quijano (an early riser and a keen huntsman) together with his dry appearance suggest, initially, a choleric temperament. But his health is damaged: 'through little sleep and much reading his brain dried up' (I, 1; i, 73). 'Adustion', or burning up of the choler, would turn his yellow bile black and result in an unnatural melancholy. 'He is, then, a melancholy madman of choler adust, and afterwards, when the humour has cooled, a melancholy type, of melancholy adust; of hot and dry, then cold and dry qualities' (Kong, 1980D, p. 234). His imagination is affected, not his other faculties. As Burton noted of melancholics in his *Anatomy of Melancholy*, 'their memories are most part good, they have

happy wits, and excellent apprehensions' (Kong, 1980D, p. 203). Most
of Quixote's symptoms and his physical type can be checked in Burton
or other authorities of the age, and not exclusively in Dr Juan Huarte de
San Juan's celebrated *Examen de ingenios* to which Cervantes has long
been considered peculiarly indebted, though given the fame of this work
in and out of Spain it is likely enough that he knew it. In the title of the
book Don Quixote is called *ingenioso*, which is probably best translated
here as 'imaginative', with connotations of subtlety in the word 'ingenious'. Whatever else Cervantes may have intended by it, the term calls
attention to his hyperactive imagination clearly enough.[6]

The summer heat, lack of proper meals and loss of sleep attendant on
his chivalresque mode of life combine to aggravate his condition.
Prescribed therapy included 'humouring' the patient with 'some feigned
lie, strange news, witty device, artificial invention'.[7] This is just what
the Priest and Barber and, in Part II, the Salamanca graduate Sansón
Carrasco do. The best-intentioned of Quixote's friends overstep the
mark at times, however. The danger of overdoing such treatment is
obvious: humouring the patient easily becomes leading him on, and can
end in baiting. Luis Vives wrote with compassion in *De subventione
pauperum*:

> Such a deterioration in this most noble of faculties is to be pitied and
> whoever has suffered it should be treated with such care and
> gentleness that his madness is not increased or even given nourish-
> ment, as happens with the raving when they are irritated and
> provoked, and with the foolish when their inane words and actions are
> approved and assented to, or when they are incited to babble with
> even greater absurdity, as if to foster and feed dim-witted folly itself.
> What greater inhumanity can be named than that of making someone
> mad give occasion for laughter and turn such misfortune into matter
> for amusement?[8]

The degrading treatment of the insane throughout Europe is well
known. They were regarded as objects of mirth even by the most
humane. But it is hypocritical to go to the other extreme and pretend
that deranged behaviour is never funny. The antics of Don Quixote are
the prime source of the book's comedy. The reader joins the numerous
other characters in the novel who laugh at them – which precludes
neither him nor them from pitying Don Quixote on occasion.[9] It is
interesting that there is never any suggestion that Don Quixote ought to

be locked up in an institution, which is what happens to the Quixote of Avellaneda's sequel. Nor is there any mention of witchcraft in connection with him, in spite of his preoccupation with enchanters. One must conclude that Cervantes wished to avoid the associations which lunatic asylums and necromancy conjure up.

After the initial data about Don Quixote's material circumstances and person, Cervantes briskly describes how the romances of chivalry become his obsession. This introduces the rich world of Feliciano de Silva's intricate prose, the battle-scarred Don Belianís and discussions with the Priest and Barber over Palmerín, Amadís and the rest, whose relative merits are discussed as those of football stars or cricketers might be today. For a moment we see how Don Quixote might have played a more normal part in this milieu as a writer: he often contemplated writing a conclusion to the unfinished romance of *Don Belianís*. But his addiction drives him over the edge.

> His imagination became filled with all that he read in the books, with enchantments, quarrels, battles, challenges, wounds, gallantries, amours, storms and impossible extravagances; and so fixed did it become in his mind that the whole contrivance of those famous fanciful inventions he read was true that for him there was no history in the world more authentic.

> (Llenósele la fantasía de todo aquello que leía en los libros, así de encantamientos como de pendencias, batallas, desafíos, heridas, requiebros, amores, tormentas y disparates imposibles; y asentósele de tal modo en la imaginación que era verdad toda aquella máquina de aquellas sonadas soñadas invenciones que leía, que para él no había otra historia más cierta en al mundo: p. 73.)

He has come to believe that the fabulous fictions of the romances of chivalry are historical fact. This is the irreducible core of his madness, and all the rest grows out of it. The next sentence makes it clear that he sees no distinction between a historical hero, Ruy Díaz, el Cid, and a fictitious one, the Knight of the Burning Sword (Amadis of Greece), except inasmuch as he is more impressed by the feats of the latter.

The second aspect of Don Quixote's madness is a major consequence of the first and follows hard on its heels.

> So, having completely lost his wits, he fell into the strangest notion that any madman in the world ever had, and this was that it appeared

to him suitable and necessary, both for the increase of his honour and the service of his state, to become a knight errant and go about the world with horse and armour in search of adventures and the exercise of all that he had read that the knights errant engaged in, redressing every kind of wrong, and exposing himself to situations and dangers with the overcoming of which he might earn eternal fame and renown.

(En efecto, rematado ya su juicio, vino a dar en el más estraño pensamiento que jamás dio loco en el mundo, y fue que le pareció convenible y necesario, así para el aumento de su honra como para el servicio de su república, hacerse caballero andante, y irse por todo el mundo con sus armas y caballo a buscar las aventuras y a ejercitarse en todo aquello que él había leído que los caballeros andantes se ejercitaban, deshaciendo todo género de agravio, y poniéndose en ocasiones y peligros donde, acabándolos, cobrase eterno nombre y fama: pp. 74–5.)

If story-book chivalry is historical fact, then it is not illogical to become a knight errant, whether chivalry has gone out of fashion or not. Honour and renown, public service, adventures, the righting of wrongs – not a highly organized programme perhaps, but the essentials of chivalry. Whatever had happened to the age of chivalry, Don Quixote's mission to restore it in some sense confirms its immanence in the world.

The third aspect of his madness is not really demonstrated until the second chapter. This is when his mind's eye imposes on external reality images from the world of chivalric romance, turning inns into castles, country wenches into princesses, windmills into giants, sheep into armies and so forth. His susceptibility to sensorial illusion reaches its height in the night scene with Maritornes at the inn, when his sight, hearing, touch and smell are all affected (I, 16). It is noticeable that all such delusions of Don Quixote's have a physical origin: he does not conjure hallucinations out of thin air, except when he is or has just been asleep and dreaming (e.g. I, 7). When real people and things comport themselves and conform closely enough to chivalresque pattern, Don Quixote accepts them without introducing any significant distortion. Such is the case with the adventures of the boy Andrés (I, 4), the funeral procession (I, 19) and the galley slaves (I, 22), for instance. When other people knowingly play up to his fantasies, there is an elaboration of the situation.

These are, as it were, the bare bones of Quixote's lunacy as Cervantes unequivocally establishes it at the start of the novel. It is not a capricious or all-encompassing madness, but inclined only in the direction of his chivalric obsession, as is remarked in the course of the story (e.g. II, 43). When distracted from this, he can talk and act as normally as anyone else, and other people marvel at the sense and intelligence of his words. He is called a madman with 'lucid intervals' (II, 18; ii, 173). The mixture particularly intrigues other characters, such as the Canon of Toledo (I, 49), and others in Part II.

For the most part it is a straightforward matter, from a common-sense point of view, to distinguish what is mad from what is sane in his behaviour, even when the combination is quite intricate (Close, 1978[1]D). However, this does not mean that his madness does not have any of the problematical implications which readers over the last two centuries have found in it. Nor can Cervantes have been blind to all of them. It is not only since the development of modern psychiatry that there has been a more complex view of mental states than the rough-and-ready distinction which law-prescribing social interests require. Erasmus made a simple distinction which shows up the difficulty of drawing lines, when he wrote:

A shortsighted man who thinks a mule is an ass is not considered insane; nor is someone who thinks that a trite poem is a very good one immediately thought to be insane. However, if a person is continually and extraordinarily deceived not only by his senses but even his judgment, then people will think him, at least, very nearly mad.[10]

(Cervantes, incidentally, plays with the first of these two examples on a number of occasions, as we shall see; and with the second when the narrator comments with sly amusement on how Don Lorenzo preened himself on Don Quixote's lavish praise of his indifferent poem: II, 18.) *The Praise of Folly*, in which the above observation occurs, is the most famous book of the age on the complex and paradoxical natures of folly and madness, wisdom and common sense.

It would be rash to assert that Cervantes had read *The Praise of Folly* or other works of Erasmus, given that after the Indexes of 1551 and 1559 Erasmus' writings were largely proscribed in Spain. However, that did not put a complete stop to their circulation, still less to their continuing influence. A generation earlier, particularly in the late 1520s and 1530s, probably no country in Europe had given a more enthusiastic reception to the doctrines of Erasmus. They were espoused at the court of Charles V, put to the service of imperial policy, and they made a profound mark on intellectual life and on literature which was still visible well after the Council of Trent. To no other major ideological current of the century do the writings of Cervantes look more attuned than Erasmianism.[11]

The Erasmian notion of the 'wise fool' clearly percolates into *Don Quixote*, though more in association with Sancho than with his master. Don Quixote's madness, like anyone else's, shows grey areas in certain places when you try to set precise limits to it. His actions and words exhibit deceptions of the senses and errors of judgement which range from palpable lunacy to the trivial and excusable.

His insanity has what may be called a public and a private face. From the former point of view, his missionary zeal often brings him into conflict with the norms of organized society, and on occasion makes him a public menace. Like the *picaros* he is at odds with society, but unlike them he seeks to reform it. The most spectacular clash occurs when he sets free the chain-gang of convicts, justifying his action by a sublime appeal to the Christian precept of forgiveness not punishment (I, 22; i, 273, and I, 30; i, 371). Not surprisingly, the Holy Brotherhood (predecessor of the Civil Guard) are soon after him. There is a touch of the fanatic about him, like any Utopian activist, when he puts himself outside the law. The members of his profession, he says, are ministers of God on earth and the arms that execute His justice (I, 13; i, 173); and who, he asks, does not know that knights errant are exempt from all judicial authority, that their law is their sword, their charters their courage, their statutes their will? Which one ever paid tax, duty or toll – or paid his tailor or castle warden (I, 45; i, 547–8)? This rather Byronic side of Don Quixote endeared him to nineteenth-century Romantics, one of whom, the poet Espronceda, apparently took the second speech seriously (to judge from his epigraph to the first part of *El estudiante de Salamanca*), which of course no seventeenth-century reader would have done. However, righting wrongs, and even arrogant proclamations are one thing; threatening to beat up innocent travellers on the road if they won't admit that Dulcinea or some other lady is unsurpassably beautiful (I, 4, and II, 58) is another. The unacceptable face of chivalry perhaps.

Incompatibility between private and socially accepted norms leads the behaviour of an individual to be judged mad or criminal. From Don Quixote's point of view there is a not merely justified, but an inspired logic and consistency in the criteria by which he seeks to regulate his career. This is well argued by Edwin Williamson (1984D, p. 144). It was a premiss of medieval culture, of which the chivalric romance was an integral part, that everything was charged with meaning. The symbols of a transcendent order of divine truth were built into the world we inhabit. (One might add that in *The Quest of the Holy Grail* this is made almost painfully explicit, with saintly hermits repeatedly explaining the meaning of events to the participants, who are thus very conscious of living allegorically, in no mere literary sense of the term, but literally.) In taking up chivalry Don Quixote is reverting to a code designed to bridge the gap between the visible world and this transcendent order. By reviving the practice of chivalry he wants to renovate the degenerated world where appearances no longer correspond to the hidden reality – to abolish the discrepancy between the actual and the potential. For this reason Dulcinea is more real for him than Aldonza Lorenzo. From a public and practical point of view his single-handed efforts to implement his beliefs are inevitably mad and laughable. But the substance of his beliefs is not funny.

Deeply serious as Don Quixote's motives are to him, his enterprise has another aspect, private – at least, to begin with – which is that of a game. It is important to recognize that there is no discrepancy here. As Huizinga showed in his classic study *Homo ludens*, 'the contrast between play and seriousness is always fluid' (1970E, p. 27). There is a strong resemblance to children's games of 'Let's pretend' in many of the adventures contrived by Don Quixote in Part I. A psychologist has understandably found infantile regression to be a part of his madness (Deutsch, 1965D, p. 221). A child of course is not regarded as suffering delusions while he plays; he believes and he does not believe simultaneously, and he is often deeply serious about it in his own special way. He has entered a parallel and magical realm, known also to 'primitive' cultures and to romance, where a special set of rules applies.[12]

Don Quixote shows frequent signs of being in this childlike state of mind, particularly in Part I. Thus in chapter 1 when he first thinks up names for himself, his horse and his lady with intense seriousness, taking days over the business. Or when he proclaims to the neighbour who reminded him who they were:

I know who I am, and I know that I can be not only the ones I've named, but all the Twelve Peers of France and the Nine Worthies as well

(Yo sé quién soy . . . y sé que puedo ser no sólo los que he dicho, sino todos los doce Pares de Francia, y aun todos los nueve de la Fama: I, 5; i, 106)

We see it again and again in his relations with Sancho, whom he inducts as a bewildered playmate. When the fulling-mills adventure does not turn out as he had hoped, he retorts hotly:

> You just turn these six hammers into six giants and send them at me one by one or all together, and if I don't lay every one of them flat, you can make as much fun of me as you like.

> (Si no, haced vos que estos seis mazos se vuelvan en seis jayanes, y echádmelos a las barbas uno a uno, o todos juntos, y cuando yo no diere con todos patas arriba, haced de mí la burla que quisiéredes: I, 20; i, 249.)

Later other people join in his game, for one reason or another, as when the Priest, the Barber and Dorotea invent the adventure of Princess Micomicona in order to get him home. In Part II, at the ducal castle and elsewhere, this sort of thing happens on a scale that has consequences of some moment. The gap between Don Quixote's private world and that of other people narrows.

In a novel so long and crowded with incident, figures and talk, it is not always easy to pick out moments which show something new in the conduct of the hero, some modification in the state of mind in which he embarked on his career. Progress from self-confident, extroverted madness to cautious and doubt-prone introspection is perceptible mainly in Part II. However, in Part I there are some early signs symptomatic of the subsequent trend towards disillusionment and sanity.[13]

We find him protecting his illusions as early as chapter 1 (p. 75), as again for example in chapter 18 (p. 224); accepting the innkeeper's advice about travelling with money, clean shirts, medication and a squire (ch. 7); recognizing the second innkeeper as such (ch. 17, p. 213); conceding that there was nothing supernatural about the funeral party (ch. 19, p. 233); laughing when Sancho laughs at the mistake over the fulling mills (ch. 20, p. 248); expressing a doubt about chivalry in modern times (ch. 20, p. 251, and again in ch. 38, p. 471). The outcome of the galley-slaves adventure shakes him a little and he readily accepts Sancho's advice that they retire into the Sierra Morena (ch. 23). The decision to do penance there produces a new twist when he takes a deliberate decision to go – or at least act – mad, and another when he admits the distinction between Dulcinea and Aldonza Lorenzo (ch. 25, pp. 305, 311).

As the stories of the subsidiary figures engage narrative attention, Don Quixote takes a back seat. He surrenders initiative to those who are conspiring to lure him home, but he manages one or two attention-seeking interruptions (chs 37–8, 43). Frustration begins to make itself felt as the consequences of two earlier adventures catch up with him: he defends himself hotly for setting loose the convicts (ch. 30, p. 371, and ch. 45, p. 547), and he is upset when he is blamed by the boy Andrés for interfering (ch. 31, p. 391). He rages at the humiliation of being ignored (ch. 44, p. 532). Intermittently he shows a new readiness to accept that other people may experience things differently. Finally he prefers not to weary himself relating his misfortunes to persons unversed in knight errantry (ch. 47, p. 561).

Against these instances can be set many others testifying to the continuing vigour of his madness in all its aspects, which, together with his optimism and self-confidence, is virtually unimpaired until he leaves the second inn for the first time (ch. 17). When he arrives home, he is put to bed, wild-eyed and unable to make out where he is, a little chastened but very mad still (I, 52). The moments I have singled out, however, show a different thread in the pattern, and point towards the 'cooling' of Don Quixote's 'humour' and to developments in Part II.

The relative complexity of Don Quixote owes something to the fact that he embodies the basic opposite qualities of *cuerdo* and *loco* ('sane' and 'mad') which other characters often comment on and marvel at (thus II, 17; ii, 166). This virtually guarantees that he could never be such a psychologically simple character as most figures in romance. It is interesting to find a practitioner of the modern love romance, Claire Ritchie, author of *Bright Meadows*, *The Heart Turns Homeward* and *Hope Is My Pillow*, making the same point:

Some people have two or more equally strong – and possibly conflicting – character traits. These are usually the characters in the straight, as opposed to the romantic novel, because that inner conflict in their natures will necessarily make them rather too complicated for the protagonists in a relatively simple and straightforward story, such as a romance.[14]

Some other character creations of Cervantes show the same kind of basic dualism very clearly. Sancho Panza is one and he is developed on a scale comparable with Don Quixote himself. Less elaborate compounds are found among the lesser figures, such as the promiscuous and mischievous, but kindly and Christian Maritornes (I, 16–17) and the ferocious but gentlemanly bandit leader Roque Guinart (II, 60–1). An outstanding example outside the *Quixote* is that fascinating mixture of obsessive jealousy and generosity, Carrizales of *El celoso extremeño*. This is only to mention characters where the compound is markedly binary, not those whose traits are more numerous, diffused and less strongly accented (Sansón Carrasco, Don Diego de Miranda, the Duke and Doña Rodríguez, for example). The former may or may not be less sophisticated characterizations than the latter, but they exhibit a clear interest on the part of their creator in the complexities of human personality as such. And this cannot be unconnected with that decisive shift towards interest in character which distinguishes the novel from romance.

Don Quixote is much more humanly interesting than any mere paradox of madness and sanity would be. Like any real person he combines strengths and weaknesses and tendencies which are divergent and even contradictory. Courage, courtesy, generosity, vanity, irascibility, temerity, pedagoguery and others. There are constants in his character. A major one is singled out in the last chapter of the novel, where it is remarked that when he was plain Alonso Quijano (that is, sane) and when he was Don Quixote of La Mancha (mad) he was always of a pleasant disposition and agreeable company, for which he was well loved by all (II, 74; ii, 589). On the other hand there is an intriguing unpredictability about him, too. Once or twice he puts his famous valour in reserve and deems it prudent to flee, or at least 'retire'. And when at the inn argument over the barber's basin reaches a pitch of uproar reminiscent of the discord at the camp of Ariosto's Agramante it is none other than Don Quixote who, in commanding but reasonable tones, brings everyone back to his senses.

Despite all this, inner conflict on any significant scale is lacking from Don Quixote in Part I, something rarely absent – though it is not indispensable – in the major figures of the great realistic novels. Having gone overboard out of his mind, the conflict is projected in external combats with very material objects and beings: windmills, sheep, muleteers, wineskins and so on, as far as the rest of us are concerned; giants, wicked knights and the dark powers of enchantment for him. In Part II the struggle will move back into the mind of the Knight.

Sancho exists as an idea before he materializes as a person in chapter 7. The need for a squire was pointed out to Don Quixote by the first innkeeper (I, 3). So, in a way, Sancho owes his existence to Don

Quixote's need for him – as Dulcinea and Cide Hamete Benengeli do, too, in other ways. This poor but worthy peasant without many brains in his head, as he is first described, is more easily identified as a type both in life and in literature than his master. He must have been observed from life (the touch of Old Christian prejudice rings very true); at the same time he has a much clearer literary pedigree than Quixote. In the romances of chivalry there had been a few roguish squires – Ribaldo in the *Caballero Cifar* and Hipólito in *Tirant lo Blanc* – although there significant similarity ends. More important was the *bobo*, or simpleton, of the sixteenth-century *comedias* and *pasos*, and perhaps a certain imprecise notion of rusticity associated with the name Sancho in proverbial folklore.[15] The associations with the well-fed figure of Carnival are more pronounced than the Lenten ones in Don Quixote's case, mentioned earlier. He also has something of the court jester about him; and, indeed, he virtually becomes one at the Duke's castle.

Though initially he appears simpler than his master, Sancho in time evolves as a creature of comparable complexity. His stupidity and ignorance are more than counterbalanced by a special kind of shrewdness which recalls the servant types in *La Celestina* and its literary progeny. Flashes of natural wit spark out from a compound of practical sense and native wisdom which owe little or nothing to formal education. He has a firm moral anchorage, for all his frailties, and Christian-humanist ideas about the blessed ignorance of the uneducated are latent in Cervantes's conception of him. He is in part a derivation of Erasmus' 'wise fool'. He combines folly and sense, as does Don Quixote in quite a different way.

His incentive in leaving his home and family to follow a madman is initially material gain, or, to put it with less opprobrium, a natural urge to better himself. The second time, however, it is also very much for the fun of it. Don Quixote's promise to reward Sancho with the governorship of some island highlights Sancho's credulity of course, but it may be remembered that many Spaniards, some of quite humble origins, did make their fortunes in the Spanish American empire. Simplicity, ambition and an innate respect for those in a more authoritative station in life can largely be held to account for Sancho's (on the face of it) implausible decision; for the rest, Cervantes makes other characters and the narrator express their astonishment at his almost Quixotic gullibility from time to time (for example, I, 29; i, 363).

Sancho is easily persuaded by persons of authority, which is a modest acknowledgement of his own limitations, and he is apt to believe anything outside the range of his personal experience. When left to himself, he usually bases his judgements on the evidence of his senses. These circumstances, together with the special pressures of self-interest, largely account for what seems at first sight the rather puzzling inconsistency in his behaviour over the affair of the Princess Micomicona. At times he is confronted with plain evidence that a hoax is in progress and notes the fact (for example, I, 27, 36 and 46). At others he appears to be quite taken in (for example, I, 29 and 30). On examination his reactions are less enigmatic. When he doubts or disputes the story, he has witnessed something that goes against its credibility; but, helped by a strong dose of self-interest, he will accept correction from supposedly responsible persons. The physical reality of one experience he refuses to doubt: he will not accept that his being tossed in a blanket at the inn (I, 17) had anything to do with enchanters or was anything but the ordinary uncomfortable experience it seemed. It is a bit like Dr Johnson refuting Bishop Berkeley's idealism by kicking a stone.

Don Quixote later gives one of the best summaries of his character:

Sancho Panza is one of the most amusing squires that ever served knight errant. Sometimes his simplicities are so shrewd that thinking out whether he is simple or shrewd gives no small pleasure. Acts of malice show him up as a rogue, and indiscretions confirm him as a fool. He doubts everything and he believes everything. When I think he is going to reach the depths of stupidity, he comes out with some judicious remarks which raise him to the skies.

(Sancho Panza es uno de los más graciosos escuderos que jamás sirvió a caballero andante; tiene a veces unas simplicidades tan agudas, que el pensar si es simple o agudo causa no pequeño contento; tiene malicias que le condenan por bellaco, y descuidos que le confirman por bobo; duda de todo, y créelo todo; cuando pienso que se va a despeñar de tonto, sale con unas discrecciones que le levantan al cielo: II, 32; ii, 293.)

He does not reach his full potential or complexity until the second part, but events and the influence of Don Quixote and others can be seen working on him from quite early on – at least from chapter 15. He lies to protect his master's reputation when they arrive at the inn (I, 16), but the most conspicuous development is on the night of the fulling mills (I, 20). In an access of fright at the thought of being left by himself in the dark wood, Sancho pleads with his master in a speech of unprecedented eloquence, even resorting to the archaic Spanish of the romances in desperation (i, 239; see Mancing, 1982D, p. 62 ff.). Here he is really forced to play Don Quixote's chivalresque game, as he will do in future, off and on, but with increasing readiness. This makes his reactions harder to judge. For the first time Sancho seriously deceives his master when he immobilizes Rocinante (p. 240). This is taken a stage farther when, prompted by the Priest and the Barber (ch. 27), he lies about having visited Dulcinea (chs 31–2), which has tremendous consequences in Part II. While affecting modesty, his vanity is tickled at the thought that his deeds may be recorded in a book with Don Quixote's (ch. 21). Although more than once he is ready to pack up and go home, when he does return he is waxing enthusiastic about the pleasures of their wanderings and looking forward to the next excursion (I, 52).

Together, Quixote and Sancho add up to a whole greater than the sum of the two parts. Kafka in his little parable *The Truth about Don Quixote* saw them as originally one single being. Their companionship and their countless conversations on every kind of subject reveal and build up their personalities bit by bit (see Close, 1981D).

The long gaunt figure and the short fat one are effectively the prototype pair of a number of relationships in literary fiction and comic entertainment, even though the idea was older than Cervantes, as the Carnival figures and the comic duo of Ganassa and Bottarga illustrate. There are modern variations on the theme which we often continue to think of as Cervantine, even when properties of the roles are switched or altered: Joseph Andrews and Parson Adams, Mr Pickwick and Sam Weller, Sherlock Holmes and Dr Watson in literature; Laurel and Hardy, Abbott and Costello in comic entertainment. The latest encapsulations of the two 'originals' revert to type quite remarkably, both visually and in other respects. They are the robots C3P0 and R2D2 of *Star Wars*. I doubt that even they are the end of the road.

NOTES: CHAPTER 5

1   See, e.g., I, 32; i, 396, and II, 70; ii, 567; also *Comedias y entremeses* (1915–22A), Vol. 1, dedication, p. 11.
2   'It would be hard to find a book in which the psychological repercussion of happenings had a greater importance' (Brenan, 1969D, p. 21). Nevertheless, a notable fact about the first modern Spanish novels such as *Lazarillo* and the *Quixote* is their lack of character analysis. Characters reveal themselves very largely by their words and actions rather than by narrative descriptions of their condition. See Bell (1982D), pp. 326 ff. This seems to be connected with the anti-generalizing,

experiential approach to character in the work (Forcione, 1982D, pp. 166, 264). Estimations of Don Quixote's character are far too numerous and diverse to discuss. Perhaps the most influential in this century has been Madariaga's (1961D).

3 The type had already been described by Antonio de Guevara in *Menosprecio de corte y alabanza de aldea*. He refers to 'a lance behind the door, a hack in the stable, a shield in the living room' (Murillo note, i, 70).

4 Structural components of their interrelationship are studied by Ferreras (1982D).

5 The remarks which follow are based on the conclusions of Deborah Kong (1980D, pp. 201–34). They amend or amplify those of Green (1970D) and Avalle-Arce (1976D), pp. 124 ff. See also Halka (1981D).

6 For a summary of views, see Percas de Ponseti (1975D), Vol. 1, pp. 34 ff.

7 Burton, cited in Babb (1951E), p. 46.

8 Vives (1947–8C), Vol. 1, p. 1396.

9 As they do, e.g., in I, 38; i, 471. Attitudes to mental illness were relatively enlightened in Spain, which, since 1409, had boasted the well-run Hospital de los Inocentes in Valencia, a pioneering model for other asylums later (see Márquez Villanueva, 1980D, pp. 99 and 111 n.).

10 Erasmus (1964C), p. 127.

11 Forcione (1984D), pp. 223–4, gives the most recent summary of the question.

12 'The child is quite literally "beside himself" with delight, transported beyond himself to such an extent that he almost believes he actually is such and such a thing, without, however, wholly losing consciousness of "ordinary reality". His representation is not so much a sham-reality as a realization in appearance: "imagination" in the original sense of the word' (Huizinga, 1970E, pp. 32–3). G. Torrente Ballester devotes a book (1975D) to the theme in *Don Quixote*. There is of course a clear element of play in chivalry itself, as the author of *The Waning of the Middle Ages* knew very well.

13 Howard Mancing (1982D) shows this process getting more fully under way in Part I than had been thought. The decisive movement does not seem to me to start until Part II, however. See also Allen (1969D), Vol. 1, pp. 33 ff.; and, for a quite different reading, Williamson (1984D), pp. 92–9.

14 Claire Ritchie, *Writing the Romantic Novel* (London, 1962), pp. 45–6, quoted by G. D. Martin (1975E), p. 160.

15 The name of the governor of Firm Island in *Amadís de Gaula* was Ysanjo. On the literary ancestry of Sancho, see Close (1973[2]D), Márquez Villanueva (1973D), pp. 20 ff.; Molho (1976D), pp. 217 ff. on the folkloric connections; Urbina (1982D) on both and on the literary parodic aspect in particular; Flores (1982[2]D) on views of Sancho Panza through the centuries.

CHAPTER 6

Literary Theory in Action

And how is it possible [asks the Canon of Toledo] for a human mind to persuade itself that there have ever existed in the world such an infinity of Amadises, such a horde of famous knights, all those emperors of Trebizond, all those Felixmartes of Hircania, those palfreys, those errant damsels, those serpents, dragons, giants, unheard of adventures . . . and finally [he concludes], all those many ridiculous events found in the books of chivalry?

(Y ¿cómo es posible que haya entendimiento humano que se dé a entender que ha habido en el mundo aquella infinidad de Amadises, y aquella turbamulta de tanto famoso caballero, tanto emperador de Trapisonda, tanto Felixmarte de Hircania, tanto palafrén, tanta doncella andante, tantas sierpes, tantos endriagos, tantos gigantes, tantas inauditas aventuras . . . y, finalmente, tantos y tan disparatados casos como los libros de caballerías contienen?: I, 49; i, 577–8)

To which Don Quixote presently retorts:

Well, for my part . . . I consider that the one who is enchanted and out of his wits is yourself, for presuming to utter such blasphemies about something so accepted and held to be true throughout the world . . .

(Pues yo . . . hallo por mi cuenta que el sin juicio y encantado es vuestra merced, pues se ha puesto a decir tantas blasfemias contra una cosa tan recibida en el mundo y tenida por tan verdadera . . . : p. 579)

Since this conviction of Don Quixote's is the core of his madness, a theoretical literary question about the relationship of chivalric fiction and true history is embedded at the heart of the novel. If he is to be dissuaded from his belief, as the Canon tries vainly to do, the arguments must contain a sizeable measure of literary theory. This entirely justifies the inclusion of the literary discussions in Part I (chs 6, 32 and most of 47–50).

The second aspect or phase of his madness, the decision to be a knight errant and live a romance, has literary-theoretical consequences of another sort deeply ingrained in the work. His imitation of exemplary heroes had the most venerable humanistic authorization. Emulation of the virtues of heroes and saints was prescribed in education. Not only that, a good many Renaissance biographies were written with the aim of supplying models for imitation (Kristeller, 1965E, p. 27). Young gentlemen were enjoined to cultivate the qualities of Scipio and Alexander, young ladies those of the chastest Roman matrons and Christian martyrs. In the Middle Ages the practice and the literature of chivalry were inextricably fused. There were Spanish as well as French and English knights in the fifteenth century who deliberately imitated romance heroes and episodes. In the sixteenth century twelve of Cortés's men banded together with vows of chivalry in emulation of the Twelve Peers of France. This kind of thing could be taken to extravagant lengths. The vow of a fifteenth-century Catalan knight, Miguel d'Oris, to wear a bodkin pierced through his thigh until he had fought with an English knight was by no means an unparalleled piece of exhibitionism.[1]

When you look to great figures for inspiration, it makes no difference whether your models are historical or fictitious. As Sir Philip Sidney remarked, 'A feigned example hath as much force to teach as a true example'.[2] This is an unspoken major premiss behind Don Quixote's answer to the objections of the Canon. He is simply not concerned whether the sources of his inspiration were fact or fiction, but at the end of the discussion he claims that since he became a knight errant he has been brave, courteous, liberal, well bred, generous, and so forth (I, 50; i, 586). Imitation as a doctrine may nowadays be dead, but the power of popular literary fiction, and still more of the visual media, to inspire and influence for better or worse is very much alive. Only the heroes change, and those of film, television, video and comic strip have the same, if less edifying, fascination for the young. This real-life fascination in turn continues to offer a fertile subject for artistic expression. In Godard's film *A bout de souffle* Poiccard, inspired by Hollywood movies, acts at being a gangster more than he really is one.

Don Quixote is not the only figure in the book to imitate literature. Notably, there are the ladies and gentlemen playing shepherds and shepherdesses (II, 58); the difference is that for them it is consciously a game. Don Quixote is an extreme case in whom heroic emulation goes over the brink into lunacy: first, because he chooses impossibly fabulous heroes as models – supermen who defeat vast armies single-handed, sink fleets, slice ogres in two as though they were made of marzipan, and outwit wicked enchanters; second, because his imitation tries to be impossibly literal and complete. It is not enough for him to try to be as brave and courteous as they, in a different milieu; he aims to transform that milieu in conformity with the pristine order of things which underlies it. This is impracticable, to say the least. Reality may not always be what it looks like on the surface, but it hits back, making of his imitation of romance an involuntary comic parody.

He sets about it with a care and deliberation which in view of the outcome make it more comic still. The effort he puts into it is consciously artistic even while it is childlike.[3] Imitating models with a view to equalling or excelling them was prescribed for art, literature and oratory no less than for conduct. The principle, laid down by Horace and Quintilian, was much invoked in the Renaissance. Don Quixote's impulse may be mad, but it is also both artistic and heroic – the two are not unconnected. Even at a less exalted level the idea of putting art into living was well known to the age: it was required of the courtier in Castiglione's *Il Cortegiano*. Don Quixote's preparations involved the studied choice of names. His formal speeches are gems of self-conscious rhetorical improvisation, clearly intended to be listened to, admired and recorded. His most consciously artistic act is his penance, before which he carefully debates whether to imitate Amadis or Roland (I, 26), and before this he actually invokes the classical artistic precept of imitating great models (I, 25).

'An artist is one who is inwardly full of images,' said Dürer. But he also has to know how to project them in his chosen medium, and here, as Sancho once or twice observes, the Knight is better with words than with deeds. The most glorious of his creations, Dulcinea, remains largely locked up in his own mind, which gives him the freedom, he confides to his squire, to depict her just as he pleases (I, 25; i, 314). Indeed, he is marvellously at liberty to imagine the whole book of which he sees himself as the hero. He gives us a specimen of it at the beginning of the first sortie, when he describes his dawn departure in language which is a splendid parody of set-piece romance rhetoric ('No sooner had ruddy Apollo . . . ': I, 2; i, 80). In so far as he can suit his actions and words to the purpose of his book, he is its author as well as its hero, simultaneously composing and performing. Up to a point he determines his own story. The trouble is that he cannot determine very much of it.

Unusual as his endeavour may seem, it is not unique. The convict Ginés de Pasamonte is also writing his own adventures as he lives them (see El Saffar, 1975D, p. 106). The chivalric author-protagonist meets his picaresque parallel. However, Don Quixote leaves the actual writing of this masterpiece to an unseen, all-seeing magician, in the best tradition of the romances of chivalry. This means that the relationship is that of historian (biographer) and his subject, from Quixote's point of view; and he has some strong words on the subject of historians who do not live up to their high calling (II, 3; ii, 64). He is, of course, absolutely right about his deeds and words being recorded in a book for posterity. The irony is that this book is not what he thinks it is.

By making Don Quixote try to live a romance Cervantes might be said to be testing this brand of fiction, matching it against a life. But, we quickly remember, this 'life' is not *really* a life, a matter of history. It is fiction on another level, of another kind. So if chivalric romance is being measured against another kind of fiction it is that of Cervantes's novel. Chivalric romance *vis-à-vis* realistic novel, substantially. Not that Cervantes knew those terms, of course. The usual word for a long prose fiction was *libro* or *historia*. Although the immediate meaning of the latter in *Don Quixote* is usually 'history', the protracted pretence that Benengeli's narrative is a history, which we *know* to be a pretence, makes for some play between the two senses of the word: 'story' and 'history' (see Wardropper, 1965D, pp. 2 ff.)

Cervantes's great originality as a theorist is his development of a substantial body of prose-fiction theory transcending the limitations of the contemporary poetics in which it is securely rooted. Probably only in part consciously, in part by intuition and the example of *Don Quixote*, he laid the foundations for a theory of the modern novel.[4] This he could not have done without making a distinction between the two genres we now call romance and novel. Most, though not all, of the major points come up in the packed but well-structured dialogues between the Canon and the Priest and between the Canon and Don Quixote (I, 47–50).

The discussion of the chivalric romances is inevitably in part descended from the anxious preoccupations or unequivocally damning opinions voiced throughout most of the sixteenth century by numerous moralists, theologians and Erasmian humanists, whose concern was mainly ethical or educational. They worried most about what effect the reading of such works might have on young and unsophisticated minds. Other kinds of fiction, including poetry, came in for criticism, too, but to a lesser degree. The mass medium of printing (introduced into Spain in the 1470s) was still new enough, in the age of the Reformation and the Council of Trent, to be a worry to responsible minds.[5]

Objections to the romances of chivalry were principally of three kinds: moral, stylistic, and because they were nonsensically untrue. The books were censured because they might inflame the passions, especially of young girls. The critical voices in *Don Quixote* insist little on this aspect, and when they do it is usually to ridicule rather than condemn, as in the fine piece of nonsense about chivalric damsels riding about the countryside loaded with their virginity, who, when not ravished by some rogue, rustic or monstrous giant, 'after eighty years, during all of which time they never once slept indoors, went to their graves as virginal as the mothers who bore them' (I, 9; i, 141).

The books were also held to be badly written. So they often were, though it is likely that allowance was not always made for the fact that their Renaissance authors cultivated an archaic style. In the *Quixote* they are roundly condemned for being incoherently constructed – 'they are composed with so many members that you would think the intention was to fashion a chimera or a monster, not a well-proportioned figure', exclaims the Canon of Toledo (I, 47; i, 565), adapting Horace and echoing Minturno and other authorities. And he is not wholly insensitive to the fact that the romances were structured on non-Aristotelian lines, as he shows in his commentary on the potential of a well-written romance.

The discussion is connected with and indebted to the sixteenth-century Italian critical debate about the epic poem on the classical model and the popular *romanzo*, typified by the *Orlando furioso*. The application to prose fiction was easily made, since 'epic can be written in prose as well as in verse' (I, 47; i, 567) – an argument applied to Heliodorus' *Ethiopica* notably by J. C. Scaliger and López Pinciano. Echoes of the Spanish theorists, El Pinciano and Carvallo, and the Italians Tasso, Giraldi Cinthio, G. B. Pigna, A. Piccolomini and Minturno are to be heard in Cervantes's theorizing. He must have read at least some of them.

The Canon's views reflect the prevailing neo-Aristotelianism of the day, like El Pinciano's; but, like him, he is no intolerant dogmatist. Although he denounces the romances, mainly for being incredible nonsense and badly constructed, he sees their possibilities and sets out his opinion of what an intelligently written work of this kind could achieve. Notably, it would please and instruct with its variety and exemplariness (I, 47; i, 566–7). He has written above a hundred pages of a chivalric romance, later abandoned, and so has some right to his opinion. It is also noticeable that his perceptive description of the functioning of verisimilitude, with its emphasis on achieving a suspension of disbelief, seems to envisage a work more like a surprise-filled romance than anything else:

> Fabulous plots must be wedded to the reader's intelligence, and written in such a way that the impossible is made easy, enormities are smoothed out, and the mind held in suspense, amazed, gripped, exhilarated, and entertained, so that wonder and delight go hand in hand

> (Hanse de casar las fábulas mentirosas con el entendimiento de los que las leyeren, escribiéndose de suerte que, facilitando los imposibles, allanando las grandezas, suspendiendo los ánimos, admiren, suspendan, alborocen y entretengan, de modo que anden a un mismo paso la admiración y la alegría juntas: p. 565)

The third and greatest objection to the chivalric romances was precisely that they were untrue and, moreover, incredible. If the second charge might seem to nullify any damage done by the first, they were still reckoned prejudicial to true history, a source of confusion to the simple (though you would have to be as mad as Don Quixote to take them literally) and an outrage to aesthetic rationale. As Vives, Tasso and El Pinciano insisted, without verisimilitude an intelligent pleasure in fiction is impossible. The Canon's arguments point towards a rationalization of chivalric romance, more than to its proscription, despite a few vehement remarks in this vein. He is fundamentally making demands of a classicist kind for good writing, with particular emphasis on credibility. There was little agreement on the precise meaning of verisimilitude, and conceptions of it ranged from very restrictive to loose.[6] Cervantes seems to have been concerned above all with the contravening of the order of nature. As the Canon's words quoted above and the example of the *Persiles* make clear, there were for him ways of making the amazing and even the incredible acceptable. They depended on admitting into their presentation an element of uncertainty corresponding to that which attends any fantastic tale in real life, such as making it a second-hand story told by an intermediary, who does not have to be believed. His idea of verisimilitude was certainly not modern realism. Cervantes could never bring himself to reject the idealization of experience, in spite of a rather shaky mistrust of the exaggeration it involves. He drew the vague line that must be drawn somewhere between idealism and fantasy close to the latter.[7] But he had a realistic respect for historical actuality, stemming from neo-Aristotelian poetics, and beyond that from those empirical preoccupations of the sixteenth century which caused the contemporary crisis in historiography[8] and a new sense of the need for art to deal responsibly with the truth (see Parker, 1967E, pp. 21 ff.).

Romance and fantasy, on the other hand, were frequently connected with dream. Cervantes makes this association in a significant number of passing references. The Priest calls the chivalric romances 'dreams dreamt by men who are awake or, rather, half asleep' (II, 1; ii, 50); the narrator speaks of 'the whole contrivance of those famous dreamed-up adventures' (I, 1; i, 73). Berganza calls the pastoral romances 'things dreamed up' (*Coloquio, Novelas ejemplares*, ii, 309) and the lieutenant referring to the *Coloquio* as fantasy speaks of 'those dreams or pieces of nonsense' (p. 295). While Don Quixote's library is being censored, the Knight is asleep and dreaming (I, 6–7), as he is again while the romances are discussed in the inn (I, 32). The association occurs once more in the adventure of the Cave of Montesinos (II, 23). Also in Periandro's tale of the marvellous island in the *Persiles*, in the play *La casa de los celos* and the *Viaje del Parnaso* (VI, 137). It is not hard to arrive at the corollary that, if romance represents a world of dreams, another kind of fiction is needed to deal with the world of waking experience.

The other, and more essential aspect of pre-modern romance, the idealistic, was much harder to deal with than the fantastic. Cervantes had reservations about it, which he usually expressed in ironic form. But his own romances make it perfectly plain that he never rejected it as he rejected unsupported fantasy. For him to have done this would have been almost tantamount to rejecting Poetry itself, which – with a capital P – he revered as 'an inner light, a clairvoyance, a transport of exaltation which lifts the soul to the realm of the essential', to use Casalduero's not excessive words (1943D, p. 58).[9] Poetic idealization comes up against the hard facts of 'history' from the viewpoint of the three friends discussing *Don Quixote*, Part I, in a well-known passage near the beginning of Part II. The Bachelor says:

'Some of those who have read the story say they would have been glad if the author had forgotten a few of the infinite cudgellings which Señor Don Quixote received in different encounters.'

'That's where the truth of the story comes in,' said Sancho.

'They could also in fairness have kept quiet about them,' said Don Quixote, 'for there is no reason to write about those actions which neither alter nor affect the truth of the story, if they are going to redound to the discredit of its hero. In faith, Aeneas was not so pious as Virgil paints him, nor Ulysses so prudent as Homer describes him.'

'That is so,' replied Sansón, 'but it is one thing to write as a poet and another as a historian: the poet can relate or sing of things not as they were, but as they ought to have been; and the historian must write of them not as they ought to have been, but as they were, without adding to the truth or taking away from it anything whatever.

(– . . . dicen algunos que han leído la historia que se holgaran se les hubiera olvidado a los autores della algunos de los infinitos palos que en diferentes encuentros dieron al señor Don Quijote.

– Ahí entra la verdad de la historia – dijo Sancho.

– También pudieran callarlos por equidad – dijo don Quijote –, pues las acciones que ni mudan ni alteran la verdad de la historia no hay para qué escribirlas, si han de redundar en menosprecio del señor de la historia. A fee que no fue tan piadoso Eneas como Virgilio le pinta, ni tan prudente Ulises como le describe Homero.

– Así es – replicó Sansón –; pero uno es escribir como poeta y otro como historiador: el poeta puede contar o cantar las cosas no como fueron, sino como debían ser; y el historiador las ha de escribir, no como debían ser, sino como fueron, sin añadir ni quitar a la verded cosa alguna: II, 3; ii, 61.)

This exchange shows clearly how much *Don Quixote* was rooted in the critical debate of the period over the relationship between poetry and history. Aristotle's distinction in the *Poetics* (1451 b) was not what started it, but it concentrated the issue as no other formulation did: 'The distinction between historian and poet . . . consists really in this, that the one describes the thing that has been, and the other a kind of thing that might be.' It was characteristic of Renaissance theory that it made no clear distinction between what 'might be' and what 'ought to be'. *Don Quixote* is the one work in which Cervantes found a satisfactory way of accommodating the poetic ideal with the representation of down-to-earth reality. Here he situates the former in the mind and heart of his hero. He internalizes it, just as the romances of chivalry, animated by the same idealism, are made part of the historical reality represented in the novel.

In his argument with Don Quixote the Canon is the very voice of reasonable, enlightened, modern opinion. It has such obvious force to anyone in his senses that it would be foolish to underrate it. Cervantes knew as well as we do what an edge historical fact (or, as Borges reminded us, what we *judge* to be historical fact) has over fiction. But, as Forcione has clearly shown (1970D, pp. 91 ff.), it is a mistake to see Cervantes as siding exclusively with the Canon. Here as so often he shows his capacity for seeing both sides of things. In comparison with the Canon's, Don Quixote's argument is medieval, but for all its muddled thinking it contains a spark of inspired insight and a kernel of hard fact. It deserves some attention.

The Knight produces a farrago of examples drawn higgledy-piggledy from fiction and history. The Canon makes a rather feeble effort with these to sort out fable from truth and half-truth, but his nice discrimination makes no great headway against dogmatic conviction. He is right – how can we not agree? – but he is not quite right enough. He fails to see a curious inference, unstated by Don Quixote and which, indeed, Cervantes himself may not have noticed, but which Unamuno (1967D, p. 131) picked up from another part of the book, and which a few other modern writers have discovered in their own novels. This is the odd fact that there is ultimately nothing whatever to distinguish a fictitious character from someone who once lived and is now dead and belongs to past history, as far as posterity is concerned. Indeed, there are characters – Hamlet, for example – who have meant more to posterity than countless historical ones. A historical figure exists solely as a matter of record, and any record can be faked or invented. There is thus no incontrovertible proof that any of us has ever existed once we have ceased bodily to do so. George Orwell noticed it:

Comrade Ogilvy, unimagined an hour ago, was now a fact. It struck him as curious that you could create dead men but not living ones. Comrade Ogilvy, who had never existed in the present, now existed in the past, and when once the act of forgery was forgotten, he would exist just as authentically, and upon the same evidence, as Charlemagne or Julius Caesar.[10]

But as this chilling inference is not explicitly drawn by Cervantes it would be improper to dwell on it further.

The remaining objection returned by Don Quixote to the Canon swallows up the question of veracity in the (for him) greater principle of artistic pleasure. The books are read with delight by one and all, great and small, poor and rich, learned and ignorant, common folk and gentry, he says. How can they be lies when they *look* so true in all their abundance of factual detail? 'Read them, and see what pleasure you get from their reading' (I, 50; i, 583–4). Without a pause he plunges immediately into the splendid parody fantasy of the Knight of the Boiling Lake. He puts all he has got into the telling of this adventure, the visual intensity of which is unusually marked. We never learn the Canon's reaction, but it is hard not to feel that Don Quixote has probably scored a point by switching from dialectic to demonstration of the deeply pleasurable irrational impact romance can have, and which it shares with fairy-tale and myth.

Perhaps the Canon is Cervantes speaking with his head and Don Quixote is Cervantes speaking with his heart on the romances of chivalry. But even that may be to oversimplify. There are strong indications that his sympathies are divided, and that is the best one can say with reasonable certainty.

NOTES: CHAPTER 6

1 See Riquer (1967E), pp. 66 ff., 123. On the surprising diffusion of influence of the romances of chivalry, see Leonard (1949E). California owes its name to a fabulous island in Montalvo's *Sergas de Esplandián*, fifth book in the Amadis series. See Eisenberg (1982E) on the Spanish chivalric romances in general.

2 Sidney (1904C), Vol. 1, p. 169.

3 Riley (1962D), pp. 64 ff.; Avalle-Arce (1976D). Freud said: 'The creative writer does the same as the child at play. He creates a world of phantasy which he takes very seriously – that is, which he invests with large amounts of emotion – while separating it sharply from reality' (cited in Storr, 1972E, p. 14).

4 For fuller accounts, see Forcione (1970D), esp. ch. 3; Riley (1962D) and (1973[1]D), pp. 310 ff.

5 There were a few attempts to get the books banned in Spain and several, rather less successful, to prohibit their importation in the Americas.

6 See Nelson (1973E), pp. 50–1; Weinburg (1961E), Vol. 1, pp. 435 ff.

7 There is a notable passage on the subject in the *Viaje del Parnaso*, VI, 138: 'for my pen has always shied away from things that smack of the impossible; those with a glimmering of possibility, which are sweet and mild and sure, explain my harmless scribbling. Never does my narrow wit open its doors indiscriminately [*a disparidad*], but those things which are concordant [*consonancia*] find them always wide open.'

8 See Domínguez Ortiz (1971E), pp. 249 ff.; Wardropper (1965D), pp. 7 ff.; Nelson (1973E), pp. 41 ff.

9 There are four great eulogies of Poetry in Cervantes: in *Gitanilla*, *Novelas ejemplares*,

i, 90–1; in *Parnaso*, IV, 106–10; in *Don Quixote*, II, 16; ii, 155; and *Persiles*, III, 2, 284.

10 Orwell (1950E), p. 51. Similarly, the author of *Monsignor Quixote* writes in an earlier novel: 'What did the truth matter? All characters once dead, if they continue to exist in memory at all, tend to become fictitious. Hamlet is no less real now than Winston Churchill, and Jo Pulling no less historical than Don Quixote' (Greene, 1971E, p. 67). Borges has elaborated on the idea in several of his stories.

CHAPTER 7

The Structure of Part I

(i) THE MAIN STORY

There are many ways of looking at the manner in which *Don Quixote* is 'put together' and what it 'consists of'. Any method that purports to explain everything will tend either to founder under the sheer weight of detail or dissolve into abstraction. So what follows here is simply considerations on aspects selected because they seem important. Inevitably one focuses on the work as a completed whole, a static though intricate entity. But one must remember two separate processes in time as well: that of Cervantes composing the book, and that of the reader reading it for the first time. A novelist engaged in the first process always has the second process in mind.

At least since 1905 it has been commonly thought that Cervantes began his book as a short *novela*.[1] The brevity of Quixote's first sortie, without Sancho, is clearly what gave rise to the idea. But if Cervantes did begin like this and changed his plan when he saw the possibilities he covered his tracks so well that it is very hard to see what the original would have looked like, and especially how it would have ended. In our novel the Knight goes home to equip himself as the innkeeper advised and is nowhere near being restored to his right mind. A more searching analysis than has yet been made of Cervantes's short-story technique might help; at present this putative *novela corta* looks at least as inconclusive as *Rinconete*. So, though there is no inherent objection to the theory, I see nothing more in its favour than against it, and it seems more useful to study the novel we have than the *novela corta* we do not.

This does not mean that Cervantes did not change his mind about the form of his work while he wrote. There is overwhelming evidence of at least one major alteration of plan. The pioneer work of Stagg (1959D), carried on by Flores (1980[2]D) makes it possible to reconstruct this part of an earlier design with some confidence. Cervantes evidently went back and transposed the Grisóstomo–Marcela episode to its present location in chapters 11–14 from an earlier situation in the Sierra Morena chapters (beginning in chapter 23). As well as a few passing inconsistencies, there is a sudden change of scenery from open country on or near the highway to mountainous and rocky terrain. The goatherds of chapter 10 are probably those who tell Don Quixote about Cardenio in chapter 23. A motive for the change is easily found. Cervantes could very well have decided to thin out the cluster of extraneous stories crowding the central section of Part I.

This change entailed adjustments, one of which he mishandled, probably as a result of working at speed with interruptions. It is the notorious case of Sancho's disappearing ass. In Cuesta's first edition of 1605 the animal is present in chapters 7–25, then it is suddenly treated as absent until chapter 43, in which the trappings it wore are mentioned as present again. The ass itself reappears in chapter 46. In Cuesta's second edition and all the others of 1605 two short passages were inserted, one relating its theft by Ginés de Pasamonte and the other its recovery. Unfortunately, they were put in the wrong places (chapters 23 and 30), making nonsense of existing allusions to the ass as being present up to chapter 25 and absent from chapter 30 onwards. Cervantes is unlikely to have inserted them wrongly himself. When he came to write Part II, where the anomaly is discussed (chs 3–4), he made no mention of the amendments, but his own explanation, entrusted to Sancho, uses and elaborates on some of the information they contain. Cervantes is adept at exploiting anything that might make matter for his novel, as he does even this asinine confusion.

He is also thought to have decided rather late in the day to divide Part I into chapters and parts, subsequently abandoning the latter. The arguments here seem more conjectural but, whenever the chapter division was done, it was carried out with a usually admirable sense of underlying narrative rhythms and a sense of humour.[2] Then there is Benengeli, who materializes with some éclat in chapter 9, to receive only four more mentions after that and disappear entirely in Part I after chapter 27. Most surprisingly, he is not named when his 'manuscript' comes to an end (see Flores, 1982[1]D). Not until Part II does he really come into his own.

Obvious inconsistencies apart, an untidy-looking narrative may be complex rather than carelessly constructed. Conversely, writing to a neatly patterned formula need not imply a great deal of thought. Like an organism, *Don Quixote* has both symmetries and irregularities. It also shows clear traces of distinct pre-existent literary forms. Apart from chivalric romance and the intercalated *novelas cortas*, the literary discussions reflect critical treatises, often dialogues, of the time. There are also, for example, *burlas* (jests and practical jokes),[3] serious colloquies, proverbs and anecdotes, of the kind collected in miscellanies, including items of folk origin.[4] But, visible as these traces are, a major difference between *Don Quixote* and all the picaresque novels which immediately preceded it is the superior manner in which Cervantes assimilates and subordinates them to the central concerns of his novel.[5] The only exception to this is provided by the extraneous stories, and that exception is less complete than might be supposed.

It is not difficult to find certain structural features showing formal symmetries and thematic regularities. The Knight's two expeditions in Part I are based on the pattern of outward journey, stay at an inn, return. The work can be seen as a series of burlesque chivalric adventures, love-stories, literary discussions and dialogues, freely recurring. It is 'framed' between the burlesque prefatory verses and those in the last chapter.[6] There are Don Quixote's two discourses (I, 11 and 37–8), with an explicit link between them and thematic connections with adjacent episodes. Don Quixote keeps vigil twice in the courtyard of an inn: once over his arms (ch. 3) and once guarding the ladies at the inn (ch. 43). What could be more chivalrous? The six extraneous episodes consist of four in the middle of the book, preceded by one pastoral episode earlier and followed by another pastoral episode later. And so on.

Since the 1950s critical emphasis has been on Cervantes the highly conscious artist. Before that the prevailing view of him – and it has remained the popular one – was as the facile improviser and careless genius. The truth lies somewhere between the two extremes, but unquestionably on the side of the conscious artist.[7] We sometimes forget how much he must have been feeling his way in the *Quixote* with problems whose solution we now take for granted. It was probably for this very reason that one of his major principles was that the writer should be thoroughly aware of what he is doing. There is plenty of evidence of the importance he attached to this principle, although he did not state it directly in so many words. The best illustration is the twice-told anecdote (II, 3 and 71) of the inept painter Orbaneja, the subject of whose painting was 'Whatever it turns out to be' ('Lo que saliere'; see Riley, 1962D, pp. 20 ff.).

Apart from a few obvious textual errors, two or three things particularly contribute to the impression of improvisation. Don Quixote's lack of set destination is one – which does not necessarily mean that the author does not know where he is going. Another is the episodic nature of the narrative. A novel that relates travels entailing a succession of separate events and encounters along the way is almost bound to be episodic, and is none the worse for that. In so far as 'episodic' implies that episodes might be removed or transposed without detriment, then Part I is only episodic up to a point. One could shift or remove, say, the incident of Don Quixote and the religious procession (I, 51), with negligible consequences; the same would not be true of the adventure of the fulling mills (I, 20), though. There is less room for such manoeuvres than at first appears.

A third reason for the sense of improvisation is Cervantes's way of letting the reader glimpse – or think he is glimpsing – him in the very act of creation[8] We are prepared for this from the very start by that picture he gives of himself in the prologue, resting his cheek on his hand and wondering what to say. Then there is the totally unexpected interruption when the story dries up in the middle of the fight with the Biscayan squire, and is resumed again with Benengeli's manuscript (I, 8–9). On another level, comments on prolixity, on digression or on the suprising nature of events function in a similar way. By alerting us critically Cervantes makes us feel that we are following not just the events of the story but also the actual writing of it.

In Part I are the beginnings of an interplay of character and events, and character with character, that develops more strongly in the sequel. This gives the work a subtler kind of articulation than anything so far referred to, where outer cause and effect interact with the characters' inner intention and response, reproducing something like the stuff of experience. Don Quixote and Sancho repeatedly discuss and interpret what happens to them. More often than the narrator, they assess its significance, and the reader, whether or not he concurs, is repeatedly exposed to their view of events. It is particularly in the conversations about them that events start to overflow the limits of their actual occurrence, though once again it is in Part II that this really develops.

The structure is bonded with links of cause and effect and a loose but pliant web of anticipations and reminiscences such as any good novel has. Some of them here contribute considerably to the appearance of improvisation. Synchronically viewed, they simply connect different portions of the work; considered diachronically, as one reads the book from start to finish, they function rather like some organic process of germination and growth. There are obvious connections, such as those provided by the reappearances of Andrés (I, 4 and 31) and the barber who owns the basin (I, 21 and 44). Much more subtle is the origin of the train of connections underlying the great motif of the enchantment and disenchantment of Dulcinea in Part II. This is tucked away in an instruction by the Priest and Barber to Sancho telling him 'that if he [Don Quixote] should ask, as he is bound to, whether he gave the letter to Dulcinea, to say yes' (I, 27; i, 328). Sancho tells the lie and is forced to embroider on it (I, 31). This puts him on the spot when they visit El Toboso (II, 9–10), with massive consequences for both of them. The reason why the Priest and Barber told Sancho to lie can be traced back to that first cause in the novel, Quixote's madness.

Many of the connections invite us to infer not only some authorial decision about a turn or development in the story, but also that an idea has taken root in the mind of a character, later to burgeon into action or a role. The Niece tells the Knight that a wicked enchanter, Frestón, spirited away his library (I, 7); Don Quixote then makes him responsible for the disaster with the windmills (I, 8), and thus the first of the malevolent horde who persecute him later. Don Quixote mentions the penance of Amadis in I, 15; the episode where he imitates it occurs in I, 25. In chapter 10, Sancho imagines Dulcinea dressing flax or threshing wheat in the barn; in the invented story of his visit to her he represents her as winnowing corn in the yard (ch. 31). When Sancho confers on Don Quixote the title of the Knight of the Sorry Countenance (ch. 19), his master sees it as a happy inspiration put into Sancho's head by the magician in charge of writing their story.[9] But shortly before this he had mentioned Amadis of Greece bearing the title of the Knight of the Burning Sword, which could equally well be inferred as the source of the idea. The incident is a curious example of the interplay of characters and author. The famous descent into the Cave of Montesinos in Part II (chs 22–3) is prefigured in allusions to three otherworld adventures, one subterranean in Part II (ch. 14) and two subaqueous in Part I (chs 32 and 50).

Generally, the first mention may be said to lie more or less dormant in our minds in the interim and we infer that it has done likewise in the mind of the character and, very likely, of the author. In fact, the finished product offers no certain guide to what went on in the writer's mind while composing, and the possible effects of revision are incalculable. All the same, with or without the medium of a character, we can often hardly avoid thinking that we are watching the author at work, perhaps preparing the ground for a later event, perhaps just betraying his own thought processes. Whether we are not, this fictional linking of bits and pieces of earlier and later experience, of thought and action, so very like what we all know in our own lives, is a verisimilar and satisfying form of novelistic articulation, which reaches its ultimate development in Joyce's *Ulysses*.

The same cannot be said of the chronological structure of *Don Quixote*. A decent respect for the calendar is assumed of any realistic modern novel. It prevails in *Guzmán de Alfarache*. The chronology of events in the *Quixote* is by comparison anarchic, with respect to days, months and years. Commentators since 1780 have racked their brains trying to make sense of it. The subject has been fully explored and explained by Murillo (1975D). Briefly: Don Quixote's first departure from home is at dawn on a morning in July; the adventures of the first part then cover a few weeks before he returns home and is put to bed. Nearly a month elapses between this and his getting up at the start of Part II, ready for another journey, this time to the jousts due to be held in Zaragoza on St George's Day (23 April). The jousts are still imminent as late as chapter 52, even though the letters in chapters 36 and 47 are dated 20 July and 16 August respectively. Trapped, it seems, in some spring-and-summer cycle, Don Quixote, having changed course for Barcelona (II, 59), arrives there at sunrise on St John's Day (24 June). The best explanation of this is that a chivalric-romance time-scale, tied to the great seasonal festivals and based on the period from spring equinox to Midsummer's Day, has been loosely superimposed, as Murillo argues.

As to the year, the many historical allusions in the Captive's tale make it possible to fix the date of its narration at 1589; but the books in Don Quixote's library (the modernity of some of which is openly commented on: I, 9; i, 141) make it some year after 1591. Yet the letter in Part II, chapter 36, is dated 1614. Temporal verisimilitude is outraged. Where sheer heedlessness gives way to calculated indifference or mystification is anyone's guess, but it is impossible to believe that Cervantes did not notice the anomalies at some stage. At first sight they are surprising, but Cervantes is in fact often vague, mocking or mystifying when numerical precision is invited. The truth is that the precise dates of Don Quixote's doings (a typically modern preoccupation) do not matter to the story. Moreover, as we are reminded openly once or twice, the reader should not give any more credence to the story than the judicious do to the books of chivalry (I, 52; i, 604). The temporal analogy with the latter, particularly in the triumphal midsummer-morn arrival in Barcelona (II, 61), looks too striking to be other than parody.

In making his novel a travel account Cervantes is also using a favourite romance structure. But, although this fortifies the role of chance in events and works against a more mundane causality, the lucky and providential coincidences on which so much depends in romance are noticeably absent where the affairs of Quixote and Sancho are concerned. There is nothing of this kind to strain the credulity of the modern novel-reader. The Priest and the Barber run into Sancho at the inn (I, 26), but since they have come expressly looking for Don Quixote to bring him home there is nothing very surprising in that. The reappearance of Andrés is prepared for in a similar manner. It is quite different where the characters of the extraneous stories are concerned, as we shall observe.

Artistic unity was without doubt one of Cervantes's major critical preoccupations. References to digression are common, and occur at more length in the literary discussions; the Canon criticizes the romances of chivalry for being shapeless. But *per tal variar natura è bella*: Cervantes was also keenly aware of the pleasures of variety, and it is on these grounds that he justifies the 'tales and episodes'of Part I as being 'no less agreeable, well made and true than the story itself' (I, 28; i, 344). They continued to worry him all the same, and in his sequel he would apply more rigorous criteria. To express concern for unity the way Cervantes did was exceptional for a Spanish prose-fiction writer of his generation. Alemán, for instance, introduced several short stories into his novel without evidently worrying about them at all.

The six in *Don Quixote*, Part I, need a section to themselves, although to do them justice would require another book.

(ii) THE EXTRANEOUS EPISODES

By 'extraneous episode' I mean a story of more than anecdotic length, with a certain coherence, and of which the origin and development, but not necessarily the conclusion, have nothing to do with Don Quixote or Sancho. This therefore excludes the fantasies invented by Don Quixote or on account of him, or an incident like the simulated Arcadia (II, 58) which has no 'story' in the usual sense of the word. It covers the tales of Grisóstomo and Marcela (I, 11–14), Cardenio and Dorotea (I, 23–4, 27–9, 36), *El curioso impertinente* (I, 33–5), the Captive Captain (I, 39–41), Doña Clara and Don Luis (I, 42–3 and passim), and Leandra (I, 51).[10]

The sad little story of Grisóstomo and Marcela is related to the affair of Galercio and the disdainful Gelasia in the *Galatea* (IV–VI). It is the first of the episodes, and its pastoral stylization may be disconcerting to the modern reader. Nevertheless, with admirable skill Cervantes brings us gradually into this very 'literary' ambience via the realistically rustic goatherds, the oration on the mythical Golden Age, Antonio's ballad, Pedro's narrative with its mispronunciations, and arrives at the funeral scene with its much grander language and dramatic attitudes. There is another concession to the realism of the surrounding narrative context in the pointed references to the characters being dressed up as shepherds, though no attempt is made to explain why they should do such a thing. The story begins with the news of Grisóstomo's death, and the events leading up to this are narrated by Pedro, who is not involved in them. The denouement is then enacted on the main narrative level, and is the *raison d'être* of the story.

It is much less the account of a tragic love affair than it is an account of the effect of Grisóstomo's suicide on Marcela.[11] Like so many pastoral stories it centres on a *cuestión de amor*, which in this case is: if one is passionately loved by someone, is one under an obligation to respond? Marcela answers this question in a dazzling display of eloquence with an emphatic No. Her spirited defence of the inalienable rights of womanhood make her one of the most interesting of Cervantes's many independent-minded young women. Her defence is inviolable; but, as has been pointed out, her want of compassion and tact alienates much of the sympathy her case arouses (Hart and Rendall, 1978D).

The intertwined stories of Cardenio and Luscinda, Dorotea and Don Fernando comprise the second episode, which threads in and out of the main action, and which has a comically distorted reflection in the invented chivalric fantasy-tale about the Princess Micomicona. Its characters, especially Dorotea, who doubles as the Princess, become more involved in Don Quixote's affairs than do those of any other, but it is none the less a complete and detachable *novela*. A trail of mysterious discoveries leads to the goatherd's account of the madman of the mountains and then to the appearance of the distracted lover Cardenio himself. He tells his story in two instalments, each to a different audience, Dorotea adds a third, and the conclusion, which sorts out and reunites the couples correctly, takes place later at the inn. The ravelling and unravelling of the tangled fortunes of Cardenio and Dorotea, with the help of Providence and some more feminine eloquence (Dorotea's), would doubtless have been the features of most interest to Cervantes's contemporaries, but the personalities of some of the characters are by no means uninteresting.

Cardenio is a study in cowardice and indecision.[12] Helpless at moments of crisis, he is brought by Don Fernando's treachery and his own remorse to the point of a nervous breakdown. Dorotea, in contrast, has great determination and prudence (*discreción*), and her involvement with Don Quixote brings out the additional quality of humour (*donaire*). Her social status – her parents are well-to-do peasant farmers – is important because Don Fernando is the second son of a duke. He is a basically uncomplicated compound of selfish sexual appetite and noble generosity. His betrayal of a friend, seduction, broken vows and abduction of Luscinda make him at first the complete 'cad', not to mention practically a bigamist. The modern reader may well feel incredulous when he surrenders and outraged at the way he escapes even poetic justice, but the point is that his liberality – the word is used several times – overcomes his lust and his remorse is genuine.[13] This redeems him completely. The wedding with the weak-willed Luscinda is rendered invalid by the betrothal to Dorotea, whose precautions had invested this with the solemn sanctity of marriage.

El curioso impertinente is presented as a piece of fiction read aloud by the Priest to the company at the inn. Don Quixote's farcical attack on the wineskins comes as an interruption just when the edifice of illusion Anselmo has built for himself is complete, only to collapse in ruins around him as soon as the story is resumed. With its concentrated, intricate plot it is highly theatrical in the best sense of the word. Indeed, it is perhaps the nearest thing to pure tragedy Cervantes ever wrote, with a Shakespearian quality about it. Events move inexorably and, though an accident leads to the discovery of Camila's infidelity, some such mischance was inevitable sooner or later. There is turn and turn-about of deception, yet each permutation of the plot has a terrible plausibility. The sustained double movement whereby events move in one direction and illusion in another is symbolized in a vividly kinetic mannerist image: 'With every step that Camila descended to the deep centre of her degradation, she mounted in her husband's eyes to the pinnacle of virtue and esteem' (I, 34; i, 423). What sets everything in motion is Anselmo's obsession with his wife's purity.

Commenting on the story later, the Priest finds it hard to accept that a husband would get his best friend to put his wife's chastity to the test. But this has to be accepted, and the reader today should have no difficulty in doing so the moment he realizes that Anselmo is a psychiatric case. Cervantes makes this perfectly clear at the start. He is the victim of a compulsion, the irrational and dangerous nature of which he is entirely aware of. It is 'a desire so strange and out of the ordinary' that he is amazed at it, and reproaches himself and tries 'to suppress his own thoughts' (I, 33; i, 402). He even compares it to one of those irrational cravings of (pregnant) women 'to eat earth, clay, coal and worse things' (p. 411). He insists and pleads with the shocked Lotario, and thanks him with unnatural effusiveness when, to humour him, his friend at first pretends to give in. It is clear that Anselmo unconsciously wants what he consciously dreads most: namely that his friend should go to bed with his wife. In the fact of their great friendship – he and Lotario had been known to everyone as 'the two friends' – there is a suggestion of homosexual relationship. He has a complex about power and more than a touch of the voyeur in him as well.[14] When he gets his way, conventional values are upset, dishonour is sought, there is neurosis in the air and the whole house is infected.

It would be quite wrong, though, to treat the story as a case-study of abnormal psychology. Both the tragedy of human relations and the intellectual argument are more heavily emphasized. Anselmo's aberration is simply the premiss from which everything follows with remorseless logic. Except at the beginning and the end, the focus is mainly on the adulterous couple caught in their own web of deception. Anselmo tried to make an abstraction out of a human relationship and the result is both tragic and a paradox. Camila's virtue proved illusory when put to the test, which it would not have done if he had not tested it. But how could he be certain without the test? The message is clear. There are things which must be taken on trust if they are to be accepted as truths. They are not open to empirical proof or rational demonstration, and to try them is impertinent curiosity. Some things have to be believed in, rather than believed.

For Cervantes, impertinent curiosity also underlies jealous fears.[15] Anselmo suffers from the same pestilential malady – an obsession with his wife's purity – as Carrizales, the *celoso extremeño*. The form it takes is diametrically the reverse, but the starting-point is the same, and the calamitous end. In both *novelas* the husband eventually realizes that he is the cause of his own dishonour – which is refreshingly different from the usual line taken by those outraged husbands, the Spanish Othellos who figure in seventeenth-century plays.

The topic of the two friends and the idea of a husband testing his wife's fidelity have long histories, going back to the *Gesta Romanorum*, to look no farther.[16] More immediately, the story is a descendant of the Timbrio–Silerio story in the *Galatea* and a collateral of the *Celoso extremeño*.[17] Like the latter, it is more novel than romance, although because of its rhetorical features this may not be immediately obvious. Nicholas Baudouin published a French translation of the *novela* as early as 1608.

The story of the Captive Captain follows the fictional *curioso* and the dramatic 'real-life' conclusion of the Cardenio–Dorotea story. It is set in a contemporary historical setting, and like Cervantes's plays *Los tratos de Argel* and *Los baños de Argel* makes much use of his personal experiences in north Africa. But it is a curious amalgam, for even though the most novelesque parts are known to be based on fact to an unusual degree[18] there are clear analogies with folk-tale.[19] The Captive is everyone's idea of a hero: stalwart man of action and considerate lover. As teller of the story, he depicts Zoraida, his Moorish maiden, as all ingenuous charm and touching devotion. But she has been seen as a more ambivalent figure, ruthlessly single-minded in her determination to escape with him to Spain and embrace the Christian faith (Percas de Ponseti, 1975D, Vol. 1, pp. 226 ff.; Márquez Villanueva, 1975D, pp. 116 ff.). The absence of a visible and plausible motive for the author to discredit Zoraida works against this interpretation, but it is true that the focus of interest shifts in the course of the tale from the drama of the Captive's escape to Zoraida's separation from her anguished father.

An epilogue outside the Captain's narrative serves to rivet it on to the central structure of the novel. By happy chance the Magistrate who presently arrives at the inn is a brother of the long-lost Captain (I, 42). This is artistically prefigured earlier when a member of the audience turns out to be a brother of one of the persons named in the story (I, 39). The Magistrate has come with his daughter Doña Clara, and she and her sweetheart Don Luis are the protagonists of the next episode, which just qualifies by our definition. It is a mere sketch, part narration, part action, an episode of a juvenile love-story, not much more than an escapade, which is brought by adult intervention, in stages, to a vague but hopeful conclusion.

The last external episode in Part I is pastoral like the first one. But the fair Leandra is the opposite of the beautiful Marcela and loses her honour if not her virginity. The milieu and events of this brief story, narrated in its entirety by Eugenio, one of the lovelorn suitors, are more realistically rural. Only after the girl has been packed off to a convent do her disappointed lovers take to the woods and fields, turning the place very purposefully into Arcadia. There is a gently ironic note which places the tale in an indeterminate area between pastoral parody and comic realism.

The variety and scale of this miniature anthology of stories is a sufficient reminder that *Don Quixote*, Part I, is still not all that far removed from the traditional collection of *novelle* set in a framework of storytellers. But they are more firmly embedded in the novel than appears at first sight. All kinds of thematic and structural connections have been found – kinds of love and passion, heroism, mental aberration, obsession, deception, truth and illusion, and others, including some of mind-numbing ingenuity. Without going below the surface of events at all, a significant link with the central action can be found. With the exception of the *Curioso*, all these extraneous episodes are, from the viewpoint of any character on the main narrative level, real happenings remarkable enough to 'make a good story'. Though mostly of love, they are adventures – but *true* adventures as contrasted with the *fantastic* ones imagined by Don Quixote or invented for him by others.

The Knight's reactions to them and the extent to which he (or Sancho) intervenes in them thus constitute an indication of their relevance. Quixote is immediately interested in the affairs of Grisóstomo and of Leandra, and he even imitates the lovers of Marcela in a small way (I, 12; i, 167). Likewise, he is intrigued by Cardenio and offers to help or console him (I, 24; i, 291). But, if he heard the Captive's tale, he shows no interest in it. He does not really wish to know the true story of Dorotea (I, 37). He apparently knows nothing of Doña Clara's. The *Curioso impertinente* he never hears at all. He makes a sort of late intervention after Marcela disappears and even goes off after her (I, 14; i, 188–9), and he offers to abduct Leandra from the convent (I, 52; i, 596). Nothing comes of this either time. Ironically, three of the true adventures simply pass him by, which in the case of the heroic Captain and of Dorotea, a genuine damsel in distress, is remarkable. The inference is that he is too absorbed in his own inner world; he is too mad to notice. Things will be different in Part II.

Leaving aside the *Curioso*, each of these stories contains clear elements of romance, which have bothered readers from Charles Sorel to Thomas Mann[20] and since. The most conspicuous of these elements are, first, the relative idealization of the main characters;[21] and, second, the intervention of accident, usually in the form of providential encounters. As soon as figures from these episodes are around, dramatic appearances and surprising recognitions are liable to occur unexplained. Thus Marcela (I, 14), Cardenio's reappearance (I, 27), Dorotea's meeting with him (I, 28–9), their meeting with Don Fernando and Luscinda (I, 36), the Captain and his brother (I, 42). And these things happen on the main narrative level, especially at the inn, which for this reason has sometimes been seen as tinged with the magical glow of romance. In the Cardenio–Dorotea story idealization of character is decidedly limited, to say the least, but divine providence plays a decisive role in bringing events to their happy conclusion. The persons present recognize this explicitly, referring directly to heaven's intervention no less than eight times.[22] As readers, we are witnessing a small irruption of romance into the novel, the brief intersection of two fictional worlds.

In this particular story romance also breaks through in other ways. Cardenio and Dorotea each withdraw into the wilds like courtly or pastoral lovers in distress, although, interestingly, we catch them only on the frontiers of Arcadia. Meeting Don Quixote and his friends keeps them out, so to speak. Cardenio is briefly bathed in chivalric light a couple of times. First, when he meets Don Quixote: 'the Ragged One with the Wretched Face' (*el Roto de la mala Figura*) and 'he of the Sorry Countenance' embrace as though Don Quixote 'had known him for a long time' (I, 23; i, 290). Later he addresses Dorotea in exactly the terms our Knight might use – 'I swear to you as a gentleman [*caballero* also means "knight"] and a Christian not to forsake you until I see you restored to Don Fernando . . . ', and he even employs the chivalresque phrase 'by reason of the unreason' (*en razón de la sinrazon*; cf. I, 1) (I, 29; i, 360–1). The reminiscence is pastoral when the Priest and Barber meet him: they find him singing sad verses like any shepherd-courtier (I, 27). So it is again when Dorotea makes her first appearance, dressed as a rustic youth and revealing her true gender as she bathes her crystal-white feet in the stream and lets down her sun-gold hair (I, 28).

The scene of reunion between all four at the inn, however, recalls not so much romance as high romantic drama, which Cervantes plays for all he is worth. He spins out the theatrical pleasure with the artificial concealment of identities and protracted recognitions (I, 36). Something very similar occurs again when the Captive and the Magistrate meet as long-separated brothers. Don Quixote puts this down to the prodigies of knight errantry (I, 43; i, 520), but of course there is nothing supernatural about it: such things do happen. Now and then.

Is Cervantes writing tongue-in-cheek? A straight answer to this question hardly seems possible. Not a little depends on the reader's frame of mind. But even when Cervantes gives a providentially free rein to coincidence I see not the slightest indication that any parodic intention there may be is derisive. Nor is it likely that he was unconscious of what he was doing. The proportions of romance and realism vary in the different *novelas*. Modern readers have naturally tended to find the traditional romance elements irritating, and of more interest those in the stories in both parts of the novel which, as Edwin Williamson says, point to an area of reality, the inner life of the characters, beyond the reach of traditional romance procedures (1982D, p. 66).[23]

NOTES: CHAPTER 7

1 Menéndez Pidal (1964D), p. 57; Hatzfeld (1966D), p. 113; Stagg (1964D). Casalduero (1949D), p. 64, and Gaos (1959D), pp. 95 ff., reject the notion.

2 See Willis (1953D). There is some precedent in earlier prose fiction for unexpected and effective chapter breaks: e.g. *Amadís de Gaula*, III, 33–4; IV, 94–5; IV, 131–2.

3 See Joly (1982E), a fundamental study; and Welsh (1981E), pp. 81 ff., on their function in novelistic realism.

4 See Guilbeau (1962D) and Barrick (1976D).

5 Segre has observed that 'Il *Don Chisciotte* è una specie di galleria dei generi letterari del suo tempo' (1974D, p. 192).

6 Pierre Ullman describes a deeper structural function of the poems (1961–2D).

7 Diverse approaches to the whole question of structure are found in: Casalduero (1949D), Parker (1956D), Togeby (1957D), De Chasca (1964D), Hatzfeld (1966D), pp. 7 ff., Castro (1967[1]D), Bell (1968D), Segre (1974D), Percas de Ponseti (1975D), Vol. 1, pp. 156 ff.

8 'The novel is a powerful example of the process of the growth of a work of art in a writer's mind, and of the luck of writing' (Pritchett, 1965E, p. 170).

9 See Atlee (1982D), on the interpretation of the title 'Caballero de la Triste Figura'.

10 Much has been written on these episodes. In addition to the studies mentioned in note 7 above, see: Madariaga (1961D), pp. 86 ff.; Immerwahr (1958D); Dudley (1972D); Márquez Villanueva (1975D), pp. 15 ff.; Avalle-Arce (1975D), pp. 91 ff.; Martínez Bonati (1977D); Herrero (1981[2]D); Williamson (1982D); Johnson (1982D).

11 On the debated question of the suicide, see Inventosch (1974D).

12 On the lost play by Shakespeare and Fletcher, based on this story, see Muir (1960E), pp. 148–60.

13 See Herrero (1976–7D) on the association discernible between Don Fernando's lust, the giant Pandafilando de la Fosca Vista and the wineskins attacked by Don Quixote (I, 35) first noted by Casalduero.

14 'Some male homosexuals who are still predominantly fascinated by the male may yet admit to fantasies in which their favourite man is observed to be having intercourse with a woman. Sometimes the subject himself is watching the procedure with interest' (Storr, 1981E, p. 116). For examples of the theme of irregular sexuality in Golden Age drama, see Bradbury (1981E). We may note the occurrence of male friends in other episodes: Grisóstomo's close friend Ambrosio, Cardenio's treacherous friend Don Fernando, the goatherd Eugenio's friendly rival, another Anselmo. The relationships vary a good deal in kind (see Andrist, 1983D), and there is no call whatever to read notions of physical homosexuality into contemporary ideals of male friendship. But Anselmo, who tells Lotario that he would never have married Camila if he had thought this would mean he and his friend would see less of each other (I, 33; i, p. 400), is surely an aberrant case.

15 See *Galatea*, III; i, 228, and *Casa de los celos* (*Comedias y entremeses*, 1915–22A, i, 181).
16 See Avalle-Arce (1975D), pp. 157 ff., Percas de Ponseti (1975D), Vol. 1, pp. 125 ff.
17 All three share similarly rhetorical phraseology at a comparable climactic moment: 'Vi a Nísida, a Nísida vi, para no ver más, ni hay más que ver después de haberla visto' (*Galatea*, II; i, 143); 'Leonora se rindío, Leonora se engañó y Leonora se perdío' (*Celoso extremeño*, *Novelas ejemplares*, ii, 129); 'Rindióse Camila; Camila se rindío' (*Don Quixote*, I, 32; i, 420).
18 Oliver Asín (1947–8D), as updated especially by Canavaggio (1977D, pp. 73–6, and 1981[1]D).
19 Márquez Villanueva (1975D), pp. 102 ff.; Chevalier (1983D).
20 'I cannot but shake my head over the single tales scattered through it, so extravagantly sentimental they are, so precisely in the style and taste of the very productions that the poet had set himself to mock' (Mann, 1969D, p. 56).
21 Cervantes gets into a difficulty when the lovely Doña Clara arrives at the inn. Had the people there not already seen Dorotea and Luscinda and Zoraida, we read, they would have thought beauty like hers hard to find (I, 42; i, 515)! Irony offers a way out, but not a very suitable one.
22 *Don Quixote*, I, 36; i, 449–50, 453, 454, 456, and ch. 37, p. 456. Similar allusions may be found occasionally in some of the realistic *novelas*, where they tend to take on a manifestly ironic note. 'Heaven ordained' that Carrizales should wake up in spite of being drugged (*Novelas*, ii, 130). Rinconete and Cortadillo met 'by chance' (*acaso*) at the Inn of Molinillo, but Rinconete refers to the meeting as being 'not unmysterious' (*Novelas*, i, 191, 194).
23 Compare another modern novelist who did not shy away from coincidences:

. . . 'that those two young men should have met last night in that manner is, I say, a coincidence – a remarkable coincidence. Why, I don't believe now,' added Tim, taking off his spectacles, and smiling as with a gentle pride, 'that there's such a place in all the world for coincidences as London is!'
'I don't know about that,' said Mr Frank; 'but—'
'Don't know about it, Mr Francis!' interrupted Tim, with an obstinate air. 'Well, but let us know. If there is any better place for such things, where is it? Is it in Europe? No, that it isn't. Is it in Asia? Why, of course it's not. Is it in Africa? Not a bit of it. Is it in America? You know better than that at all events. Well, then,' said Tim, folding his arms resolutely, 'where is it?'
'I was not about to dispute the point, Tim,' said young Cheeryble, laughing. 'I am not such a heretic as that. All I was going to say was, that I hold myself under an obligation to the coincidence, that's all.'
'Oh, if you don't dispute it,' said Tim, quite satisfied, that's another thing . . . '
(Charles Dickens, *Nicholas Nickleby*, ch. 43)

CHAPTER 8

Don Quixote Continued

At the end of Part I, Cervantes introduced a rumour or legend about a third sortie of Don Quixote's, thus leaving a convenient opening for a sequel if this seemed to be called for. In case it did not, he concluded with a set of commemorative epitaphs for Don Quixote, Sancho and Dulcinea. In this way he hedged his bets, leaving his novel suspended between the possibility of a continuation and the suggestion of a conclusion.[1]

Just when he started work on Part II is little more certain than it was in the case of Part I. Estimates range from 1606 to 1612 or later, but those which suggest about 1609 seem more likely. Cervantes first announces it as forthcoming in the prologue to the *Novelas ejemplares* (1613); but the *Parnaso*, the *Persiles* and the compiling of his dramatic works were all competing for his attention. He had written about half the eventual book a year later, if the date of 20 July 1614 on Sancho's letter in chapter 36 represents the day Cervantes wrote it. Be that as it may, he was given cause to hurry in the latter part of that year.

A second part of *Don Quixote*, licensed on 4 July for the diocese of Tarragona, was published probably in September under the name of one Licenciado Alonso Fernández de Avellaneda. His true identity is still unknown despite the quantities of research and conjecture devoted to it from the middle of the nineteenth century on. All that can be concluded as reasonably sure is that he was Aragonese, a rather narrow Catholic, knew the University of Alcalá de Henares, was hostile to Cervantes by whom he felt in some way offended, and was a fervent admirer of Lope de Vega.[2]

Oblivious of paying Cervantes the supreme compliment of imitation, he insults him in the prologue, deriding his age and lack of friends, and accusing him of spite and offensiveness to himself and Lope de Vega. The last accusation was not wholly without foundation, of course, and it is also the case that some of Avellaneda's gibes are not unperceptive. He describes *Don Quixote* as 'almost a *comedia*' and most of Cervantes's *novelas* as '*comedias* in prose' (prol.; i, 7, 12). Whether he was referring to Cervantes's use of dialogue, the theatrical character of some of his writing, or something else, the remarks have often been picked up by critics and variously utilized. With some insight Avellaneda also observed that he was of an 'opposite humour' to Cervantes (p. 13). A little more reflection, however, might have told him that incompatibility of temperament was a good reason for not trying to write in the same vein.

It is not necessary here to say much about the characteristics and qualities of the work.[3] Because comparison with the original is inescapable they are easily underrated. The book is quite funny now and again, it has a kind of unity which appealed to the eighteenth century, and it shows a certain narrative fluency which recalls some of the picaresque novelists. But Avellaneda lacks the subtlety and sympathy of Cervantes and works in a very much cruder way. His Quixote gives up Dulcinea, raves, irrationally attacks Sancho, is a public spectacle and ends in the madhouse. Avellaneda seems more interested in Sancho, whom he exploits but does not often raise above the level of buffoon. Running through the book is an unpleasant streak of cruelty mingled with vulgarity, another aspect of which is found in the sensationalist violence and piety of the two extraneous stories, which are well told all the same.

After the 'authentic' continuation came out, almost nothing was heard of Avellaneda's until Lesage took it up and adapted it into French (1704). This gave it a certain prestige which in the next three years sparked off English, Dutch and German translations. The second Spanish edition followed in 1732.

Cervantes probably first saw a copy about September 1614. Since his first mention of Avellaneda occurs in chapter 59 of his own Part II, it is usually supposed that this was the point he had reached at the time. However, there is not the slightest reason why he should not have heard of it before that and waited for a convenient moment in his narration. From chapter 59 to the end there are some half-dozen allusions to it.

There are a few rather curious points of similarity between the two Parts II, which have given rise to speculation (see Riquer, 1962A, introduction, pp. xxxiv ff.), although when all proper allowances are made not much mystery is left. Discounting any correspondences which occur in Cervantes from chapter 59 onwards (because from there one is obliged to accept it as probable that Cervantes was imitating Avellaneda for his own purposes)[4] there is only a little which is not easily attributable to mere coincidence and to the fact that both books have the same starting-point. For instance, Avellaneda's Quixote sees a play performed, gets carried away and interrupts the performance (ch. 27) like Cervantes's Quixote at the puppet show (II, 26). But the coincidence is unsurprising; given the nature of the hero's aberration, it even seems likely that such an event would occur to any author having a Don Quixote to invent episodes for. Sancho's role of buffoon at the house of the 'Archipámpano' (Avellaneda, chs 33 ff.) is like that of the other Sancho at the Duke's castle (Cervantes, chs 31 ff.). The nature of the character, his appearance now in elevated social circles, and the author's wish to capitalize on Sancho's popularity with readers of Part I account for either case easily enough.

But what of Sancho's letter to his wife in Avellaneda (ch. 35) and the other Sancho's letter to his Teresa in Cervantes (ch. 36)? The two missives do not have more in common than one would expect, nor do they have less. But the fact that Sancho should send a letter to his wife at all does not seem to me to carry such a weight of built-in probability as the two cases previously mentioned. This raises the question whether one author followed the lead of the other, though of course pure coincidence can not be ruled out. It is not very likely that either writer had detailed knowledge of the other's work before publication. The possibility remains, therefore, that Cervantes added to or modified his own work after reading Avellaneda. Presumably any such addition or modification would have been very minor; Cervantes cannot ever have *needed* an Avellaneda. But whether the letters were linked or independently conceived it was a good idea, which in Cervantes initiates a brief run of diverting correspondence involving the Panza family.[5]

The most interesting, certainly the most unconventional coincidence is the faint suggestion in Cervantes of the existence of a fictitious or pseudo-Quixote and pseudo-Sancho before Avellaneda's rival heroes ever cast their shadows over the real ones, as they do in chapters 59–72. The aptly titled Knight of the Mirrors (Carrasco) claimed to have defeated in combat a Don Quixote who was not the real one (II, 14); and Sancho introduces himself to the Duchess, a little oddly, as the Sancho Panza who figured in Part I 'unless I was changed in my cradle – I mean in the press' (II, 30; ii, 270). One can hardly believe that Cervantes wrote the passages in later. Rather, these obscure premonitions seem to highlight the brilliance with which he later integrated Avellaneda's work into his own, thereby elaborating on a theme that had already been suggested in his own novel.

Cervantes starts his prologue to Part II by explicitly refraining from indulging in the slanging match the reader might have expected (ii, 33); he replies to Avellaneda here in a comparatively dignified fashion. This is not to say that he does not take his revenge, though. He does so principally by enshrining his criticism of Avellaneda in his own novel, for ever, as part of his own story of *Don Quixote*. Alemán had done the same, though in a somewhat different way, with Martí's sequel in *Guzmán*, Part II. There can be no doubt that Cervantes was angered and upset by what had happened, as may be deduced from passages like the one in Part II, chapter 70. The anecdotes about the madmen maltreating dogs, personally addressed to Avellaneda in the prologue, are rather enigmatic. But, whether or not they mean more than they seem to, their nastiness aptly conjures up an aspect of his rival's work.

As Avellaneda was careful to remark in his prologue, there was nothing new in a writer taking over the creation of another and continuing the story. Alemán and Cervantes both had occasion for some personal resentment at the way it was done to them but, even so, there is something modern in their concern. It is a premonitiòn of the proprietary hold of the professional writer on his work. There was no law of copyright yet, but the essential anonymity of the medieval writer was a thing of the past. The two novelists show a kind of self-identification with their work, shared, too, in different ways, by Tasso with his *Gerusalemme liberata* and Montaigne with his *Essais*. At the end of *Don Quixote* Cide Hamete's pen is told to proclaim

> For me alone Don Quixote was born, and I for him; he knew how to act and I how to write; only we two are as one, despite the fake Tordesillescan scribe . . .

> (Para mí sola nació don Quijote, y yo para él; él supo obrar y yo escribir; solos los dos somos para en uno, a despecho y pesar del escritor fingido y tordesillesco . . . : II, 74; ii, 592)

And because of Avellaneda and others like him there must be no doubt this time that Don Quixote is finally and for ever laid to rest (p. 593, and prol., p. 37). 'My valorous knight', 'my true Don Quixote', he calls him (pp. 592–3).

These vigorous expressions of attachment to his hero indicate the complete confidence Cervantes now had in his creation. It shows through the annoyance with Avellaneda, and through the jocularity of the dedication to the Conde de Lemos (with its joke about *Don Quixote* being used as a college text in China). It was no doubt boosted, too, by the unusually warm terms in which the *aprobación* of the Licenciado Márquez Torres is couched. Indeed, Márquez Torres is so much in tune with Cervantes that there is reason to suspect that Cervantes had some connection with the writing of it (Rivers, 1960D; Riley, 1976D, pp. 194–5). He tells of the fame of the *Galatea* and the *Novelas ejemplares* in France and of the poverty of their author.

This *aprobación* is dated 27 February 1615. The book, licensed for all the dominions of Spain, came out at the end of the year. Cervantes had less than six months to live. This year 1616 saw another edition published in Brussels and another in Valencia; 1617 one more in Libson. Parts I and II were published together for the first time in Barcelona, 1617, commissioned by the publishers who brought out the *Persiles* there in the same year (Moll, 1979E, 105).[6]

NOTES: CHAPTER 8

1 Apart from this, the conclusion of Part I reads rather like the prologue to a putative sequel, as Mario Socrate notes (1974D, p. 71).

2 These are basically the conclusions of M. de Riquer in the introduction to his edition of Avellaneda (1972C), i, p. lxxx.

3 See ibid., pp. lxxx ff.; Durán (1973D), pp. 357 ff.; Gilman (1951D).

4 This is undoubtedly the case with Sancho's comic exchange with the landlord about the supper he orders, in ch. 59 itself: compare Avellaneda, chs 23, 24. At the same time the passage belongs to a popular tradition of jokes about the catering in inns (Joly, 1982E, pp. 533 ff.).

5 It is possible that the date on Sancho's letter, 20 July, with the year 1614, which is so extremely out of step with the existing disorder of the chronology, might have been prompted by Avellaneda. It clearly predates the publication of Avellaneda's *Quixote*. Cervantes could have put it in either to advertise the genuine priority of his own letter, or else maybe to disguise that it was a later insertion. This is, of course, pure hypothesis, occasioned by the unique mention of the year.

6 On the work of the compositors this time, see Flores (1981D). He concludes that, together with an apprentice, there were four compositors, each with 'his own distinct spelling and punctuation preferences and his own peculiar setting habits' (p. 43).

CHAPTER 9

The Structure of Part II

(i) THE MAIN STORY

Don Quixote, Part II, comes near to being the perfect sequel. Dependent on the earlier book without repetition, developing and diversifying without sacrificing familiarity, it is a richer and profounder work. Though leisurely in its unfolding, and despite a hiccup in the middle, it is more tightly wrought and centres more firmly on Quixote and Sancho. To achieve any fruitful new development Cervantes had to introduce some significant new factor or exploit some elements present in the first part. He did both.[1]

There are two new factors of major importance. First, he modifies one aspect of Don Quixote's madness: not his basic belief in the historicity of the chivalric romances, not his essential belief in the rightness of his chivalric mission, but his *spontaneous* misreading of physical appearances – the very basis of so many of his early adventures. Whatever the presumable explanation for the change – and a month's rest in bed since the first expedition would be sufficient reason – henceforth he no longer takes inns for castles, sheep for warriors, and so on. There is one major exception to this, which will be dealt with later. But apart from that relapse his mental health has in an important way improved. When he does misinterpret the reality behind the appearance, it is either because other people mislead him (over Dulcinea and at the castle, for example), or because the illusory aspect is abnormally intense or theatrical (Carrasco disguised as a knight, the puppet show). One of the amusing ironies of Part II is that reality itself starts living up more to Don Quixote's earlier expectations of it. His encounters, without being fantastic, are now often distinctly out of the ordinary. He meets, for example, costumed actors on the road, lions, a duke and duchess, bandits, corsairs and several persons disguised for one reason or another.

The second new factor is a highly original idea: nothing less than the incorporation into the fiction of Part II of the extraneous but indisput-

able fact of the publication and success of Part I.² Don Quixote and
Sancho meet people – first Sansón Carrasco, then the Duke and
Duchess, and others after that – who have read the account of their
earlier adventures. The heroes are therefore known about in advance by
certain other characters who on several notable occasions fabricate
situations for them to react to. These include the most elaborate
deceptions in the whole novel. So if we are tempted to complain that
these adventures in Part II are often highly contrived, which they
undeniably are, we should remember that it is the characters who appear
as immediately responsible for the contriving, not the author.

Less fundamentally a new factor, but a new agent exerting an
influence on events, is the Bachelor, Sansón Carrasco, who takes over
the initiative previously exercised by the Priest and the Barber. He
'humours' Don Quixote by encouraging him to set out on his travels
again (II, 4 and 7), and then goes out in pursuit to fetch him home by a
trick. Since the first attempt to do this ends in total failure (II, 14), he has
to do it all over again (II, 64). The two combats between Don Quixote
and the Bachelor, disguised each time as a rival knight errant, are thus
nodal points in the central action of Part II. The first is a triumph for
Don Quixote and the second a disaster, each having the effect on him
that might be expected.

As well as these new things, Cervantes develops as major motifs two
'elements' in the *Quixote* of 1605, which were just possibilities there.
Both of them involve Sancho, which does much to account for his
greater prominence in the sequel. One of them is that Sancho actually
acquires the governorship of what he is given to suppose is an island, just
as his master had promised when they first set out together. This event,
the most elaborate hoax in the book, is the high point of Sancho's career.
The Barataria episode (chs 44–53) shows us a side of Sancho which we
had only glimpsed before, diversifies the narrative with new kinds of
material, and openly presents questions of a political and ethical kind.

The other development springs out of the lie Sancho told his master,
at the bidding of the Priest and the Barber, about his embassy to
Dulcinea (I, 31). Sancho finds himself in an embarrassing position when
his master now decides that they should call on her in El Toboso (II,
9–10). He extricates himself temporarily by telling another lie, giving
Don Quixote to believe that Dulcinea is bewitched to look like a coarse
farm girl. This alleged enchantment is henceforth a constant source of
anxiety to Don Quixote and a major strand in the story, out of sight
much of the time, surfacing occasionally, but always there. No decep-

tion or ruse in Part I, not even that of Princess Micomicona, is so consistently sustained, or has anything like the same impact on Don Quixote's feelings. It is an important structural link between external action and internal. Dulcinea's enchantment can also be read, with entire psychological plausibility, as the major cause of Don Quixote's dream in the Cave of Montesinos, an episode seen to be preoccupying him on more than one subsequent occasion (see II, 25, 41 and 62).

Connected with Don Quixote's normal freedom now from ocular delusion is the fact that a higher proportion of encounters and events can not be classed as 'adventures' in the old sense at all. There are more casual meetings and ordinary conversations. Quixote and Sancho are seen moving in society and being much more a part of it than previously. Near the end of the book, for the first time, they enter a city.

Barcelona is the farthest point on their long journey, half across Spain. They reach it not by any whim of Rocinante's or anyone else's design, but of Don Quixote's own volition, after he has changed his mind about going to Zaragoza. For particular reasons of the Knight's they have also visited El Toboso and the Cave of Montesinos and decided to have a look along part of the River Ebro. The wanderings of Part II thus are much less undirected. The basic pattern of the previous expeditions (outward journey, stay at an inn, return) is still discernible, but it is elaborated. The protracted sojourn at a genuine castle this time (chs 30–57) replaces those at the inns which Quixote had insisted were castles previously. There are short or overnight stops at three inns and brief stays at three private houses as well.

The Knight and Squire dominate Part II more than they did Part I. They are more involved even in the external episodes. The greater cohesion does not prevent the work falling into recognizable sections (chs 1–7, 8–29, 30–57, 58–65, 66–73, 74), but the divisions are determined by the course of events affecting the two heroes, not by the external episodes. In Part I these episodes cause the narrative to split and branch right in the middle of the novel, while in Part II they are more spaced out. The only notable syncopation is when the story zigzags between Don Quixote in the castle and Governor Sancho, plus a quick excursion to the latter's family back home (II, 44–55).

It is quite often supposed that, because of Avellaneda, Cervantes finished *Don Quixote* in a hurry. This is very possible, but very hard to show. At any rate, I doubt that it has anything to do with the obviously repetitious features in the last dozen chapters or so. The talking bronze head (ch. 62) echoes the fortune-telling monkey (ch. 25), for example,

and Quixote's pastoral project and the herd of pigs (chs 67–8) recall the
simulated Arcadia and the herd of bulls (ch. 58). There are several more.
However, one may rate their effectiveness, these narrative reprises are
not the procedures of an author in a hurry. A single chapter would have
sufficed to bring the heroes home. There was already a tendency to
devise parallel incidents or group episodes with something in common.
Don Quixote descends into the Cave of Montesinos (chs 22–3), and
Sancho falls into an underground pit (ch. 55),[3] Chapters 24, 25 and 27
give us braying aldermen and a talking monkey; chapters 19–21
variations on the theme of Art versus Nature (see Casalduero, 1949D,
pp. 260 ff.).

Except for the subordination of the extraneous episodes, the second
part of *Don Quixote* is not constructed in any essentially dissimilar way
from the first. It is another account of a journey, still basically episodic
with many unexpected encounters. The improvised look is still there
(nowhere more so than when the Knight changes his destination from
Zaragoza to Barcelona: II, 59), but so are a few clear signs of planning.
Thus the defeated Sansón Carrasco is left musing on his revenge and we
are warned (II, 15) that the history will be returning to him in due
course, as indeed it does, almost fifty chapters later. Naturally, we can
find more of those subtler links behind different portions of the novel,
too. Something very like the adventure of the 'enchanted barque' (ch.
29) had already come into the mind of Don Quixote (II, 1; ii, 48). And
long before Sancho asks Don Quixote to be paid for his whipping (ch.
71) he had speculated over what he would have earned had he been paid
four *maravadíes* for every blow he had received on the previous trip (II,
4; ii, 69).

The main ingredients of the earlier book are found again here, though
not necessarily in the same proportions. A few additional kinds of
miscellaneous literature make their presence felt: notably in Don
Quixote's counsels to Sancho on the duties and attributes of a good
governor, and also in the clever judgements of Sancho in Barataria.
Indeed, the heterogeneous generic elements in the whole Barataria
sequence are quite easily spotted. In this same part of the novel, between
chapters 47 and 52, six letters are also dispersed. There are signs around
here, if not of a crisis in the composition of the work, at least of a
disturbance, or a hiccup, in the inventive flow.

Even so, and despite the continuing absence of a central intrigue or
plot, the sequel coheres better than the work of 1605, and what focuses
the reader's attention more than anything else is the concentration on

Quixote and Sancho. But at this point, a little more than halfway through, Cervantes complains through one or other of his intermediaries of finding it a strain to be tied to

> such a dry and limited history as this one of Don Quixote; for it seemed to him that he must always be talking of him and Sancho, without daring to expatiate in other more serious and more entertaining digressions and episodes. And he said that to have mind, hand and pen always restricted to a single subject and to speak through the mouths of so few characters was an intolerable hardship in no way rewarding to the author.

> (una historia tan seca y tan limitada como esta de don Quijote, por parecerle que siempre había de hablar dél y de Sancho, sin osar estenderse a otras digresiones y episodios más graves y más entretenidos; y decía que el ir siempre atenido el entendimiento, la mano y la pluma a escribir de un solo sujeto y hablar por las bocas de pocas personas era un trabajo incomportable, cuyo fruto no redundaba en el de su autor: II, 44; ii, 366)

This, he goes on, is why he had resorted to *novelas cortas* like the *Curioso* and the *Capitán* in Part I.[4] He must eschew them now. Extraneous episodes must grow naturally out of the main action and be limited in length. The author, he concludes, begs to be given credit not for what he has written but for what he has refrained from writing. The preoccupations of Cervantes in this notable passage rest on neo-Aristotelian epic theory (Minturno, Tasso, El Pinciano come to mind), but they point in the direction of the modern novel. It is a far cry from the comparable moment in Part I when he justifies the inclusion of extraneous tales by the pleasures which variety gives (ch. 28); a far cry, too, from the Canon of Toledo's prescription for the ideal romance.

(ii) THE EXTRANEOUS EPISODES

Having relayed strong doubts as early as Part II, chapter 3 about the propriety of including *novelas* like the *Curioso impertinente*, Cervantes promptly goes on to include exactly the same number of external episodes (by my previous definition) in Part II. But even the longest of them is quite short, and he is at some pains to splice them into the main narrative, though they are all separable entities. In fact, he does it so successfully that two of the six extraneous episodes are not usually recognized for what they are. Three or four of them can also be paired quite easily with external episodes in Part I. This is especially true of the first.

The pastoral story of the rich Camacho's wedding (II, 19–21) is related to the incident of Daranio and Silveria in the *Galatea* and to the comic affair of Rústico and Clori in the play *La casa de los celos* as well as to the Grisóstomo story, although to the last mostly in a contrasting sense. That story concerned a suicide and a rustic funeral, and was tragic; this one concerns a wedding and a fake suicide, and ends happily. Basilio dramatically interrupts the ceremony, as Marcela did. There was a *cuestión de amor* in the other story; here there is the moral question of whether Basilio's gross deception can be justified. Don Quixote answers it firmly – 'Quiteria belonged to Basilio and Basilio to Quiteria by the just and favourable decree of heaven' (II, 21; ii, 201) – explaining later that what has a virtuous object 'cannot and should not be called a deception' (II, 22; ii, 203). Chapter 20 here begins as Part I, chapter 13, had done with an allusion to the dawning day in terms which gently parody pastoral style.

In many other respects the two episodes are very different, however. The sumptuousness of this rustic wedding, with its almost painfully relevant allegorical masque, the elaborate artifice of Basilio's deception and the moral casuistry that justifies it, the picaresque touches, the shifts of focus between protagonists and spectators, the deliberate uncertainty over whether Quiteria had advance knowledge of Basilio's trick or not (she is not telling and neither does the narrator): all combine to make this the most 'baroque' piece of pastoral in Cervantes. Quixote and Sancho remain in the foreground throughout the episode and change their allegiances in the course of it: Don Quixote from Camacho to Basilio, and Sancho from Basilio to Camacho.

By interposing their reactions and by underlining the artificiality and Rabelaisian scale of the festivities, Cervantes contrives to make the extraordinary nature of the proceedings a little more acceptable. The socio-economic reminders are strong, yet idealization has not been subverted by material considerations. Cervantes maintains something resembling the knife-edge equipoise of Góngora in his poem 'En los pinares de Júcar', or Velasquez in 'The Wine-bibbers'.

The brief, farcical and abortive episode of the braying villagers (II, 25, 27) is clearly of folk origin and unlike any of the other external episodes in Part I or II. Its exemplary value is obvious. A host of men are prepared to do battle for a cause as ludicrous as any that Don Quixote ever took up arms for. This is the closest thing to a pitched battle which Don Quixote ever encounters, so it is all the more ironically absurd that he and Sancho are forced to take to their heels. There is a suggestion of chivalric travesty. From the realistic point of view the episode is as inherently improbable as Camacho's wedding.

The third external episode is that of the daughter of Doña Rodríguez, duenna at the ducal castle (chs 48, 52, 56, 66). In many ways it is the most singular one in the novel. Alone among all the theatrical japes and fantasies perpetrated and staged at the castle, this is a true story. That is to say, Doña Rodríguez genuinely is a distressed widow and mother, whose daughter really has been dishonoured by a scoundrelly neighbour. She comes truly seeking help to compel the young man to make honourable amends. Thanks to the Duke, the climax of the episode is masked in chivalric fantasy, but even then True Love intervenes when Tosilos the lackey claps eyes on the girl, and the duel is called off. The Duke is very annoyed, but all is ripe for a happy ending. Only ten chapters later do we learn that the lackey has been given a thrashing, the duenna dismissed and the daughter sent to a convent. Never did Cervantes seem more sure of his narrative skill than in this comic story where the peripeteias come thick and fast and our expectations of the outcome are completely upset.

There is an explicit connection with the preceding adventure, the fantasy about the 'Dueña Dolorida'. Doña Rodríguez is 'the second Afflicted Duenna' (II, 52), but not a bogus one. Not for the first time in the book 'life' is found imitating 'art' – or artifice, anyway. Duennas were stock targets for satire and ridicule, and those in Cervantes's writings are no exception. Doña Rodríguez, one of his best comic creations, is a little different, though. She is a vulgar, snobbish, malicious old woman, and above all a silly one, but there is a certain pathos in her tribulations. She is the only person in the whole novel who seriously seeks Don Quixote's help, other than in a fleeting moment of necessity. Cervantes even makes her slip into the archaic language of the romances of chivalry as she formally implores the Knight's help in the presence of the Duke and Duchess (II, 52; ii, 434). Is this rather simple woman actually touched in the head by the grotesque goings-on in the castle? one wonders.

The story reverses the finale of Camacho's wedding in that wealth and power triumph over love in the end. Of course, the loves of lackeys and duennas' daughters are not in the same socio-stylistic bracket as those of the idealized peasants of pastoral. Love's frail flower is nipped in the bud by the Duke, who has been exercised by material interests in the affair from the start. According to Doña Rodríguez at least, he had been unwilling to take action against the girl's seducer because he owed money to the young man's father, his vassal (II, 48; ii, 402). There are limits to his fondness for knightly games, and he breaks the rules here. The extravagant behaviour of Doña Rodríguez shows up, as nothing else does, the emptiness of the chivalric charades at the castle. They disintegrate when they come up against the social and economic facts of the seventeenth century. In this thematic respect, no other extraneous episode in Part II is more firmly connected with the fortunes of Don Quixote than this absurd but significant story.

The next of these episodes involves the young daughter of one Diego de la Llana and her brother, who play truant from home in Sancho's Barataria (II, 49). Like the story of Doña Clara and Don Luis in Part I, it is exceptionally brief, and no more than a sketch of a story about a childish escapade. It is similarly ended by adult intervention – Governor Sancho's in this case – and fades out with the suggestion of a happy ending, as the Butler accompanying Sancho falls in love with the girl, thus constituting another interestingly embryonic version of a romantic *novela*. It shares with the Doña Rodríguez episode the distinction of being a true story amid a series of prearranged and fabricated ones. Though complicated by a dual transvestism and a good deal of fib-telling, the affair is genuine.

Claudia Jerónima (ch. 60) provides the only overtly tragic episode in Part II, a story as melodramatic as it is brief. In a misguided moment of jealous fury Claudia has shot her lover and ruined her own life – the exemplary note is unambiguous. In her marriage to the expiring Don Vicente there is an echo of the story of Basilio and Quiteria but there is no trick this time. For the first time, here and in the company of Roque Guinart and his bandits, where this event is situated, Don Quixote and Sancho meet real death and bloodshed. There is no doubt that their adventures are changing.

The sixth story, that of Ana Félix, the daughter of Ricote the Moor (II, 54, 63, 65), corresponds to that of the Captive and Zoraida. The historical background this time is provided by the expulsion of the Moriscos from Spain (1609–14). This was the 'final solution' of the problem of the large unassimilated minority of Moorish inhabitants left in Spain after the fall of the Kingdom of Granada in 1492. Unassimilated and resentful, they had been driven by inept and inconsistent national policy to serious insurrection in the Alpujarras region of Granada in 1568–71, and not even the naval victory over Turkish imperialism at Lepanto had quietened old fears of an onslaught by Islam at once from within and without. The extremists prevailed over moderate voices in the ears of Lerma and King Philip III, and about 275,000 persons were forced into exile. The loss of artisans and peasant labour was damaging (seriously so in Valencia), although it is a myth that the expulsion precipitated national economic ruin.

The episode contains some staple ingredients of adventure romance: the chase on the high seas, the girl dressed as a Moorish captain, her lover in disguise in the harem (as in Cervantes's play *La gran sultana*), the providential appearance of Ricote at the right moment. For the contemporary reader it is likely that the romantic story was enhanced by the intensely topical context. Never did Cervantes bring contemporary public events and even personalities into his fiction with more immediacy. With an event such as the Morisco expulsion it is not too surprising that he should put some unlikely sentiments into the mouth of Ricote, whose plight and that of his family feature prominently in the first instalment.

The question of Cervantes's personal attitude to the expulsion is a particularly difficult one, because we want to believe he detested it. A degree of irony is virtually certain. That he accepted the measure as a regrettable political necessity is quite possible; that he deplored the suffering it brought to innocent families and individuals is evident.[5] The open-endedness of the story is uncharacteristic of a tale of this kind. It has nothing to do with generic convention as such, but is a necessity imposed by political reality. Anyone knowing that reality would be aware that the chances of father, daughter and lover being allowed to remain in Spain were negligible.

Again the extraneous episodes are relevant to the story of Quixote and Sancho inasmuch as they represent true adventures. But this time the heroes become involved in them to an unprecedented degree. I refer not just to their presence as audience or spectators but to their actual or proffered intervention every time. Don Quixote leaps to Basilio's defence when Camacho's understandably incensed supporters start to turn ugly (II, 22). He tries to bring the army of asinine villagers to their senses, only to have his efforts ruined when Sancho puts his nose in (II, 27). He is invited to settle the affair of Doña Rodríguez' daughter, but events take another turn (II, 56). He promptly undertakes to help the distressed damsel Claudia Jerónima; then Sancho chips in and no one takes any more notice (II, 60). Similarly in the Ana Félix adventure he offers to rescue Don Gregorio from Barbary (II, 64), but other arrangements are set in train and then his final defeat disqualifies him anyway.

On the previous journey he was too absorbed in his own fantasies to pay much attention to other people's real-life adventures unless they had a strong flavour of literary romance about them. Now he does not fail to recognize any that comes his way, but his attempts to intervene effectively are foiled by circumstances or by Sancho or, worse still, are simply ignored. It is left to Sancho alone to intervene decisively in any of them. This he peremptorily does in the case of the two adolescents on his 'island'.

Four of the episodes are still sufficiently tinged with romance to be distinguishable from the narrative mode of the main action. The two exceptions are the story of the village brayers and that of Doña Rodríguez' daughter, the second of which resembles the main action in that events are dressed up in a parodic simulacrum of chivalric romance by the figures involved in them. Here there is open parody, thanks to the simplicity of the duenna and the frivolity of the Duke. The Duke (with his major-domo) might be compared, indeed, with Maese Pedro as another manipulator.

In the other cases, estimates of parodic intention on the author's part are subjective in the long run. It seems to me that suspicions are aroused more strongly by these stories than they are by the external episodes of Part I. Nevertheless, parody, burlesque and travesty are kept on a very short leash, and only allowed to signal their presence at moments or in indirect ways. The outrageous artifice of Basilio is narrated 'straight' in the sense that suspense and surprise are clearly meant to prevail over any subversion that might be caused by a sense of the ridiculous.[6] Yet, while no one could doubt that Quiteria is really beautiful, the description of her when she first appears on the scene is conveyed in burlesque fashion through the expostulations of Sancho (II, 21; ii, 196). Cervantes still wants to have it both ways. The dramatically sudden effects of true love on the lackey Tosilos are not less real for being described in burlesque mythological terms, though they may not be very lastingly profound. There is a joking allusion also to the Butler's love-smitten reaction to the beauty of Diego de la Llana's daughter. In his estimation she was weeping not tears 'but seed pearls or meadow dew, and he even raised them a point higher and likened them to oriental pearls' (II, 49; ii, 413). As long ago as the *Galatea* Cervantes had remarked on the comic side of love-affairs when viewed with an impartial eye.[7] These moments of amusement do not imply attempts to undermine the love-story through mockery. If the inclusion of two comic stories among the extraneous episodes of Part II suggests the sense of a need to bridge the gap between them and the central narrative better this time, the presence of the occasional note of undisguised humour points to a wish to lubricate the junctures of romance and novel with a few drops of comic parody.

Cervantes pushes romance-based fiction as far as it will go in the realistic contemporary ambience of *Don Quixote*, Part II. Social differences and political realities were features of Dorotea's story and that of the Captive, but they were not allowed to impinge on the harmonious resolutions of the love-stories. Nor do they in the Basilio–Quiteria story of Part II, though at the expense of some credibility. It is entirely otherwise in the Doña Rodríguez episode, however, and by implication in that of Ana Félix. As Williamson has noted (1982D, pp. 63–4), Cervantes takes romance to its limits in this story, showing it incapable of dealing with political realities of the magnitude of the Morisco expulsion. It ends inconclusively with the protagonists left to await the outcome of Don Antonio's promised efforts at Court to bring about a judgement favourable to the lovers – a judgement about which the old Moor Ricote is under no illusions. Don Antonio answers that he will take every step he can, one by one, 'and leave the rest to the will of heaven' ('y haga el cielo lo que más fuere servido': II, 65; ii, 540). We must surely take this as said in a spirit of resigned acceptance, at most a pious hope. Not even the most impassioned writer of romances would have felt able to rest the denouement of this story on an appeal to an ever attentive Providence, and get away with it.

NOTES: CHAPTER 9

1   See, e.g., Rosales (1960D), Vol. 2, pp. 325 ff.; Allen (1969D), Vol. 1, pp. 42 ff.; and, for a different reading, Williamson (1984D), pp. 170 ff.

2   'I know nowhere else in literature where the hero of a novel lives on his own fame, as it were upon the reputation of his reputation' (Mann, 1969D, p. 55).

3   Anyone preferring a more baroque schema can triangulate the figure by capping the subterranean adventure of each individual hero with their joint 'flight through the heavens' on Clavileño (ch. 41).

4   To quote Graham Greene again: 'And so the short story for the novelist is often yet another form of escape – escape from having to live with a character for years on end, picking up his jealousies, his mannerisms, his dishonest tricks of thought, his betrayals' (1980E, p. 273).

5   The best examination of the whole question is in Márquez Villanueva (1975D), pp. 229 ff.

6   On the resemblance with the gory trick in Achilles Tatius, see Zimic (1972D), p. 882.

Less commented on is the slight but explicit echo of the story of Pyramus and Thisbe (Ovid, *Metamorphoses*, bk IV), noted by Casalduero (1949D), p. 259.

7 'When the affairs of love are observed with an impartial eye, lovely Nísida, they reveal so many absurdities that they arouse as much laughter as compassion' (*Galatea*, II; i, 149).

CHAPTER 10

The Return of the Heroes

Early in Part II the Knight and the Squire are found discussing with the Bachelor Sansón Carrasco whether there will be a Part II or not. The Bachelor reports that there are those who advise against it, but also some jovial folk who say: 'Let's have more quixotries, let Don Quixote go charging in and let Sancho Panza talk, and come what may, we'll be content with that' (II, 4; ii, 68). Even if this was not everybody's view, nor a very sophisticated response, it would have been enough for Cervantes to capitalize on. And so he did, duplicating the fact of his heroes' popularity within the fiction of Part II. He thus built into the story an audience reaction which helped to determine its course. In so doing he could hardly have failed to discern how much the appeal of his book lay in the persons and personalities of the heroes. Their early appearance as carnival figures suggests the same thing. It could well have been an incentive to develop Quixote and Sancho as characters.

By itself, public success is less likely to promote characterization of depth and subtlety than it is to produce imitation or extension of a work. One sees this most clearly in television series and serials. It seems broadly true to say that a successful formula for the action is likely to result in imitation; and when it is the characters (combined with the human presence of the actors) which most appeal the result is likely to be prolongation. Or of course it may be both. The interesting fact about the appeal of characters here is that there need not be anything profound about them for the process to work. To some extent it also happens in detective fiction where formula is supreme. One reads another Sherlock Holmes story, Hercule Poirot or Philip Marlowe novel very much for the sake of seeing the familar character in action again.

The Bachelor Carrasco's opinion sample, quoted above, points to the success of both formula and characters. And, while this certainly is not enough to explain the more subtle and dynamic characterization of the heroes in Part II, it could have been just enough to ensure that it happened. The bases had been laid in the work of 1605 and their development already begun.

Both of the new factors mentioned at the start of Chapter 9 above are directly relevant. The Knight in particular is lured into a succession of invented situations which are a comic parody of what, thanks to Part I, he is popularly supposed to expect. Don Quixote becomes the victim of his own celebrity. This irony is compounded with another, for what the jokers do not know, or do not care about, is that he is not quite the same man as he once was. In one major respect he is less mad.

The other principal new factor in Part II is, of course, precisely this. He is now almost never spontaneously deluded simply by the physical appearance of things the way he was in the earlier book. This naturally affects the nature of the adventures and involves Sancho.[1]

It is not clear whether the change in Don Quixote's condition is attributable to the month's rest, with nourishing food, which he has had since being brought home in the ox cart (II, 1; ii, 41), or to the first adventure after he and Sancho set out again, or to some other unnamed cause. At all events, that first adventure gave him a profound emotional shock. It is when Sancho swears that the peasant wench passing by on a donkey is Dulcinea in all her radiance, and forces Don Quixote against the evidence of his eyes to accept this as fact. Here is a total reversal of the usual situation of Part I, where Don Quixote's was the transformed vision and Sancho's the prosaic view of reality. The whole episode is one of some psychological subtlety. When they first arrive in El Toboso, Don Quixote, having first put Sancho on the spot, then makes it as easy as possible for his squire to trick him. It is almost as though he wanted to be deceived – if not in precisely this way (see Rosales 1960D, Vol. 2, pp. 100 ff.). To account for Dulcinea's new appearance the Knight has to postulate a fiendish work of enchantment. It is dramatic proof that appearances are not to be trusted, and good reason for the caution he shows from now on in interpreting them.

There was a perceptible progression in Don Quixote's state of mind through the ups and downs of his adventures in Part I, but it was only intermittently apparent and not pronounced. In Part II a steadier development is evident, although he does not recover full possession of his wits before he is on his deathbed. Until the last chapter he is liable to do and say things which are mad by ordinary human standards. But he is less obviously insane more of the time because his behaviour is less dependent on visual delusions. He is a more complicated figure, because doubt, which was only a passing cloud before, now casts a more constant dark shadow. The happy equanimity of Don Quixote's lunacy has been disturbed. Basically mad still, he remains basically comic, mostly by the same token (though in subtler ways, too), as Russell (1969D) and Close (1978[2]D) have reminded us. Nevertheless, the effect in general is a sobering one. Don Quixote is no exception to one of the few reasonably reliable rules in literature: namely that in proportion as a character learns from experience he becomes less comic.[2]

The change which gathers way in him is consistent with his medical history. Growing caution, signs of loss of confidence and depression are symptoms of the gradual cooling of his hot dry passions, which ends in cold melancholy. His condition is aggravated by further neglect of proper food and rest. The logical culmination of the process is death, which follows his quartan fever, heavy sleep and final brief return to sanity.[3] The doctor who attends him at the end diagnoses the cause of oncoming death as 'melancholy and depression' ('melancolías y desabrimientos': II, 74; ii, 587). The fever and the sleep help to restore the balance of his mind but do not save his life.

The exact state of Don Quixote's mind is of considerable interest to other people in the book on more than one occasion, starting in chapter 1 when the Priest and the Barber pay a visit to find out how he is. The answer emerges in the course of their conversation on national affairs of the day. Cervantes characteristically establishes the position without narrative comment. Rumours and speculation over a possible Turkish invasion were still a popular topic of conversation in Spain. Don Quixote's proposal for dealing with the threat reveals that he is as much as ever gripped by his chivalric obsession. At the same time, however, his private fantasy is linked with the contemporary world in a way we had not seen before. Indeed, the Knight is quite clearly being classed here with the numerous *arbitristas* who thrived in the country at this time (the words *arbitrio* and *arbitrante* are used in the passage).[4]

Arbitristas were a symptom of the troubled state of the nation, for whose many problems, especially the economic ills of the day, they proposed all kinds of remedies. They bombarded the king's ministers and officials with memoranda, of which a considerable number are preserved. While many were cranks, a number had ideas in advance of their time, which historians today take very seriously. In the popular mind they were generally identified as crackpots, and as such they had begun to appear in literature – starting, it seems, with the eccentric figure who makes a brief appearance in Cervantes's *Coloquio de los perros*.

Although Don Quixote's proposal shows that the core of his madness is still intact, the satirical equation with the *arbitristas* narrows the gap between Don Quixote and contemporary society. This is to be a constant feature of Part II. There is less of the fanatic and more of the merely eccentric about him now.

So how much of the old windmill-basher and sheep-fighter is left? How much of the intrepid adventure-seeker? Not a lot, but something is. It turns out that on the occasions when he is roused to action in the old way, without being obviously or deliberately solicited, either the stimulus is exceptionally theatrical or else there is a clear analogy with some situation in chivalresque literature.

The adventure with the boat on the River Ebro (II, 29) is unique in being the sole occasion in Part II on which Don Quixote acts as if his senses were spontaneously deluded by entirely undeceptive physical appearances in the way they used to be. The empty boat, an oft-used property of Arthurian romance, triggers off one of the most delightfully childlike adventures in the whole novel. It was ready and waiting in his mind, as an earlier reverie makes quite clear (II, 1; ii, 48). Cervantes offers no explanation for this exceptional reversion to old behaviour, but permits us to draw inferences. He carefully indicates that the sight of the water has plunged Don Quixote into amorous-bucolic reverie and set his mind racing with memories of the Cave of Montesinos (p. 261). Under the impulse of an excited imagination he now responds to the chivalric signal offered by the boat and fabricates an adventure of the kind we have scarcely seen since the early days of his madness. It is a reasonable inference that he is trying to recapture that carefree time now. When it ends in comic disaster, just as those adventures did, he exclaims, whether in exasperation or despair it is hard to tell: 'I can do no more' ('Yo no puedo más': p. 267). His offer to pay for the damage is accompanied by brief relapses into fantasy as also occurred when he paid Maese Pedro for damaging his puppets (II, 26). He and Sancho return to their mounts, melancholy and out of humour. It is the end of the first stage of the third expedition and it marks the end of a phase in Don Quixote's career.

At the Duke's castle Don Quixote takes no such initiatives, but is the target of other people's fantasies. The literary basis of his whole madness is evoked for the last time when the crudely painted epic legends of Helen of Troy and Dido of Carthage on the wall-hangings of an inn revive in him impossible longings of heroic intervention (II, 71).

Several allusions to his sadness at moments when there is nothing immediately to account for it point to an underlying melancholic condition. When Sancho goes into El Toboso to seek Dulcinea, Don Quixote remains outside the village 'full of sad and confused fancies' (II, 10; ii, 105). There is a similar reference to melancholy when he is with Don Diego (II, 16; ii, 154) and another when he first speaks after emerging from the Cave (II, 22; ii, 210). We may infer that he finds his stay at the castle ultimately depressing. We see him low-spirited in the absence of Sancho and suddenly, in his solitude and poverty, Cide Hamete shows him to us as a seedy gentleman of advancing years (II, 44). He is glad to get away (II, 58). After being run down by the bulls he is almost in despair (II, 59), unable to sleep and plagued with troubled thoughts (II, 60). And all this is before his final and irremediable defeat by the Bachelor disguised as the Knight of the White Moon. After that his intensifed depression is obvious and explicit.

Two specific problems preoccupy Don Quixote on this third expedition. One is the spell supposedly laid on Dulcinea, and how to remove it. The other is the nature of his experience in the Cave of Montesinos. These two connected events are of such central importance in Part II that we must look at them separately later. What may be noted here is that both Dulcinea herself and the Cave adventure are in origin and essence mental creations of Don Quixote, and that doubt intrudes into each of them under different guises. The centre of dramatic conflict in the novel has shifted away from the contest of Don Quixote versus the material world of external reality, and moved into the mind of the Knight. The effect is limited – this is not Proust or Henry James – but it largely accounts for the enhanced psychological interest of Part II.

Doubt intrudes in several forms. It plays a part in the Knight's new-found caution over identifying things and people by their appearance. This begins in El Toboso and reaches a culmination in the River Ebro adventure. Sancho perhaps began it when he spoke of searching for Dulcinea's 'house, fortress or palace' (II, 9; ii, 103), but it is his master who gets the shock on this occasion. In the next episode Don Quixote addresses the driver of the cart carrying the travelling actors by a set of alternatives as 'Carter, coachman, devil, or whatever you are' (II, 11; ii, 116). In the adventure in the boat Quixote's vacillation almost causes the whole fantasy to fragment: all he seems to know for sure is that there is someone he must rescue from oppression. He cries out to Sancho:

'Do you see? Over there, my friend, appears a city, castle or fortress where some afflicted knight must be, or some luckless queen, infanta, or princess, for whose assistance I have been brought here.'

('¿Vees? Allí, ¡oh amigo!, se descubre la ciudad, castillo o fortaleza
donde debe de estar algún caballero oprimido, o alguna reina, infanta
o princesa malparada, para cuyo socorro soy aquí traído': II, 29; ii,
265; similarly on pp. 262, 266)

In the old days the Knight would never have prevaricated like this. His
imagination is surrendering to the fact that the possibilities are multiple.
It is true that Cervantes does not show much more of this hesitancy of
Don Quixote's. Instead, and unexpectedly, he carries it over into
Benengeli's narration in this section of the book (chs 8–30), as we shall
see later on. Meanwhile the Knight's caution has at any rate been
established. At the ducal castle his generally polite and passive
behaviour in unusual confrontations is at least consistent with caution if
nothing more. By the time he is in Barcelona he is sceptical enough to be
'on the point of not believing' Don Antonio Moreno's account of the
talking bronze head (II, 62; ii, 511).

Another way in which doubt betrays its presence is in Don Quixote's
new wariness over omens. From start to finish of this third journey (chs
8–73) he is on the lookout for auguries and signs, and he pays attention
to them seven or eight times.[5] Occasionally, like a good Christian, he
dismisses them as superstitious nonsense; more often, he does not. In
any case, they figure in his consciousness as they never did before and
point to a self-confidence less than rock-firm.

It seems to be fundamentally for the same reason that he is anxious to
know the meaning of his dreamlike experience in the Cave of Montesinos. He consults two 'oracles' about it; Maese Pedro's fortune-telling
monkey (II, 25) and the bronze head. But whereas the hero of romance
or epic might use oracles, dreams and omens as an astronaut today would
use computer readings Don Quixote seems to require confirmation that
he is the man for the job. Had this been true of the first sortie, rather
than the third, one could draw a different conclusion, but it is not. There
is a major change in Don Quixote's intentions in Part II. He does not
now concentrate directly on the task of restoring the age of chivalry, but
rather on a quest for proofs that he is destined to do so. He needs
endorsements of a transcendental kind: the blessing of Dulcinea, the
visionary experience in the Cave. He knows now that it is not enough
just to proclaim the nature of reality. There are hostile enchanters at
work confusing the look of things. (See Williamson, 1984D, pp.
110–11.)

Enchanters are another mental creation of Quixote's playing a major role in Part II. They derive, of course, from the romances of chivalry. The great majority of them plague the Knight maliciously. (Benengeli, who is by and large benevolent, may be left out of account, since his role as chronicler of Don Quixote's history is unique.) In a moment of unusually sombre vehemence Don Quixote exclaims:

> This cursed breed, born into the world to obscure and obliterate the deeds of the good, and to light up and exalt the deeds of the bad. Enchanters persecute me, have persecuted and will persecute me until they bring down me and my lofty deeds of chivalry into the deep abyss of oblivion; and they hurt and wound me where they see I feel it most.

> (Esta raza maldita, nacida en el mundo para escurecer y aniquilar las hazañas de los buenos, y para dar luz y levantar los fechos de los malos. Perseguido me han encantadores, encantadores me persiguen y encantadores me perseguirán hasta dar conmigo y con mis altas caballerías en el profundo abismo del olvido, y en aquella parte me dañan y hieren donde ven que más lo siento: II, 32; 289–90.)

This outburst is caused by the transformation of Dulcinea, the most diabolical of their deeds. Enchanters are nearly always invoked by the Knight to account for things which are not to his liking, but it would be asking too much to expect them to play a wholly consistent part in his scheme of things; nor do they. However, in general, Don Quixote holds enchantment responsible for making the marvellous things of his fantasy look like the common everyday things that other people – and the reader – perceive (see Predmore, 1967D, p. 40). His sorcerers do not – as might at first thought have been expected – turn windmills into giants, but giants into windmills, and knights into sheep, a helmet into a basin, Dulcinea into a country bumpkin, the Knight of the Wood into the likeness of Sansón Carrasco, a champion into a lackey. From our point of view Don Quixote is using them to explain why things look the way they do. By a curious coincidence they are thus rather like Descartes' *malin génie*, the hypothetical demon who might exist and be capable of falsifying all the information we have, or of distorting the faculties by which we judge it, so preventing us from apprehending the world as it really is – the ultimate weapon in the armoury of scepticism (*Meditations on First Philosophy*, I).

Don Quixote's greater passivity in Part II is another symptom of his cooling humour. He no longer strives even to convince others of the historical authenticity of the chivalric literary heroes, his most deep-seated conviction. He admits to the Priest that he was not always successful in this in the past (II, 1), and he tells Don Lorenzo that he has given up trying to correct the widespread error in this regard (II, 18). Nor is he the free agent he once was. Now other people set the pace and play his game. Worst of all, he is reduced to humiliating impotence in the matter closest to his heart. Not he but Sancho is the one who is ordained to lift the spell on Dulcinea.

Yet Don Quixote still often seems to be indulging almost wilfully in something like make-believe. The chivalresque game goes on in Part II – with a new development. This is supplied by the intervention of many other people and Don Quixote's consequent loss of control over the thing he started. Three sets of characters are chiefly involved. First, there is Sancho. Previously a rather reluctant playmate, he had been showing signs that he was starting to enjoy himself (for example, I, 52; i, 603). Now he becomes deeply committed by the solution he contrives to his dilemma over Dulcinea. As Mancing observes (1982D, p. 141), Sancho does not take Don Quixote's hints here, but invents his own scenario. His motivation is not at all playful in this case. Indeed, he strikes a blow at Don Quixote that changes the nature of the game between them, bringing in an element of rivalry, if not of contest. His advantage over his master is further secured when he is made responsible for disenchanting Dulcinea and when he gets his governorship from the Duke and not from Don Quixote. The Knight is too good a sport not to comply with anyone who makes a show of joining in and observing the rules, and he gives no sign of suspicion over Sancho's disgraceful cheating at the end (II, 71). Sancho is always apt to overdo things. Playing the game for all he is worth, he tells the ludicrous lie about dismounting from the wooden horse Clavileño in mid-space flight. To level the score Don Quixote whispers in his ear that he will believe Sancho in this if Sancho believes him about what he saw in the Cave of Montesinos (II, 41; ii, 355).

Second, there is the Bachelor Carrasco, who is moved to participate partly out of concern for Quixote's best interests, but who is liable to get rather carried away. When urging the Knight to set out on his adventures without delay, he overdoes the linguistic parody, and Don Quixote, while recognizing the goodwill in the Bachelor's complicity, replies in a tone of burlesque irony very difficult to imagine in the Quixote of Part I (II, 7; ii, 89–90). Later Carrasco introduces the major contest, twice challenging Don Quixote as a rival knight. In this he keeps strictly to the rules, losing the first round and winning the second. He plays a passably creditable game.

Whether the same can be said of the Duke and Duchess and their retainers is another matter. They far outdo everyone also in the scale and variety of the chivalric fun they organize. In addition to the amateur dramatics with dressing-up and disguises, there is a wealth of ludic variations: ritual, practical jokes, tests, combats, riddles and, in Barataria, a strong suggestion of carnival. The extravagance of the ducal goings-on may verge on the incredible to the reader of today, but it is less improbable than it looks when compared with some of the festive occasions celebrated in royal and noble palaces in seventeenth-century Spain, complete with theatricals, processions and masques, often with chivalric literary motifs.[6] The aim is simply amusement; there is little or no question of humouring Don Quixote for his own good. He and Sancho become figures of fun much of the time, and play teeters on the brink of mockery. It is as though older and better-equipped children have taken over. Don Quixote becomes noticeably more passive, is often silent, and before he leaves shows signs of having had enough (II, 51; ii, 429).

It is not Don Quixote's madness which is infectious, but his playfulness, in so far as it is possible to discriminate between them. But there is one group of persons found at play quite independently of the Knight: the gentlefolk innocently engaged in pastoral charades in their simulated Arcadia (II, 58). Once more the gap between Don Quixote and other people is narrowed slightly. However, there still is a clear difference, which is highlighted when he responds with a totally inappropriate show of chivalric bravado. This is a breach of decorum for which he pays when the herd of bulls leaves him flattened.

This 'playfulness' runs right through the novel and is an integral part of Don Quixote's mental make-up, whether we call it infantile regression or not. It is obvious when he and Sancho discuss taking up a pastoral life (II, 67). It colours much of his behaviour and influences that of others, because it is a part of theirs, too. The phenomenon is complex and not easily pinned down, and Cervantes's depiction of it in operation shows considerable psychological insight. Van Doren (1958D) and Torrente Ballester (1975D) have pointed out the element of playacting which it gives rise to in Don Quixote's conduct. But it is a mistake to try to distinguish too precisely between playacting and madness in his attitude to chivalry. Playing a role is not in itself indicative of either madness or sanity; it may partake of one or the other by dint of associated circumstances. One man's pastime may be another man's obsession.

In a sense Don Quixote's credulity, his readiness to fall for other people's deceptions and disguises, even when evidence to the contrary is overwhelming, is a measure of his 'good sportsmanship'. He refuses to spoil the game, whether it is going his way or not. But, as I have just intimated, Don Quixote's playacting cannot be equated with that of the rational person who disbelieves in the fundamental reality of the roles assumed and events enacted. Don Quixote believes in his hoaxers, who are playing his game but doing so in a different spirit from his. This has moral implications. The alternative to accepting that the peasant girl is Dulcinea, that the Knight of the Wood (or Mirrors) is an enchanter's facsimile of Sansón Carrasco, that the adventures at the castle are genuine is to conclude that Sancho is a liar, the Bachelor an imposter, the Duke and Duchess frivolous jokers. These accusations are not without substance, but the Knight's refusal to admit such notions is to his credit. It raises him in our eyes and lowers them correspondingly. Even Carrasco, the best motivated of them, does not come too well out of it when Don Quixote wonders to Sancho why their friend would come out after him, armed to the teeth, and pick a fight. What reason, grudge or rivalry could explain it (II, 16; ii, 148)? However simple-minded it may be to do so, he trusts and believes in his friends (see Parker, 1956D). There is a redeeming benevolence in Quixote which underlies his madness and overrides his petty faults.

Throughout the novel he shows a self-awareness which also is intensified in Part II. Having pretensions to heroism from the moment he became 'Don Quixote', a degree of self-consciousness was inevitable. But he also believed he was actually being commemorated in print, which was distinctly unusual. When, amazingly, this belief comes true, and he is given evidence of the fact (II, 2–3), his self-conceit is inflated. We find him boasting later to Don Diego of his literary fame. A tendency to vainglory was always a weakness of his, and it has something more to feed on now. So was personal vanity, which reaches new heights in his complacent assumption that the mischievous Altisidora finds him desirable as a lover (II, 46). There is a rich vein of humour here which Cervantes exploits brilliantly in the night scene with Doña Rodríguez (II, 48). Some other comic moments are supplied by the Knight's acute embarrassment at the indiscretions, actual or potential, of his Squire. He shows this embarrassment from the moment of Sancho's first reappearance (II, 2). This implies a new sensitivity to other people's reactions; and in view of his close partnership with Sancho his embarrassment may be seen as an extension of his self-awareness. The most remarkable case of his intensified self-consciousness is in his encounter with Don Diego de Miranda. It has implications which must be kept for later consideration.

This greater self-awareness, while still intimately enough connected with Don Quixote's role-playing to be a source of comedy – a more subtle sort than that which derives straight from his mad antics – also indicates a new and more rational seriousness in his character, if self-knowledge is the beginning of wisdom. The second of his famous counsels to governor-designate Sancho, after that of fearing God, is that he must seek to know himself (II, 42). Quixote will not be able to live up to his own precept before he returns to his right mind at the very end of his life, but the man who says 'Up to now I do not know what I have been conquering by the force of my labours' (II, 58; ii, 473) has made progress.

We have in Don Quixote a would-be hero aware of himself as an individual and of his own continuing existence in time. As readers, we are made aware of his awareness, and see how he sees himself, as well as seeing him from without as others do. These two views are basic to the novel, which revolves on the axis between them.

The resemblance between Don Quixote and Sancho as companions in folly was remarked on more than once in the course of Part I. Clearly this had to persist if the sequel was not going to take a very different direction. At the outset of Part II the Priest says: 'It is as if they had been cast in a single mould' (ch. 2, p. 54). As though to underline it, Cervantes then depicts Sancho talking to his wife Teresa in a manner so remarkably like his master's that doubt is cast on the very authenticity of the chapter (II, 5). As the fortunes of Quixote and Sancho become more closely entwined and their interdependence more intricate, the balance shifts. Previously Sancho had depended on Don Quixote for his hoped-for island. Now Don Quixote is dependent upon Sancho for the disenchantment of Dulcinea. This imposes on Sancho an obligation which he does not manage to wriggle out of until very late in the day. From the moment he decides to play Don Quixote's game on his own terms, deceiving him over Dulcinea, he starts, however, to assert a relative independence which develops through much of the book and reaches its zenith when, with ironic fortuity, he gets his island not from his master but from the Duke.

To the words quoted above, the Priest adds what sounds more like the comment of a reader than of a participant in the story, to the effect that the master's madness would not be worth tuppence without the follies of the servant (p. 54). The exploitation of Sancho after his particular success with readers of Part I is unsurprising. What is unexpected is the way the character now consciously plays up to his reputation – often plays to the gallery, indeed. He is more garrulous, more apt to butt in, answer back and show off than before. At the ducal castle he behaves very like a court buffoon, and is treated like one, being both mocked and conceded special privileges. Here Cervantes exploits a basic aspect of Sancho's personality, as did Avellaneda, whose Sancho ended his career in this very role.

The Squire stands somewhere between his master and the rest of the world in being sometimes deceived and sometimes deceiver (Alonso, 1962D). He touches new heights of discernment and new depths of slyness, but as before he is dupe as well as sceptic. He evidently accepts Quixote's assertion that the Knight of the Mirrors was not the real Sansón Carrasco (II, 14), yet he disbelieves his story of what occurred in the Cave of Montesinos. Having tricked his master into believing that the girl on the donkey was Dulcinea, he lets himself be persuaded by the Duchess that it was really Dulcinea after all (II, 33). There is no way of clearly distinguishing between his gullibility and his readiness to play the chivalric game which everyone seems to be playing at the castle. The only plausible explanation of his lie about what he saw and did on the supposed flight of the wooden horse Clavileño is that it was a mischievous and clumsy attempt to join in. He has become thoroughly immersed in his master's world of adventure, and seems to be enjoying himself, most of the time, from the start when he bids Don Quixote to hasten their departure on their travels (II, 4) to the finish when he begs him not to die of melancholy but to go on living – with his illusions (II, 74). Despite grumbles, threats to opt out and go home, and signs of a certain sober awareness, from around the time of Barcelona, that the game is nearly over, Sancho's loyalty and affection towards Don Quixote may be eroded but are not destroyed. As he told the Duchess:

That was my lot and my bad luck; I can't help it; I must follow him: we are from the same village, I've eaten his bread, I love him well, he is grateful and gave me his donkeys, and above all I'm faithful.

(Pero ésta fue mi suerte, y ésta mi malandanza; no puedo más; seguirle tengo: somos de un mismo lugar, he comido su pan, quiérole bien, es agradecido, diome sus pollinos y, sobre todo, yo soy fiel: II, 33; ii, 298.)

However, had Don Quixote been less guileless, the partnership, one is made to feel, could hardly have lasted to the end. Because the Knight is so innocent, their friendship survives the two gross deceptions over Dulcinea, and even the appalling moment when they come to blows and Don Quixote lies pinned to the ground with Sancho's knee planted on his chest (II, 60). If there is any discrepancy in Sancho's attitude to his master in Part II, it seems less an inconsistency produced by faulty art than a natural inconsistency in human behaviour.

His *discreción*, whether native or rubbed off from his master (II, 12; ii, 121–2), issues not only in droll remarks or astuteness but also occasionally in moral pronouncements which would do credit to a bishop. But he also has lessons to learn. One of the hardest is that involvement entails responsibility, like it or not. Even he might have recognized the comic poetic justice in his having to suffer physically so that the spell on Dulcinea should be lifted, but why ever should he suffer for Altisidora (II, 69)? Trying to get out of the Trifaldi–Clavileño adventure, he protests: 'What have squires got to do with their masters' adventures?' (II, 40; ii, 342). And when they have been run down by the herd of pigs he cries bitterly: 'What have the Panzas to do with the Quixotes?' (II, 68; ii, 554). Commitment to his master's service means sharing even the worst of his misfortunes – something Sancho never openly assents to.

The biggest lesson he does learn, and admit to, is the practical import of Don Quixote's counsel to know himself (II, 42; ii, 357), which means to know his own limitations. This causes him to win a victory, effective if not total, over his material ambitions. The lesson and the victory spring from his one week's experience as governor of the 'island' of Barataria. This illusory experience yields up a moral commonplace about the trumpery nature of all human dominion, reminiscent of Calderón's *La vida es sueño*. But just as the test of Segismundo was real enough, so is the test of Sancho's judicial abilities. On the nine occasions when he adjudicates, and the one when he legislates (II, 45–51), he acquits himself astonishingly well, and to that extent turns the tables on his hoaxers.[7]

The entire episode of Sancho's career as district justice could be held to impose a threefold strain on the reader's credulity. One might wonder at his success rate; at his impeccably moral reasons for ultimately giving up this most cherished illusion; third, one might be sceptical about the whole thing taking place at all. But Cervantes is careful to maintain a foundation of credibility. Sancho has shown wit and wisdom at unexpected moments before, so none of his Solomon-like judgements – essentially practical and based as they are on experience of human nature, or his master's recent advice – is grossly out of character. The ground is carefully prepared for his change of heart, quite apart from the fact that the governorship is materially very unrewarding. As for the artificiality of the whole set-up, we have already seen the Duke's servants going to great lengths to construct theatricals around Don Quixote and Sancho. There is something else, too, however.

The apotheosis of Sancho represents the most extreme development of Don Quixote's chivalresque game. It not only involves the intervention of other participants on an unprecedented scale, and completely takes over Sancho himself (until he opts out), but it moves right away from Quixote the originator. Indeed, the game now ceases to have anything much to do with chivalry at all. As Cervantes's first readers would have recognized more quickly than we do, Barataria is filled with the spirit of carnival. This is an important contribution to its credibility. The carnivalesque inspiration throughout the Barataria chapters seems unquestionable (Redondo, 1978D, pp. 50 ff.). It is there in the burlesque exaltation of Sancho as ruler, the Mardi Gras abundance of dishes whipped away by the penitential figure of Dr Pedro Recio of Tirteafuera ('Take-em-away') (II, 47), the final battle recalling that between Carnival and Lent (II, 53), the burlesque tribunal of popular justice (II, 45), the grotesque wedding figures (II, 47), transvestist disguises (II, 49) and riddles (II, 51), not to mention any symbolic associations with the death of Sancho's delusions of grandeur and his rebirth into good sense.

There is no indication that Barataria is meant to be part of genuine carnival festivities. The date of the Duke's letter in chapter 47, 16 August, rules that out, and his known predilection for festive events is explanation enough. Nothing in this sequence of chapters cannot be realistically accounted for. Nevertheless, as, with Sancho, we enter this curious world, so very close to the carnivalesque 'world upside-down', where the tables are turned and the humble exalted for a while, it is hard to avoid the feeling that Cervantes has crossed generic boundaries. Erected on the realistic foundation is a construction of burlesque, satire, symbolism, disputational topic and moral apologue, disposed between chapters 42 and 55. It begins with the moral truth about the insignificance of worldly dominion, springing from Sancho's ridiculous fiction about his ride on Clavileño (p. 355), followed by Don Quixote's didactic advice on the qualities of a good governor. It ends with Don Quixote's rescue of Sancho from his fall into the pit or catacomb.[8]

The didactic part is not restricted to Don Quixote's advice to Sancho on being a good governor, but is built into the story. The particular question is: will Sancho be a good governor? Behind this is visible the general academic question: are the qualities of good governorship innate or are they acquired by education and training? It is one among a number of practical applications of the Renaissance concept of Nature versus Art. At the political level the governorship question belonged to the theory of statecraft and princely education. The idea of the rustic as wise ruler was an associated topic which, in slightly variant forms, appeared not uncommonly in Golden Age literature. Behind all this ran strong lines of humanist thought both on natural, common-sense government and on the need for training. Thus, as the scholar Simón Abril observed, even in villages 'those who served His Majesty in a governing capacity should understand in what good government consists and so they would not embark on a thing of such weight and moment all untutored, as they do'.[9] Although the precise sources of Don Quixote's counsels to Sancho are unlikely to be pinpointed, Juan de Castilla y Aguayo's *El perfecto regidor* (1586) is cited as typical in the kind of advice purveyed. Similarly, Gracián Dantisco's *Galateo español* (1593, based on Giovanni della Casa's handbook) offers advice on good manners (including the avoidance of belching) like that of the Knight to the Squire. Polonius combined moral doctrine, worldly wisdom and rules for polite behaviour in his advice to Laertes in much the same way (*Hamlet*, I, iii).

Cervantes dramatizes comically the question of the untutored peasant's fitness to govern in his interlude *Los alcaldes de Daganzo*, and it seems to suggest itself more or less openly whenever illiterate aldermen or councillors appear in his works. He must have met some not too dissimilar municipal functionaries in his travels around southern Spain; and the whole question of a governor's qualities must have crossed his mind when he applied for administrative office in America in 1590.

In *Don Quixote* the problem is presented in terms of Sancho's character. There is advance speculation about how he would acquit himself. Sancho's own earlier confidence in his ability is tempered by more realistic considerations in Part II. Don Quixote wavers. He tells the Duchess that he sees in his squire a certain aptitude for the job: ' . . .

moreover we know from long experience that neither great ability nor much learning is needed for one to be a governor, for there are any number of them around who can scarcely read and yet they govern like goshawks' (II, 32; ii, 293). But then later we find him deploring Sancho's inability to write, and in exasperation warning him that his abuse of proverbs will assuredly drive his subjects to rebellion (II, 43; ii, 364).

Sancho's way with proverbs, indeed, is another facet of the problem. These popular sayings (*refranes*), in which Spain is so rich, were highly esteemed by Renaissance intellectuals as the inherited wisdom of collective experience. Cervantes several times defines them in such terms. Some famous collections, like the *Filosofía vulgar* (1568) compiled by the Sevillian humanist Juan de Mal Lara, were published. Sancho has an endless store and in Part II produces strings of them, however unrelated to each other and irrelevant to the occasion they may be. He has a natural facility in them which amazes his master but, to the equal irritation of Don Quixote, no conception of how to use them appropriately. In other words, he lacks the Art to employ effectively what Nature has so richly endowed him with. It is an illustration of the fact that his native peasant wisdom and wit are undirected by education or formal training ('art'). The governorship problem illustrates the same fact.[10]

However, that is not to suggest that Sancho's success and failure as governor – for he is both – fit comfortably into any abstract scheme. They do fit up to a point, but other factors complicate, dilute and ultimately humanize the tendency towards neat schematic allegory here. One of these is found in Sancho's new symptoms of concern for his spiritual health. Perhaps the fulfilment of his ambition carries risks for his soul. As early as chapter 4 in Part II he wonders about this, and concludes 'Sancho I was born, and Sancho I intend to die' (p. 71). Long before Don Quixote's famous second precept, therefore, Sancho is seen as predisposed to know his limitations, which for the conservative seventeenth century still traditionally also meant knowing his place. Being always apt to overdo things, even in stating moral scruples, he declares after Clavileño that he would prefer the smallest piece of heaven to the biggest island in the world (II, 42; ii, 355). A little later, with more engaging modesty, he is ready to give up the governorship at a word from his master – a sentiment which Don Quixote regards by itself as sufficient qualification for the job. 'You have a good natural instinct,' he tells him, 'without which no knowledge is worth anything' (II, 43; ii, 365). Sancho's cheerful readiness to relinquish the governorship thus has an edifying moral justification which would smack more of wisdom *post hoc ergo propter hoc* than it does if Cervantes had not planted such clear indications of it beforehand.

The ostensible reason for giving up is more immediately compelling. Sancho has acquitted himself brilliantly as a judge, but he fails completely as a military leader. He makes not the slightest attempt to defend the 'island' against 'attack', and when it is over he saddles his ass and steals away. He knows he cannot cope with this sort of situation. Another favourite topic is recalled here: that of arms and letters. Sancho can get by well enough, it seems, without knowledge of the latter, but not without the former. The Duke had told him that he must go dressed partly as a lawyer and partly as a captain, and Sancho had commented that whatever he wore he would still be Sancho Panza (II, 42; ii, 356). When he did set out he went dressed simply in a lawyer's gown (II, 44; ii, 368). He certainly proves to be no soldier. The outcome bears out the observation made by Don Quixote, long before, that an island governor needs understanding of how to rule and the courage to attack and defend himself in any eventuality (I, 15; i, 193–4).

To attribute revolutionary sentiments to Cervantes and invest the Barataria episode with twentieth-century political significance, as is sometimes done,[11] makes little sense. The proletarian governorship of Sancho must be seen in its proper historical context, related to contemporary Utopias, other humanist thought and the folk tradition of carnival.[12] Which, of course, is not to say that it lacks social implications or interest – any more than does the festival of Holy Innocents' Day or the *topos* of the 'world upside-down', to which the carnivalesque rule of Sancho is related,[13] Indeed, the general rise of Sancho throughout *Don Quixote*, Part II, is socially significant in a broad sense. It is of a piece with a literary phenomenon of the age which reflects a slow but sure process of social history. Across two centuries, at least, from *La Celestina* through numerous picaresque novels and comedies, via Molière to Defoe, Lesage and Beaumarchais the clever servant comes more and more into his own.

Several times after leaving Barataria, Sancho recites the lesson learned, but lest that should not be enough Cervantes makes him fall down a hole in the ground. This clearly symbolizes his plunge from the heights of fortune and power, just as his rescue by Don Quixote signals the restoration of dependence on his master (II, 55). The lapse from realism is resounding, and the effect of both incidents within the principal context of *Don Quixote* is meretricious. They are much better suited to the narrative procedure of romance and would have been well at home in *Persiles y Sigismunda* which Cervantes was writing at the same time. Nowhere else in *Don Quixote* does he handle the story in quite such a heavy-handed, not to say clumsy, way. It is undoubtedly a part of that brief disturbance of which we have noted other signs around this point in the novel.

There was a danger at this point of at least part of the novel becoming something else. But Cervantes had to bring Sancho back into line and, although he makes him learn his lesson about ambition, he is careful not to suggest that he has undergone the sort of life-transforming experience usual in fable. Sancho is much his old self again afterwards, undoubtedly a little wiser, but still with a vestige or two of his old desires. The taste of power and the thought of an earldom, though not a governorship, still have a few charms for him (II, 63 and 65). He even gets one more chance to exercise his judicial talents and he settles the difference between the village runners (II, 66).

Cervantes sometimes had trouble keeping his inventiveness in check. As a teller of stories, he was a bit like Sancho with his proverbs: finding them was no problem, organizing and controlling them was. Quite apart from the many-sided Barataria episode, he was simultaneously keeping other balls in the air. Intercut with the 'island' sequence are the fresh and comic scene where the Duchess's page visits Teresa Panza and Sanchica, the start of the Ricote–Ana Félix story and the Doña Rodríguez affair. If for a moment Cervantes falters here in *Don Quixote*, Part II, characteristically he shows that he knows it. The 'Moor's complaint' (II, 44) is a good example of the real author's articulate self-awareness. He complains, but he knows he must restrict himself to the story of Quixote and Sancho.

and so he confines himself closely within the narrow limits of his narration, while having the ability, sufficiency and wit to deal with the whole universe

(y pues se contiene y cierra en los estrechos límites de la narración, teniendo habilidad, suficiencia y entendimiento para tratar del universo todo: II, 44; ii, 366)

NOTES: CHAPTER 10

1   It is remarked three times when Don Quixote arrives at different inns that he does not take the inn for a castle (II, 24, 59 and 71). Luis Rosales was perhaps the first to

appreciate the implications of the change, though it is necessary to modify some of his conclusions (1960D, Vol. 2, pp. 360 ff.).

2 Mary McCarthy puts it the other way round: 'The comic element is the incorrigible element in every human being; the capacity to learn, from experience or instruction, is what is forbidden to all comic creations and to what is comic in you and me. The capacity to learn is the prerogative of the hero or the heroine: Prince Hal as opposed to Falstaff' (1962E, p. 289).

3 'All melancholy men are better after a quartan,' says Burton, quoted in Kong (1980D), p. 233.

4 See Vilar (1973E), pp. 68 ff., on this passage and on the subject; also Elliott (1963E), pp. 294, 312.

5 See Riley (1979D) and García Chichester (1983D).

6 A sumptuous amateur dramatic event of this kind, based on *Amadís de Grecia*, was performed before the king in the open air at Aranjuez in 1622. 'The performance began as twilight was falling, with the opening of two doors and the entry of court ladies to perform a masque, after which they took their seats on a dais to watch the play. Two triumphal cars then entered from opposite archways . . . Three trees then opened to reveal three nymphs, and the prologue was spoken by the daughter of Olivares, who came out of a wood . . . ' (Shergold, 1967E, p. 269).

7 The first three cases contrived to test him have their origin in folklore (Murillo, 1978B, 125–6). So, no doubt, did the paradox of the oath and the gallows (II, 51), though this perhaps goes back to Sextus Empiricus (Hazard, 1931D, p. 172): it is not mentioned in a recent study of scepticism in Cervantes (Ihrie, 1982D). On the Renaissance vogue of paradox, see Colie (1966E) and Márquez Villanueva (1975D), pp. 209 ff.

8 Sancho's career in Barataria has analogies with Don Quixote's chivalric career, as Allen has shown (1979[1]D), pp. 19–36

9 Cited by Maravall (1976D), p. 219.

10 Subtler implications are pursued by Joly (1984D).

11 For example, by Osterc (1963D), p. 267.

12 See in particular Maravall (1976D), pp. 216 ff.

13 Sancho's appointment of a constable to sort out genuine beggars and false ones (II, 52) reflects the same concern with the contemporary problem of mendicancy as lay behind *Guzmán de Alfarache*.

CHAPTER 11

Levels of Being

Someone has counted 669 characters mentioned in *Don Quixote*, Parts I and II. Though not urban-centred like the average picaresque novel, it probably gives as good a cross-section of Spanish society *circa* 1600 as any of them do, without being a 'social' novel in the sense that many of the great nineteenth-century works are.

One aspect of its characterization was unique in its day and remains exceptional even now. The work is peopled by figures of whom an unusually large number play or have imposed on them invented roles distinct from their basic personalities. Whereas, for example, Dorotea exists and moves on the same level as Sancho, the Priest or the Captive, she also assumes a fictitious identity as Princess Micomicona whose operative sphere lies in the paraliterary world of the imagination – that of Don Quixote, of other people and of the books of chivalry. Don Quixote himself is 'really' Alonso Quijano, who sees himself, at least potentially, as occupying the very region, to his eyes no less real, where heroes of fiction like Amadis and Roland have their being. Dulcinea is another paraliterary invention like Micomicona belonging on the same plane. There are on this level a few inhabitants (Marcela and the Arcadian shepherdesses) known only under their assumed identities. A small number of others are visible only to Don Quixote and are of non-human origin: the giants which others see as windmills or wineskins, the warriors which were sheep. This plane of invented characters hinges on the imagination of Don Quixote, but takes in the creations of other people, including those of other writers of fiction. It almost, but not quite, corresponds to 'romance fiction', while the basic level might be called 'novelistic'. Not every character is fictitious in orgin, however: Roque Guinart, the famous Catalan bandit, is historical.

So far all those referred to, except Dulcinea (the original, not the travesties), actually 'appear on the scene' in the narrative. There are others who are spoken of but do not appear: 'real' ones (for example, Cardenio's father), newly invented ones (Dulcinea), literary ones

(Amadis, Anselmo, Montesinos, Avellaneda's Quixote and Sancho). In the same general category are extratextual figures like Don Juan de Austria and Cervantes himself. Finally, there are the invented figures of Cide Hamete Benengeli and the anonymous and intermediary authors who exist in a marginal zone inside the novel but outside the story.

All this demands a diagram, which I have supplied (Fig. 11.1). It gives *examples* of characters in these zones and on these planes, with an indication of the movement there may be between them. If the taxonomy is not misconceived, it should be possible to situate any character in the book appropriately, although one could certainly elaborate the subclassification further. If it has no other value, the scheme helps to show how very permeable are these levels of being, in the work to which the modern realistic novel is generally held to owe more than to any other.

(i) QUIXOTIC REFLECTIONS

Creative writers often remark on something which critics shy away from – understandably so, since the observation does nothing to explain the creative process. They speak of a character 'coming to life' as they write, and taking over his own development, or else failing to do so. Just when the author of the *Quixote* might have made such an observation is anyone's guess; that he had every reason to make it is certain.

Few characters in literature enjoy as much autonomy as Don Quixote and Sancho seem to do. The illusion depends first on the credibility of the depiction, but also on the alleged historicity of the story, on the fiction that they existed independently of all versions of it, and on their self-awareness. The illusion derives part of its power from the paradoxical fact that Cervantes carefully destroys the autonomy and the historicity at certain moments (notably in I, 8–9; i, 137–45 and I, 52; i, 604–5). He thus exposes the literary illusion for what it is: not a deception for making new quixotes of us all, but something to be enjoyed for its own sake. Although the trick was by no means unknown before the nineteenth century, probably no writer before Pirandello and Unamuno made better use of it than Cervantes.

The idea of exploiting the previously acquired fame of literary characters had been used before Cervantes, of course, but used differently. In the late fifteenth-century romance of *Grimalte e Gradissa*, for example, Juan de Flores took over Boccaccio's Panfilo and Fiammetta for his own work. But this is quite a different matter from recycling

Figure 11.1 *Examples of Character*

appear

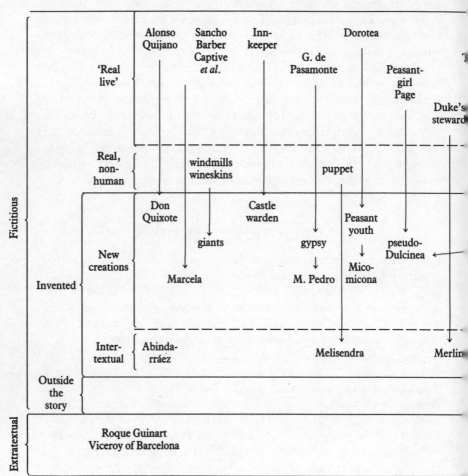

in Don Quixote *who*

are referred to, but do not appear

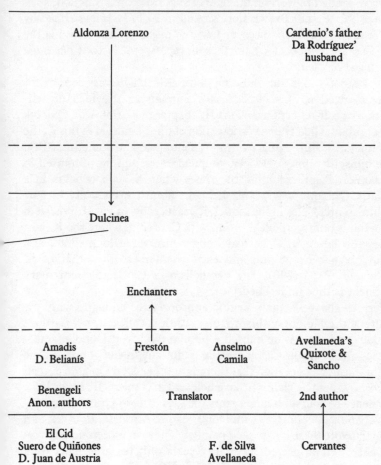

Aldonza Lorenzo

Cardenio's father
Da Rodríguez'
husband

Dulcinea

Enchanters

Amadis D. Belianís	Frestón	Anselmo Camila	Avellaneda's Quixote & Sancho
Benengeli Anon. authors	Translator		2nd author
El Cid Suero de Quiñones D. Juan de Austria		F. de Silva Avellaneda	Cervantes

one's own literary successes, so to speak. The few followers of Cervantes in this have tended to work in the field of superior popular fiction, such as Chesterton's Father Brown stories. And in *The Mysterious Island* by Jules Verne the travellers discover that the master of the island is the famous Captain Nemo of whom they have read in *Twenty Thousand Leagues under the Sea*.

The notion of a character thinking of himself in a literary context, or being recognized as one, leads easily enough to the idea of self-duplication or self-reflection. In Part II, chapter 3, we find Don Quixote wondering about Cide Hamete's depiction of him. Unusual as this is, the idea then takes a still stranger form. We glimpse, and sometimes Don Quixote himself seems to glimpse, momentary reflections of himself in other people. (I am excluding the times when Sancho behaves in a particularly Quixotic way.) This happens almost exclusively in Part II but, like so much else in the sequel, it has its roots in Part I. I mean in Don Quixote's unforgettable meeting with Cardenio, where the Knight embraces the latter 'as if he had known him for a long time', and Cardenio gazes back at him and each wonders at the other's odd appearance (I, 23; i, 290). The parallelism of Cardenio's temporary derangement is thus underlined.[1]

In Part II the reflections begin, appropriately enough, with the adventure of the Knight of the Mirrors.[2] With his alleged lady Casildea de Vandalia, not only is he himself a bit of a parody of Don Quixote – being the joker Sansón Carrasco, this is not surprising – but also he makes the explicit suggestion that there is another Don Quixote abroad in the world, whom he claims to have defeated in combat (II, 14; ii, 135). It is nonsense of course, but he plants the idea in Don Quixote's mind.

The very next encounter is with Don Diego de Miranda. Between him and Don Quixote there is a marked parallel. They have a certain physical resemblance. 'He appeared to be fifty years old; his grey hairs were sparse, his countenance aquiline' (II, 16; ii, 150).[3] They are two country gentlemen of similar age and rank, differently dressed but each in an eyecatching manner. They are unequal in wealth, however, and, as soon appears, completely opposed in temperament and lifestyle. Don Quixote certainly, and Don Diego possibly, senses the parallel the moment they meet. Don Quixote reacts by exhibiting intense consciousness of how he must appear in the eyes of the other (p. 151). And after his absurd confrontation with the lion he begins his speech of justification by anticipating Don Diego's reaction to his apparently mad behaviour (ch. 17, p. 166). Could it be that Carrasco's suggestion has given a new turn to the self-consciousness Don Quixote has always had, and made him ready for once to look at himself as others do, and not exclusively from his own deluded viewpoint? If that is the case, the Bachelor's first attempt to rescue the Knight from himself was not the total disaster it seemed to be.

The next instance obligingly springs from the depths of his own psyche. Taking the Cave of Montesinos adventure, as we must, to be a dream experience, the three major figures have some clear affinities with the dreamer and Dulcinea. Montesinos and Durandarte may reasonably be seen as projections of Don Quixote himself. Montesinos is a superannuated knight and the sage which Don Quixote might aspire to be. Durandarte is the laid-flat knight who has literally lost his heart to his lady Belerma. And she resembles the transformed Dulcinea in having lost her good looks (II, 23). These emanations from Quixote's unconscious mind can be read as views of himself and his imaginary lady: the first, potentially, as having given up his chivalric enterprise; in the second case, going on as he has been doing. They are options open to him. The fact that Cervantes did not write with the theories of Jung, Freud or anyone else in mind does not invalidate such an interpretation, of course. It is a superbly authentic-sounding dream, and as such it is amenable to interpretation in some degree.[4]

Nor is that quite the end of Quixotic reflections in this episode. The Scholar Cousin who guides Don Quixote and Sancho to the Cave resembles him strongly in one major respect: his ludicrous propensity for confusing poetic fable and empirical fact. As a man of letters he is as extravagant a figure as Don Quixote the man of arms.

Another figure who deserves brief mention in this context is Doña Rodríguez, who will be the main subject of the final section of this chapter. She is perhaps less a reflection than a complementary figure, a female counterpart. However, parallels are established from the start of their midnight encounter (II, 48). Each reacts with alarm at the other's appearance, and this is followed presently by panic as the thought of a possible assault on their chastity occurs to both of them (pp. 397–9). They are of much the same age and the same middling social status (petty hidalgo and duenna). More than this, she apparently believes in modern knights errant, in her simple-minded way. Her faith in the Knight complements his own and makes them seem a natural pair. In some ways she shares his private world.

The last occurrence of character reflection crowns the whole sequence, although it comes from a source that must have been wholly unlooked for. When the pseudo-Quixote and Sancho of Avellaneda dropped like ripe plums into his lap, Cervantes proceeded to exploit in his own novel the undeniable fact that there now existed a Don Quixote and a Sancho who were certainly not those who figured in his own Parts I and II. When his heroes learn of these rivals (II, 59), they vigorously assert their own identities, yet they show some pardonable anxiety over the impostors or whatever they are. They remain in this state of mind until they meet Don Álvaro Tarfe, who has walked right out of Avellaneda's pages. They then obtain his readily granted agreement that they alone are the authentic Quixote and Sancho, thus exorcizing the phantoms to the best of their ability.

It would not be difficult to put together and impute to the conscious intention of Cervantes a whole theory of the psychological evolution of Don Quixote, of the most impressive modernity, based on these partial but unmistakable reflections of character. Don Quixote, one might say, encountering something of himself in others, rejecting his not-self (Avellaneda's Quixote) and eventually finding his 'true' self in the sanity of Alonso Quijano. But it will not do. The sequence as a whole is almost certainly as unplanned as the intervention of Avellaneda's heroes was unlooked for. But that does not make these character reflections fortuitous irrelevancies. A good deal of the inventive genius of Cervantes in *Don Quixote* must be intuitive, if less so than used to be thought. More than once he opens up vistas of narrative possibility and human personality which modern novelistic techniques have accustomed us to view from an angle which we cannot be sure was his own.

(ii)   TWO COMIC CHARACTERS IN ACTION

The midnight scene between Don Quixote and Doña Rodríguez (II, 48) shows Cervantes at the height of his powers. Few scenes in the novel are conveyed with more graphic literary skill. The great commentators Clemencín and Rodríguez Marín both remarked on this. All the central narrative, with its two main figures, is keenly visualized – which does much to account for its popularity with artists and illustrators – but there are high points and this is one of them.[5] It was of course a natural gift of the writer's, and one of whose importance he was well aware, probably thanks in part to the romances of chivalry. Don Quixote, who claimed that he could almost say he had seen Amadis of Gaul with his own two eyes (II, 1; i, 50), certainly makes his own verbalized fantasies very vivid (I, 21 and 50).

Physical descriptions of Don Quixote and Sancho are relatively brief and infrequent considering the vividness of impression evoked. In the Knight's case, at least, Cervantes achieves much by the art of mere suggestion. His behaviour repeatedly reminds us of the difference between the way he sees himself and the way others see him. There are many tacit reminders thus given of his appearance. Now and then these are explicit. 'Put straight that chamber pot you are wearing on your head,' says one of the convict guards to Don Quixote, suddenly reminding us that he is still wearing the barber's basin (I, 22; i, 274).

In the nocturnal scene we are considering the description is as economical as it is clear-out. Lying sleepless in his room in the ducal castle, Don Quixote hears the door open and stands up in bed, 'wrapped from head to foot in a yellow satin bedspread, a woollen cap on his head, his face and moustaches bandaged up' (the face because of the scratches he had got from the cats, the moustaches to keep them from limply drooping: p. 396). The figure who enters is 'a most venerable duenna with a long white gathered headstole, so long that it cloaked her from head to foot'. She wears outsize spectacles and carries a lighted candle. The two of them together make an extravagant spectacle.

The comedy of the scene works in several ways at once, though it depends primarily on incongruity and surprise. There is the usual discrepancy between the scene as it is and the fiction-fed expectations which Don Quixote brings to it – or which by now we regularly presume he does. No seventeenth-century reader could fail to be primed with memories of, say, the Infanta Elisena visiting King Perión's bedchamber in *Amadís de Gaula*, or the attentions offered to the wounded Don Belianís by the Princess Florisbella. He would also be waiting, like today's reader, for the mischievous damsel Altisidora to come through the door. But it is the matronly Doña Rodríguez who enters – the first surprise in an episode which has one twist after another, even after we thought the end had been reached.

The mutual shock of the Duenna and the Knight is an infallible comic device. Laurel and Hardy in some dark and spooky situation come suddenly upon one another and recoil gibbering in fright.[6] The incident in the *Quixote* in fact has a considerable literary history. It almost certainly owes something to *Guzmán de Alfarache* (II, ii, 6), in which the *picaro*, hearing a noise of cats in the night, goes downstairs naked and encounters in the patio his master's wife in the same condition. She thinks he is a ghost, screams and flees. So does he. Cats scatter. Guzmán trips over one on the stairs and falls on his face. A cat grips his legs with its claws. The incident ends in a messy 'Rabelaisian' way. (In *Don Quixote* the incident with the cats had just preceded the meeting with the Duenna.)

If Cervantes here owes something to Alemán, so does the English novel to Cervantes. Near the beginning of *Tom Jones*, Doña Rodríguez' consternation is momentarily relived by the matronly Mrs Wilkins on encountering Squire Allworthy in his nightshirt, a candle in his hand (I, 3). The incident is further elaborated in *The Posthumous Papers of the Pickwick Club* when, to their mutual alarm, Mr Pickwick in his nightcap and the lady with her hair in curlers surprise each other in the Great White Horse Inn at Ipswich (ch. 22).[7]

The range of humour in the *Quixote* is wider and often less boisterous than the author is given credit for. While much of it is knockabout, especially in Part I (compare the bedroom scene involving Maritornes in Part I, chapters 16–17), there is just one clownish moment here, when Doña Rodríguez falls over her skirts. But Cervantes almost sedulously avoids the farcically obvious by *not* allowing Don Quixote, as he makes a rush for the bedroom door, to collide with the returning Duenna.

Much of the comedy comes from Don Quixote's nervous fears for his virtue, fears to which we are privy, and then his impetuous rejection of them. Those fears, which would have done credit to a virginal Galahad, become doubly ludicrous when we see him paired, not with the young and pretty Altisidora, but with an unattractive widow well on in years. The comedy of Don Quixote's behaviour here has little directly to do with his madness. It does not depend on his chivalric illusions, although it is linked with them. It depends rather on his vanity, always a weakness of his. He comes very close – and he does so even more with Altisidora – to being the comic type of the fatuous aged gallant, like Don Mendo in Calderón's *Alcalde de Zalamea*, or the superannuated suitors found again in Molière and in English Restoration comedy.

Doña Rodríguez is something more than the comic literary stereotype of the duenna, perpetual target of satirists like Quevedo and of Cervantes's Licenciado Vidriera (*Novelas ejemplares*, ii, 69). Of course she remains a comic figure and her plight is not meant to be taken very seriously. To speak of 'the enchanting simplicity of this good woman' in this 'melancholy adventure', as Unamuno did (1967D, p. 242), is overdoing it. But there is in Doña Rodríguez a complication of personality, more latent than manifest, a potential for development in a direction which is not comic. We can recognize, without sentimentalizing, that her cause is genuine and her distress not simulated, that the Duke is indifferent to it, and her helpless recourse to Don Quixote for assistance is foolish but made in good faith. Neither the comic treatment of the episode nor the less agreeable traits of Doña Rodríguez cancel out all the significance of these things.

She, too, has become in some measure the victim of the Duke, whose entire household, not to mention a dependent village, appears to be involved in a series of practical jokes, taken to inordinate lengths. Not for nothing do the odious chaplain (II, 32) and Benengeli himself (II, 70) wonder if the jokers are altogether in their right minds. We all but hear the sniggers and stifled guffaws resounding through the dark galleries. There is something rather odd about life in this castle (or palace) – and not merely odd but unpleasant. Physical pain, trivial but disagreeable, is never far away – slaps, cuffs, pinpricks, pinching, scratching, whipping. If Don Quixote's fantasies resemble children's games, the games in the castle savour of another kind of infantile regression. There is something not quite right about the inhabitants, and it is Doña Rodríguez with her dottiness who more than anyone serves to bring it out. It is she who reveals (if we are disposed to believe her) that the Duke borrows money from one of his vassals, that the lovely Duchess has 'issues' in her legs through which bad humours are purged, and that Altisidora has bad breath. Imparting this information earns her and Don Quixote the slippering and pinching in the dark with which the bedchamber scene ends (pp. 402–3).

The castle is situated in relatively feudalistic Aragon. The Duke and Duchess are gracious, charming and generous, and life in the castle has its agreeable side, but with a neurotic tinge. Don Quixote is relieved to be out and breathing the air of the open road again (II, 58). In varying concentrations and diverse settings a similar atmosphere may be perceived in other literature of the age: in *Guzmán*, in *Estebanillo González*, Avellaneda's *Quixote*, *El curioso impertinente* and in various plays of the Spanish and the English Jacobean theatre.

Looked at from Don Quixote's point of view, this castle, where absurd things over which he has no control keep happening to him, is not so far away from Kafka's. Cervantes's comedy in these masterly chapters of *Don Quixote* has a hard edge of irrationality.[8]

NOTES: CHAPTER 11

1 Faint reflections of Quixote may also be discerned in Ginés de Pasamonte as author-protagonist of his life-story (I, 22; i, 271–2); and in the Innkeeper's credulous acceptance of the romances of chivalry (I, 32; i, 396).

2   He has small pieces of reflecting glass attached to his armour. The word used is *lunas*, which also means 'moons'. In his next disguise he is the 'Knight of the White Moon'. See Pope (1983D) for some deeper speculations on the significance of the first encounter.

3   There is also some resemblance to Cervantes himself in this description. See Sánchez (1961–2D).

4   Compare, too, the description of Don Quixote's right hand (I, 43; i, 528) and Durandarte's (II, 23; ii, 214). For a fuller account, see Riley (1982D).

5   Why is the adventure of the windmills remembered and associated with Don Quixote above all others, to the point of having bequeathed a proverb to the English language? There are several possible contributory reasons. It is probably the most supremely futile of his exploits. It is an early example of the potent modern theme of man against machine. There may be some relic in our minds of an old emblematic association of windmills – or toy whirligigs at any rate – with madness (see the figure of *Pazzia* in Ripa's *Iconologia*, 1618C, pp. 399–400; and Márquez Villanueva, 1980D, pp. 105–6). And lastly there is the simple mythopoeic power of the visual image. Anyone who has seen the windmills in La Mancha will surely agree that they do look strange in the open landscape. It requires no great leap of the imagination to metamorphose them into something else – some mutation out of Hieronymus Bosch, or giants.

6   In *Don Quixote*, I, 19, the members of the nocturnal funeral party who have scared Sancho and almost scared Don Quixote take to their heels at the latter's outlandish appearance.

7   On the connections between Dickens and Cervantes in *Pickwick Papers* especially, see Gale (1973E), though he does not mention this one.

8   See Robert (1977D). There is an evocation of a similar milieu in Robin Chapman's novel *The Duchess's Diary* (1980E), with its fascinating re-creation of Cervantes's 'original' Duchess.

CHAPTER 12

Ideals and Illusions

It is not possible to sum up *Don Quixote* in the terms of a single general theme. The huge multiplicity of motifs, themes and topics which the work has been held to contain may be seen in the titles listed in any critical bibliography. The range and depth of Cervantes's novelistic invention partly account for this, but his basic choice of subject is also in part responsible – the consequences of a man going mad through reading too much chivalresque literature. Out of this it is in fact easy to abstract a whole range of related conceptual polarities: madness-sanity, illusion-reality, appearances-truth, fiction-fact, art-life, poetry-history, romance-novel, idealism-realism, theory-practice, mind-matter, spirit-flesh. They are open to such infinite speculation, however, that any temptation to ponder them here is easily resisted.

One of these concepts above all others has been especially associated with Don Quixote. Idealism – ineffectual idealism, to be exact. In the major European languages to be 'quixotic' means to pursue impracticable ideals. More or less like Cervantes's hero, the quixotic idealist takes little or no account of practical realities in seeking to implement his aims. He does not see when pursuit of an ideal becomes surrender to an illusion.

Now, although this incapacity is a distinguishing characteristic of Don Quixote, Cervantes offers no direct and explicit commentary on it, as he does, for example, on the comportment of some of the central figures in his *Exemplary Novels* and other works. His own precise attitude to his hero's deficiency has remained in part elusive. 'In part', because he obviously presents him as a figure of fun, while still leaving ample room for speculation over whether in addition he tacitly condemns, reproves, mocks, pities, sympathizes or admires. Rightly or wrongly, answers have perennially been inferred from the way Cervantes handles the story or from sources outside it. This general area of interpretation has been over the years the most contestable of the whole novel. Most people have taken Cervantes to be defending idealism; a few have thought he was attacking it. Probably he was doing neither. Unamuno canonized Quixote for his idealism ('my Saint Quixote', he calls him: 1967D, e.g. p. 212). Ruskin was inclined to rate Cervantes first 'of all powerful and popular writers [who] in the cause of error have wrought most harm to their race . . . for he cast scorn upon the holiest principles of humanity' (1855E, pp. 66–7).

While it is misguided to treat the novel as a moral or philosophical tract, many such questions of a more particular kind do insistently present themselves. Does Cervantes really tend to suggest that ideals are illusions, idealism folly? Is Don Quixote foolish or heroic to persist in his? How is it that we laugh at a man so wholly dedicated to relieving distress and fighting injustice? Has he simply got his ends right and his means wrong? There are many such questions as these and even more answers to them.[1] It is a measure of Cervantes's success in reflecting life through this least dogmatic of books that people have been so disposed to find in it the answers they would like to find there. No one is immune. Centring attention too exclusively on the ideals leads to Romantic distortions of the work; focusing too narrowly on Don Quixote's crazy behaviour eventually reduces the novel to the vacuousness of a comic strip.

The simple connection between Don Quixote's ideals and his illusions is central. The fact that he regains his sanity at the very end means that to all intents and purposes he eventually sheds his illusions, although until he is on his deathbed the separation of ideals and illusions is slow and incomplete. The process is under way at least from the beginning of the third expedition, maybe earlier, when his most obvious physical illusions – ocular delusions – almost disappear. We have also noted signs of the growth of another kind of dis-illusionment: namely his incipient recognition of the impracticality of literally and completely realizing the ideals of story-book chivalry in the world he lives in, and of doing so on his own. What happens to his idealism in these circumstances is naturally important. There can be little doubt of his intensified melancholy in the later chapters, or of the surge of disappointment after his defeat. But I do not see incontrovertible signs of loss of faith in his ideals *per se* – close though he may come to this – either before or after he regains his wits. Nothing in his deathbed conduct suggests the cynicism, bitterness or broken spirit one might expect of the frustrated idealist. He abjures the books of chivalry and their heroes and looks back on his obsession as ignorance (II, 74; ii, 587); his predominant concern now is to die a good Christian death. The emphasis is on balance of mind restored.

In this general context I shall look at one major motif of the novel and two important episodes in Part II: respectively, Dulcinea, the Cave of Montesinos and the encounter with Don Diego de Miranda. All three are rich in a variety of ways and throw light on Don Quixote's state of mind. The first two do so from within, as it were. In some degree the third does the same from a source outside it, and by means of a complementary figure provides a kind of equilibrating control for the assessment of the hero. Of course one cannot anatomize Don Quixote's entire madness by means of a simple bisection of idealism and illusion, but a careful look at the text with these central concepts in mind may help.

(i) DULCINEA

Dulcinea enters the book almost as an afterthought to Don Quixote's other preparations for his career as knight errant (I, 1), but she plays a major part in his story. She is one of the most extraordinary character conceptions in literature. She exists as pure idea in the mind of the Knight, is the professed motivation or justification for many of his actions, and the occasion for some bravura displays of eloquence. As it turns out, she is not his exclusive property, however, and moves others to action, too. She has no physical presence, but an incarnate original form as Aldonza Lorenzo, who is spoken of, but never 'appears on the scene' in Cervantes's novel (unlike various modern stage and screen versions of it). Two figures alleged by others to be Dulcinea enchanted do appear. In the circumstances perhaps it is forgivable not to attempt an exact definition of her existential or ontological status!

The contrast between the perfections she represents in spiritual form and the earthiness of her material one is a dominant feature of her persona. The earthiness is captured to some extent in the very name 'Aldonza', which has strong peasant connotations to the Spanish ear.[2] As an idealization of an individual, Dulcinea is to Aldonza rather as Don Quixote is to Alonso Quijano or Princess Micomicona is to Dorotea – only more so. The paired figures have some analogy to the twin terms of a metaphor, and it is no accident that Dulcinea is intimately connected with the metaphorical procedures of enhancement characteristic of the cultivated poetry of the age (see Rodríguez-Luis, 1965–6D, p. 387). Don Quixote envisages her as possessing

all the impossible and chimerical attributes of beauty conferred by poets on their ladies . . . such as that her hair is gold, her brow the

Elysian fields, her eyebrows rainbows, her eyes suns, her cheeks roses, her lips corals, pearls her teeth, alabaster her neck, marble her breast, ivory her hands, her whiteness snow.

(todos los imposibles y quiméricos atributos de belleza que los poetas dan a sus damas: que sus cabellos son oro, su frente campos eliseos, sus cejas arcos del cielo, sus ojos soles, sus mejillas rosas, sus labios corales, perlas sus dientes, alabastro su cuello, mármol su pecho, marfil sus manos, su blancura nieve: I, 13; i, 176.)

Similarly, when Quixote revises Sancho's prosaic (and plausible) account of his supposed visit to Dulcinea, he transforms grains of wheat into pearls, as a sophisticated poet of the day might have done (I, 31). As an idealization of womanhood, Dulcinea inevitably has some connections with the damsel Poetry who recurs in various of Cervantes's works in forms ranging from outright allegory in the *Viaje del Parnaso* to symbolic association in the gypsy girl Preciosa. Naturally, idealization on the scale of Dulcinea's invites comic deflation. Being another of Don Quixote's imitations from chivalric romance, she is a parody from the start, but she is not *in herself* a comic one. The comedy comes from the material contrast and when the metaphor is stood on its head.

There may be some doubt about Dulcinea's royal lineage (I, 13; II, 32), but there is none about her literary pedigree. A younger sister, as it were, of Oriana and other peerless princesses of chivalric romance, she is the ultimate descendant of those perfectly idealized ladies whom courtly love poets had sung and swooned over, sighed and died for, for centuries, beauties who like her had been loved *de lonh*, and *de oídas*. She is the parody version of the *donna gentile*, and the chaste adored of poets in the Renaissance neoplatonic vain. She is close kin to the Amaryllises and Dianas, Galateas and Phyllises of pastoral, whose flesh-and-blood content is negligible – as Don Quixote actually explains to Sancho in I, 25. More perfect than Petrarch's Laura, Garcilaso's Elisa or Herrera's Luz, she is the beloved whose virtues have etherialized her right out of physical existence. She is the disembodied mistress.

In Part I, Don Quixote establishes her as the conventional absent mistress, for whose sake . . . (etc.), and who alone imparts strength to his right arm (I, 30; i, 178). He admits to Sancho that he depicts her in his imagination exactly as he pleases (I, 25; i, 314), but he domiciles her in the real village of El Toboso where, in the novel, Aldonza Lorenzo lived. This gesture towards the actualization of his ideal woman, though consistent with finding giants in wineskins and so forth, is the source of all the trouble later on, when Sancho is required to make contact with her. By attaching a place-label to his ideal, Don Quixote turns it into an illusion which is vulnerable.

This is borne out in Part II, where he suffers the nightmarish experience of having a cherished dream go out of orbit, get taken over by other people and return to haunt him. The moment Sancho talks him into believing that the uncouth peasant girl is Dulcinea under a spell, he loses his freedom to depict her in his imagination as he pleases. His own beautiful parody becomes a crude travesty fashioned by Sancho. The juxtaposition of Don Quixote's beautiful courtly prose with the 'rustically boorish' language of the peasant girl has been described by Erich Auerbach as something which 'had certainly never happened before' in literature (1969D, p. 114). Sancho proceeds to dislocate totally the metaphorical picture of Dulcinea, railing at enchanters for changing 'the pearls of my lady's eyes' – as though she were a codfish, Don Quixote objects later – 'into corktree galls, and her hair of purest gold into red ox tail bristles', and so on (II, 10; ii, 112).[3] Dulcinea's recovery of her pristine state is henceforth a major preoccupation for the Knight. Small wonder that he dreams about her in the Cave of Montesinos. Then the Duke and Duchess and their attendants get involved, and the travesty becomes literal at the next appearance of 'Dulcinea', when a page, heavily veiled, burlesques the part of the enchanted damsel (II, 55). The figure of Dulcinea has been debased and transformed, first by Sancho out of self-interest, then by others for their own amusement, and Don Quixote is helpless by himself to break the spell (short of regaining his wits). Worse is to come. Her image is contaminated with money.

The Knight's attitude to money and to any kind of commercial transaction at the outset of his career had been one of superb disregard. However, the first innkeeper amiably persuaded him of the need to be basically provided (I, 3), and so on his second sortie he goes out modestly equipped for his and Sancho's needs. He continues to regard lucre as a drab requirement at times but not the sort of thing a gentle knight worries his head about. He refuses to pay the second innkeeper (I, 17) and is evasive about paying Sancho a salary. Not a few sixteenth-century gentlemen would have behaved in exactly the same way. In Part II, where he is less alienated socially, he accepts the need for money transactions almost as a matter of course, agrees on paying Sancho a salary, tips the lionkeeper and carter two escudos (II, 17), and almost meekly pays for the damage he has caused to Maese Pedro's puppets (II, 26) and to the boat on the River Ebro.

The first intimation of Dulcinea's involvement with money is an incident in the Cave of Montesinos, an incident in Quixote's dream, with symbolic prophetic force.[4] Dulcinea sends a message to Don Quixote asking for a loan of six *reales* and offering a cotton skirt as security. More humiliatingly still, the Knight has only enough change on him to oblige with four (II, 23). Not long after, the whole business of disenchanting Dulcinea, devised at the Duke's castle, takes on the sordid colours of a commercial deal, as depressing for Don Quixote as it is ridiculous to everyone else. Sancho has to 'pay' by receiving 3,300 lashes on his ample posterior (II, 13). Naturally he does not accept this without haggling. Eventually (II, 72) he gets his master to pay him so many *reales* per stroke, raises the price some more, and finally cheats Don Quixote by faking the entire punishment. Could Dulcinea be more debased?

It is hard to say what she 'stands for' precisely in Don Quixote's eyes, apart from being his professed inspiration and object of devotion. As a concept she has been likened to Aristotle's concept of God (Atlee, 1976D) and St Anselm's argument for His existence (Durán, 1960D, p. 160). I do not think she is the *symbol* of anything in particular. All the same, it is clear that her image resides close to the heart of all that chivalry means to Don Quixote. Dulcinea is obviously associated very closely with chivalry for him. In the light of this it is significant that nobody (except perhaps Sancho in moments of confusion) believes in her existence, yet quite a few people (notably the members of a ducal court) pretend to do so and pay lip-service to her. The charade of restoring her to what she once was ends in a fraudulent cash deal. Her image has become a travesty of her original self and tainted with commercialism. It is easy to draw the analogy between Dulcinea and what was left of chivalry in Spain in the early capitalist era, when the buying of patents of nobility was widespread. It was the new age of that powerful *caballero*, Don Dinero, 'the great solvent of the solid fabric of the old society, the great generator of illusion' (Trilling, 1961E, p. 209). It was the age when, as Olivares reminded Philip IV, 'Kings cannot achieve heroic actions without money' (Elliott, 1963E, p. 320).

Dulcinea's appearance as impecunious bumpkin in Don Quixote's dream implies that at the unconscious level of his mind he accepts that something has happened to his ideal mistress. She does not *look* the same to him now. This suggests that a cherished belief of his has been undermined; it points to a deep-level disillusionment, representing a painful step towards sanity. However, at the conscious level, he considers the metamorphosis to be neither fundamental nor irreversible, but a temporary aberration induced by magic. As he reminds Sancho:

> enchantments switch all things around and change their natural shapes. I do not mean that they really change them from one thing into another, but that it looks that way, as we learnt from experience in the transformation of Dulcinea, sole refuge of my hopes.

> (todas las cosas trastruecan y mudan de su ser natural los encantos. No quiero decir que las mudan de uno en otro ser realmente, sino que lo parece, como lo mostró la experiencia en la transformación de Dulcinea, único refugio de mis esperanzas: II, 29; ii, 265.)

The distinction between her appearance and her real self is all-important. When Don Quixote now asserts his steadfast belief in Dulcinea's perfections, as he resolutely does at least from the time of the discussion with the Duke and Duchess onwards (II, 32; ii, 289–93),[5] it is of course to her unchanged essential self that he refers. His resolution is strengthened by the news that the false Quixote of Avellaneda was disenamoured of Dulcinea, and he loudly proclaims his undying devotion to her again (ch. 59, p. 486).[6] But the great, the most authentically heroic moment in his whole career is when he lies prostrate beneath the lance-point of the Knight of the White Moon and

> battered and dazed, without raising his visor, as if speaking from within a tomb, he said in a low and faltering voice:
> 'Dulcinea del Toboso is the most beautiful woman in the world, and I am the most unlucky knight on earth, and it is not right that my weakness should discredit this truth.'

> (molido y sturdido, sin alzarse la visera, como si hablara dentro de una tumba, con voz debilitada y enferma, dijo:
> – Dulcinea del Toboso es la más hermosa mujer del mundo, y yo el más desdichado caballero de la tierra, y no es bien que mi flaqueza defraude esta verdad: II, 64; ii, 534.)

Don Quixote knew nothing of Sansón Carrasco's imposture: for all he did know, he risked being run through by a lance when he said this. But nothing happens to lift the spell from Dulcinea and Quixote's spirits with it. The pleasure and hope he shows when Sancho completes his whipping (ch. 72, p. 580) are short-lived. He reads the incidents with the running hare and the boys with the cricket's cage as bad omens – '*Malum signum! Malum signum!* Hare runs, hounds give chase: Dulcinea won't appear!' (ch. 73, p. 581). In a brave effort to undo the maleficence of these omens, Sancho buys the cricket-cage, symbolically associated with Dulcinea, for four *cuartos*. Her connection with money is maintained to the end.

However, Don Quixote's pessimistic words are not quite the last he has to say on the subject. All he has just said is that he does not expect to *see* her. When he mentions her next, for the last time, he restores her to all her poetical glory. Fantasizing with his friends about their going pastoral together, he calls her 'the peerless Dulcinea del Toboso, glory of these river banks, ornament of these meadows, pillar of beauty, cream of wit, and, in short, fitting object of all praise however hyperbolical it may be' (p. 584). This final affirmation of faith in her does not so much revive her illusory status as relegate her to the printed page of pastoral romance, where, as he had once told Sancho, her sister Amaryllises and Galateas were all to be found (I, 25).

The only serious doubt Don Quixote betrays over Dulcinea concerns her visible physical presence. In El Toboso he gets cold feet and avoids taking the obvious action required for them to meet face to face. Then he lets his private visualization of her be supplanted by Sancho's, which is diametrically opposed to it. Finally he decides that she will not make the appearance he wants her to. The one thing that he has become unsure about is her palpable existence as a living human being. And this is the strictly illusory side of Dulcinea, since a Dulcinea incarnate is unbelievable. Her status as a mental image, however, as a compendium of womanly perfections is secure. When Don Quixote proclaims that her real beauty is intact, despite the worst that enchanters – and the most sordid materialism of the age, one feels inclined to add – can do, he is symbolically affirming his belief in the ideal qualities she epitomizes. His faith in these does not waver.

(ii) THE CAVE OF MONTESINOS

The adventure of the Cave is the richest and most suggestive in the whole novel, thanks partly to Cervantes's fertile imagination and partly to the fact that caves have always been marvellous repositories of symbol. A modern study of the *Quixote* devotes 177 well-filled pages to the episode.[7]

The very nature of the experience Don Quixote relates is intended to be mysterious. He soon becomes unsure about it himself. Benengeli refuses responsibility and leaves it to the prudent reader to judge (II, 24; ii, 223). The really prudent reader knows that he can never know, but if he cares to put himself on the same level as the characters in the book and join in the discussion he can opt for the most plausible of four possibilities: that the events really physically happened just as they appeared to; that somebody staged them; that Don Quixote deliberately made up the whole story;[8] that it was a dream or some kind of visionary experience. The only evidence is circumstantial and it points to the last of these. Aside from which the episode reads as one of the best dreams in literature before Galdós.

Montesinos, Durandarte and Belerma are figures from a group of Spanish ballads of Carolingian chivalric derivation, closely associated with this region in La Mancha, where, close to the Cave of Montesinos, the Lakes of Ruidera are to be found and the partly subterranean River Guadiana runs. In these circumstances it is natural that the ballad figures mentioned should comprise the principal dramatis personae of the dream. But its mainspring is Dulcinea, even though she plays a smaller role in it. The dark shadow of her enchantment has clouded the otherwise auspicious beginnings of the third expedition. Lifting the spell on her is now the Knight's major preoccupation. It is little wonder that he dreams about redeeming all the inhabitants of the Cave (which include her) from the enchantment imposed on them by the arch-wizard Merlin. His account of the dream offers a unique insight directly into his mind at this point in his career.

Freud said that 'every dream deals with the dreamer himself' (1953E, p. 332). Although they originate in balladry, the main figures have affinities with the dreamer and the lady mainly responsible; they are projections of Don Quixote and Dulcinea (as we have previously remarked). Quixote's role in this wish-fulfilling yet anxious dream is that of messianic deliverer foredestined to release from bondage all the inhabitants of the Cave (some figures from Arthurian lore are mentioned, too). He is frustrated by premature awakening when his friends haul him up to the surface but, quite apart from that, the signs were not encouraging. He had fallen short of Dulcinea's financial needs, for one thing. For another, Durandarte, stretched out on his marble slab, had been disappointingly sceptical about Don Quixote's mission. 'And if it should not be so,' he says in the immortal words, 'if it should not be so, oh, cousin, patience I say, and shuffle the pack' (ch. 22, p. 217). It is not surprising that Quixote's pleasure in recalling his dream is at the same time pervaded by a tone of deep melancholy (ch. 22, p. 210).

The dream is notable for its fine touches of absurdity – the rosary beads the size of ostrich eggs, the scholar's cap and hood worn by Montesinos, the two-pound human heart pickled in brine, the outsize turbans, Belerma's looks, the caper cut by Dulcinea's maid, and so on. While quite appropriate to a dream, the inclusion of such ridiculous details, of a kind which were almost totally absent from Don Quixote's two major, consciously invented, chivalresque fantasies (I, 21 and 50), is significant for another reason.[9]

These ridiculous details puncture the fabric of his chivalric vision. They damage the imagery in which it is couched. They do not *fit*. Their oddity, empirically based (as we shall see later) is at variance with the perfectionism which idealized literary chivalry demands. It is as if his unconscious mind which engendered them were mocking him with their incongruity. And, as usual, the unconscious is well ahead of the conscious mind here. It seems right therefore to read the Cave experience in the way most critics have done, as a significant pointer towards Don Quixote's eventual rejection of chivalric fiction and his recovery of sanity. Indeed, considered in this light, his attack on Maese Pedro's puppets shortly afterwards (II, 26) might be seen as a further stage in his psychic development. They, too, are pseudo-Carolingian ballad figures, and Don Quixote wreaks destruction on them indiscriminately, 'friend' and 'foe' alike.

The dream in the Cave has some marked characteristics of myth to which also we will return later. However, one principal mythic motif is relevant here. It is metamorphosis. This affects not only the dueña Ruidera with her brood of children and Guadiana the squire, but the major characters, too. Montesinos is not the knight of the ballads now, but a wise old man. Durandarte subsists in a curious condition, intermittently dead and alive. Belerma has lost her beauty. Each one has changed a lot since the heyday of his or her existence as recounted in the ballads. Drastic change is also Dulcinea's problem. Lastly, there is the dreamer himself. Perhaps the most important change of all is taking place in Don Quixote. Something certainly seems to have happened in his innermost mind to his chivalric vision, as it happened to the figure of Dulcinea with whom that vision is intimately associated. The process of disenchantment, which, in another sense of the word, was the object of his dream mission to the other world, appears to have begun to operate upon himself.

The ludicrous details of the physical appearance and manner of existence of the figures in the Cave signal the fact that their physical embodiment as witnessed by Don Quixote is unreal, and therefore some kind of illusion. Later on, the physical reality of the experience in the Cave is precisely what Don Quixote wonders about.[10] So, just as he does with Dulcinea, he shows doubts about the physical manifestation, which is the illusory side.

Montesinos, Durandarte and Belerma nevertheless preserve a gravity consonant with their chivalric status. As Menéndez Pidal observed, although Cervantes treats them in jest this does not affect their inner nobility (1948D, p. 22). The absurdity of their manifestation in the flesh, now apparent even to Don Quixote, does not for him impair the chivalric values they embodied and exemplified in their conduct (such as valour, fidelity in love, steadfastness, friendship). As with Dulcinea again, the underlying idealism is unquestioned. In his dream he does not succeed in liberating either his lady or the other prisoners of the Cave. Similarly, his self-imposed mission to restore chivalry to the world is not destined to succeed. Unconsciously at least, he is beginning to realize this. But he says nothing to suggest that the impracticality of the task undermines the status of chivalry as an ideal in his eyes. In the Cave of Montesinos adventure he begins to separate illusion and ideal, which is the beginning of sanity.

(iii) DON DIEGO AND DON QUIXOTE

'J'ai découvert que tout le malheur des hommes vient d'une seule chose, qui est de ne savoir pas demurer en repos dans une chambre,' said Pascal (*Pensées*, no. 205). This rather dismal maxim would have been applauded by a number of figures in the novel – if not by Don Antonio Moreno, who argues quite the contrary (II, 65; ii, 536–7). But staying quietly at home is prescribed for Don Quixote's cure, and on a number of occasions expressly identified with right living by a variety of persons. The Niece gives expression to it at the beginning of the second sortie (I, 7) and the Housekeeper at the end of the third (II, 73). In between, so do Sancho (I, 18, and II, 28), the Housekeeper again (II, 2), Tomé Cecial (II, 13), the odious ducal Chaplain (II, 31), the unpleasant Castilian (II, 62) and the Bachelor Carrasco (II, 64). The Housekeeper's words are representative:

Stay at home, look after your property, go to confession frequently, be good to the poor, and on my soul be it if any harm come to you.

(estése en su casa, atienda a su hacienda, confiese a menudo, favorezca a los pobres y sobre mi ánima si mal le fuere: II, 73; ii, 585.)

Essentially the sentiment is the same as that of another phrase from a less pious source than the Housekeeper, Voltaire's 'Il faut cultiver notre jardin' in *Candide*. Since it represents a way of life diametrically opposed to Don Quixote's and is clearly equated with sanity, it would seem natural to take this stay-at-home philosophy as the 'moral' of the book, the panacea for Quixotism and Cervantes's last word on the matter, although the proponents of the view do not look very likely candidates for authorial spokesmanship. In any case, nothing in *Don Quixote* is that simple; Cervantes is too disposed to see both sides of things. It so happens that the Housekeeper's simple message is embodied in Don Diego de Miranda, a figure of many virtues but – since the well-bred gentlemen-farmer type ceased to be universally admired – a not uncontroversial one. However, it is as exaggerated to regard him with contempt as 'a commonplace man of no importance, complacently living in social and cultural stagnation' (Castro, 1971D, p. 93) as it is to set him up as 'the ethical focus for the entire novel' (Mandel, 1957–8D, p. 160).[11] He is a complex figure who must be seen, above all, within his novelistic context and not just in the light of twentieth-century social likes and dislikes.

Sancho's response to Don Diego's brief account of himself is an exaggerated but not incongruous response to the squirearchical qualities displayed (II, 16; ii, 153–4). The courtesy, generosity and other good points of Don Diego are no less evident to the reader. However, in at least two situations, his behaviour, though entirely sensible, commands something less than admiration and probably induces in most modern readers a certain sympathy for Don Quixote, despite his crazy behaviour. The first is Don Diego's disapproval of his son's passion for poetry. Don Lorenzo's enthusiasm is creative, scholarly and a little ingenuous (chs 16 and 18), but he is not at all one of those ridiculous amateurs of poetry who crop up in Cervantes's writings from time to time. The father's wish that instead he should study for a successful law career anticipates a million unromantic modern fathers. The second is Don Diego's prudence when Don Quixote insists on having the door of the lion's cage opened. Unable to dissuade the Knight from his folly, he puts himself at a safe distance, like the others (ch. 17, pp. 161–2). Nothing could be more reasonable, but there is inescapable irony in the fact that Don Diego claims hunting as his habitual exercise (ch. 16, p.

153). And it is hard not to feel a sneaking regard for Don Quixote when he tells Don Diego to attend to his docile falcon and his plucky ferret and leave this business with lions to him (ch. 17, p. 161). The Gentleman in Green really does look like an early example of the *bon bourgeois*, prudent, a bit of a philistine and, as his self-introductory speech contrives to suggest, a trifle self-satisfied in his Erasmian moderation and his complacent epicureanism.

The intense speculation engendered by the detailed description of Don Diego's mostly green clothing (ch. 16, pp. 149–50) now hardly seems warranted. It is festive enough to earn him the sobriquet of the Gentleman in the Green Coat from Don Quixote, but the outfit seems distinctive rather than exclusive. The vagaries of colour symbolism are merely confusing (see Joly, 1977D). The last word on the subject has probably not yet been said, but it is unlikely that Cervantes meant him to be such a hermeneutic target as he has become centuries later.

Don Diego de Miranda is in fact perfectly well accounted for in terms established by Don Quixote. He sees Don Diego as a 'knight about court', as distinct from himself, the knight errant out in the field and abroad in the world. His first words to him are 'Señor galán', referring to his dress, which has just been described.[12] Don Diego is not literally a courtier; on the contrary, he lives a retired life in the depth of the provinces. But it is natural enough for Don Quixote to see him this way: a knight like himself, but the inactive sort. He had pointed out the differences to his Housekeeper earlier:

> and although we are all of us knights, there is a great difference between us; for courtiers, without leaving their rooms or crossing the threshold of the court, can rove round the world by studying a map, and without it costing a penny, and suffering neither heat nor cold, hunger nor thirst.

> (y aunque todos seamos caballeros, va mucha diferencia de los unos a los otros; porque los cortesanos, sin salir de sus aposentos, ni de los umbrales de la corte, se pasean por todo el mundo, mirando un mapa, sin costarles blanca, ni padecer calor ni frío, hambre ni sed: II, 6; ii, 80.)

The encounter with the cartload of lions is a heaven-sent opportunity to demonstrate the difference between their roles, and our Knight seizes it eagerly. He follows up this somewhat abortive triumph with another disquisition, delivered meaningfully to Don Diego, on the difference between courtly knights and knights errant (ch. 17, pp. 166–8).[13] It is quite apparent that he is keenly conscious of these two kinds of knight, the former being a lot more abundant in this post-chivalric age. He brings up the topic on other occasions (II, 1; ii, 48, and II, 35; ii, 325). He is also echoed by the seguidilla-singing youth off to join the army, whom they meet on the road a while later. 'I'd rather have the king for lord and master and serve him in war than some hard-up fellow in the capital [*corte*]' (II, 24; ii, 227), says this 'venturesome page', whom Don Quixote also addresses as 'Señor galán', presumably on account of his courtly dress again (pp. 226–7). The parallel and contrast with Don Diego may well be intentional.

No 'story', much less any adventure, attaches directly to Don Diego de Miranda or his son. Although Don Quixote tries to romanticize him a little by calling him the Knight of the Green Coat, and the narrator follows this lead by suggesting that his home is a castle, which it is not, he is as remote from chivalric romances as the books of chivalry are from his portals (ch. 16, p. 153). His sanity and his excellent qualities are marked by an unpoetic, unheroic strain. And it is precisely this unromantic complication which makes him so interesting novelistically. With Don Diego, Cervantes opens a path leading directly to the nineteenth-century novel.

Don Quixote mad has great ideals and great illusions; Don Diego sane has ideals, we infer, but no illusions. Don Quixote ends up sane, as Alonso Quijano, with ideals intact and no illusions (and no time left to cultivate his garden). The equation between the two men is very finely balanced, and perhaps only the reader's personal predilection gives one the advantage over the other. It is hard not to take sides, though, whether it is with the equable Don Diego, who finds in Don Quixote an object of polite curiosity, or with the visionary Don Quixote who, though overanxious to establish a superior position, succeeds in transmitting to so many readers a degree of the scorn he feels for his counterpart.

The whole episode bristles with subtleties and diverse nuances. Don Quixote argues that true valour is a virtue poised between the extremes of temerity and cowardice, but that it is better to err on the side of excess than of insufficiency, it being easier to turn prodigality into generosity than to do the same with meanness (ch. 17, p. 167). But his recent behaviour with the lion is absurd as a demonstration of this. Analogously, the way of life embodied in Don Diego, which is undoubtedly presented as a counterweight to Quixotism, is shown as having built-in limitations.[14] Don Quixote's conduct is inexcusably excessive; Don Diego's falls short of the mark. Men can have ideals without illusions, but can men without illusions be men of vision?

Cervantes never lets us forget the foolish side of the medal which has *Heroism* inscribed on the other side. Facing the lion is one of the Knight's greatest acts of physical courage. However, it is not only superfluous and anticlimactic, but significantly prefaced by an act of pure clowning, when he unwittingly empties a helmetful of curds over his head (ch. 17, p. 158). Authentic heroic impulse constantly struggles to be realized in the face of misapplied effort, intractable material circumstance and physical inadequacy. *Don Quixote* is a comedy of good intentions confounded, of ideals misdirected, lack of *discreción*, infantile regression and other things besides. But because the Knight's aims are noble and heroic (and they are not less so because he overdoes the imitation of heroes of chivalry), and also because he learns bit by bit from experience, there is, through the zaniness of his antics, something in his character to admire.

He is admirable, too, in that he never quite gives up, despite his melancholy and even if at times despair is not far off. For a time he lives with doubts about ultimate success, even before he is forced to retire. To live thus, without throwing over his ideals, takes another kind of heroism – unexciting, humdrum and perhaps more exacting than the traditional sort. It is probably what lies behind Sancho's remark when, at their homecoming, he describes him as 'defeated by another in battle, but victor over himself' (II, 72; ii, 580) – a remark his master impatiently dismisses. Don Quixote, failing hilariously to be the kind of hero he aims to be, somehow succeeds in being the ancestor of the unheroic modern hero. As Lionel Trilling saw, Joyce's Leopold Bloom, the modern Ulysses, stands in direct line of descent from him:

In the existence of both men the ordinary and actual are prepotent; both are in bondage to daily necessity and to the manifest absurdity of their bodies, and they thus stand at a polar distance from the Aristotelian hero in the superbness of his aristocratic autonomy and dignity. Yet both Bloom and Don Quixote transcend the imposed actuality to become what we, by some new definition of the word, are willing to call heroes. (1972E, p. 90)

NOTES: CHAPTER 12

1 In recent years the whole problem has been confronted afresh by Anthony Close, who finds in Cervantes little or no room for approval of Don Quixote's brand of idealism, because his aims as well as his acts are presented as a 'madly literal mimicry of the stereotype behaviour of the heroes of chivalric romance' (1972D, p. 37; see also 1978[2]D, pp. 16 ff.). It is hard to see, however, why this should eliminate our, or Cervantes's, perception of the valid ideals transparently visible through Don Quixote's crazy behaviour.

2 As found in popular saws and phrases like 'moza por moza, buena es Aldonza' and 'Aldonza con perdón'.

3 J. Herrero (1981[1]D) pursues the debasement of the Dulcinea metaphor through to ultimately diabolical associations.

4 See Hughes (1977D), pp. 110 ff. By a not insignificant juxtaposition, Don Quixote's letter to Dulcinea in high chivalresque style and his promissory note for three donkeys, written in commercial jargon, occur together within the space of little more than a dozen lines in I, 25.

5 It now seems perfectly clear that the sentence beginning 'God knows if there is a Dulcinea in the world or not . . . ' (p. 290) has been much misinterpreted in the past, as Close (1973[1]D, p. 250) and others have pointed out.

6 See also ch. 48, p. 396, and ch. 70, p. 567.

7 Percas de Ponseti (1975D), Vol. 2, pp. 407–583. See also Barto (1923D); Forcione (1970D), pp. 137 ff.; Dunn (1972D, 1973D); Avalle-Arce (1976D), pp. 173 ff.; Hughes (1977D); Redondo (1981D); Riley (1982D).

8 Cide Hamete himself spreads the rumour that Don Quixote on his deathbed confessed to having invented the whole thing. This much misread passage contains a double qualification reducing it to mere hearsay: 'it is *held to be* true that at the end, at the time of his death, *they say* that he retracted it and said that he had invented it' ('*se tiene por* cierto que al tiempo de su fin y muerte *dicen que* se retrató della, y dijo que él la había inventado': p. 223). English translators have regularly mangled the passage, removing the uncertainty. Thus Shelton, Motteux, Cohen, Starkie. Putnam is closer. Ormsby gets it half right (see Allen, 1979D[2], p. 6).

9 Cervantes insisted on the importance of the literary absurdity being deliberate. 'How can an absurdity please, unless it is committed deliberately, guided by a seemly humour?' (*Viaje del Parnaso*, VI, 138). At the same time he was well aware that a work could in fact give pleasure and amusement for the wrong reasons – unintentionally, that is.

10 II, 26; ii, 238, and II, 29; ii, 261, and II, 62; ii, 516. On this last occasion he sees the alternatives as 'truth' and 'dream'.

11 On Don Diego, see also Bataillon (1950D), Vol. 2, pp. 417–19; Sánchez (1961–2D); Percas de Ponseti (1975D), Vol. 2, pp. 323 ff.; Márquez Villanueva (1975D), pp. 150 ff., and (1980D), pp. 97–8; Joly (1977D); Pope (1979D).

12 '*Galán.* El que anda vestido de gala y se precia de gentil hombre' (Covarrubias [1611], 1943C, s.v.).

13 His statement 'Better a knight errant aiding a widow in some deserted spot than a courtly knight wooing a damsel in the cities' (p. 167) obliquely recalls the courting of Cervantes's neighbour, the widow Doña Mariana Ramírez, by a certain Don Diego de Miranda, both of whom were implicated together with Cervantes and members of his family in the Ezpeleta incident of 27 June 1605. See McKendrick (1980B), pp. 235 ff. The possibility of some personal allusion in the figure of Don Diego in the novel cannot be discounted.

14 Though overingeniously elaborate, it seems to me, the arguments of Márquez Villanueva are basically right on this score (1975D), pp. 150 ff.

CHAPTER 13

Points of View

(i) NARRATIVE ANGLES

One reason why *Don Quixote* looks so surprisingly close to many twentieth-century novels is that it contains a built-in complication of viewpoints (other than the common one caused by first-person narration).[1] Much of the experimenting which has gone on in the postrealist novel has been in the realm of narrative point of view. The main cause of this complication is, once again, Don Quixote's madness – the part of it which transforms his physical perceptions. In such a case it is necessary to know both who and what people and things really are and also how Don Quixote perceives them.

The way in which his encounters are first presented is therefore significant. When taken in succession, the forms of presentation turn out to be neither uniform nor random but to fall into three distinct, though overlapping, phases. There is a progression evident enough to indicate structural development, but untidy enough to appear unpremeditated, and indeed to accommodate some possible revisions of structure. This progression can also be integrally related to the development of Don Quixote's state of mind. Phase one falls in Part I, chapters 1–17; phase two in Part I, chapters 18 to the end; phase three belongs to the sequel and attains greatest concentration between chapters 9–30 of Part II. The phases are cumulative rather than discrete. A new technique distinguishes the second phase, but it does not fully supplant the one previously used, which continues to occur occasionally. Similarly, in the third phase techniques one and two do not disappear with the appearance of technique number three. Furthermore there are a few premonitions of the last two phases early in the first.[2]

The basic pattern is set when Don Quixote comes to the first inn. The essential information conveyed is that he sees an inn, and 'as soon as he saw the inn he imagined it [*se le representó*] to be a castle' (I, 2; i, 82). We are first told what the object is and then how Don Quixote interprets it. However, because this is the first of many similar occasions, Cervantes is at some extra pains to fill out and clarify. He indicates just before this that the Knight was in an imaginatively receptive state of mind: he was already looking out for 'a castle or a sheepfold'. Then the wording 'saw . . . imagined' indicates a minute but perceptible time-lag between visually registering and mentally interpreting the image, which suggests that element almost of deliberation in his delusion. We also see here how he fits other pieces into his overall design. The prostitutes become courtly damsels gracing the scene, the swineherd's horn-blast a fanfare of welcome. The mode of presentation of the Knight's encounters in the first seventeen chapters follows the same basic pattern with only secondary variations. The reader may be left to fill in the details, but he is never more than momentarily in doubt about who and what people and things really are.

Phase two begins with the adventure of the flocks of sheep, quickly followed by those of the funeral party, the fulling mills and the barber's basin (I, 18–21). None of these things is presented immediately as what it is, but as a phenomenon of uncertain origin requiring interpretation: clouds of dust in the distance, a train of moving lights, fearful clanking noises, something shining like gold on a man's head. Each time Don Quixote proceeds either to misjudge the origin of the phenomenon (as armies, as Mambrino's golden helmet) or simply to decide in advance that it heralds some marvellous adventure. What is new is that the reader is not immediately enlightened. Indeed, in the case of the fulling mills explanation is withheld throughout most of the chapter. The effect is to nudge the position of the reader and that of Don Quixote closer together. He is not the only one who has to interpret what he sees and hears. And he is not the only one who could get it wrong.

The points of view of protagonist, narrator[3] and of course reader are tightly buttoned together at the start of the Cardenio episode (I, 23). First, Sancho sees Don Quixote 'trying with the tip of his lance to pick up I know not what bundle that lay on the ground' (p. 281). From this point there is a succession of concrete indications that something unusual is afoot. The nature of the objects is not here in doubt – a bag with money, a notebook with a letter and verses, a glimpse of a wild figure, a dead mule – but the significance of their presence on a trail in the Sierra Morena is. Because these finds are so promisingly out of the ordinary, they evoke no extravagant interpretation from Don Quixote. He and Sancho draw tolerably accurate inferences from each clue. As in many a modern detective story, narrator and reader remain steadily alongside the hero.

In the sequel of 1615 both of the procedures used in Part I are used again, as one might expect, with variations, but also with a noticeable tendency to maintain a narrative perspective in line with that of the two main characters, in the interests of suspense. Now that Don Quixote hardly ever misreads appearances spontaneously, his view and Sancho's usually coincide. When something unusual, surprising or mysterious occurs, Cervantes most often presents it first just as it occurs or appears to them, only explaining it to the reader later. Until he does, the reader is naturally left in suspense, mystified or obliged to guess, with the inevitable result that he is aligned with the heroes in this respect. The essential information may be withheld for a considerable time. The 'two men on horseback' first seen in chapter 12 (p. 124) are not revealed as Sansón Carrasco and Tomé Cecial until the end of chapter 14 (pp. 143–4).

Very occasionally Cervantes uses the other procedure of explaining the mystery or divulging the reality behind the appearances right from the start. When Don Quixote, out walking, hears the voice of Sancho calling from underground, like a soul in purgatory, we know the why and wherefore before the Knight does (II, 55). Similarly, the Trifaldi adventure is preceded by the information that the Duke's steward has prepared another hoax (II, 36). But in general, and apart from the fact that we are led to expect hoaxes as likely throughout the stay at the castle, this method is much more uncommon in Part II. When deliberate deception is involved, and the reader knows this in advance, he becomes, however innocently, a party to it. He is put on the same side as the jokers.

The contrast between Avellaneda's Part II and that of Cervantes here is interesting. Avellaneda usually divulges the deception in advance, so we are one up on the protagonist. Cervantes more often leaves us in doubt, or perhaps even misapprehension, with his heroes. We are consequently more likely to sympathize. When Cervantes so often chooses one procedure and Avellaneda so often the other, we may well wonder whether the difference does not say something about the attitude of each author to his creation and how he expects to be read.

In the third phase in Cervantes's *Quixote* the narrator moves closer than ever before to his heroes – to the point of absurdity in fact. He appears to become involved himself in the difficulty of identifying – naming – things. Not the major ones, which would be too confusing, but the minor ones. Though supposedly omniscient, we find him equivocating from time to time over details as doubtfully as Don Quixote is now

apt to do. Since there is really no need for this, it is very strange. There
is no doubt that he is making fun of excessive precision over entirely
unimportant details, but there is more to it than that. He is no less
certainly imitating his characters, in particular Don Quixote, just when
the latter has become most cautious about identifying people and
things. (We remarked earlier, for instance, on the way he fragments his
fantasy into multiple possibilities in the River Ebro adventure.) Sancho
perhaps started it, though. He advises his master 'que se embosque en
alguna floresta' (II, 9; ii, 103 – English loses the pun on *bosque*, 'wood')
while he looks for Dulcinea's 'house, castle or palace'. The narrator
then has Don Quixote enter a 'floresta o bosque' ('grove or wood'),
which moments later becomes a 'floresta, encinar o selva' ('grove,
oakwood or forest': ch. 10, p. 104).

Maximum comic confusion occurs very shortly after this, in the
narration of Don Quixote's traumatic experience of the enchantment of
Dulcinea. In counterpoint with this major motif runs the very secondary problem of exactly what sort of donkeys or horses the girls were
riding. I will retain the original words for 'donkey' and so forth. 'He saw
that . . . three peasant girls were approaching on three *pollinos*, or
pollinas, the author does not say which, although it is rather to be
believed that they were *borricas*, these being the usual mount of village
girls' (II, 10; ii, 107). Sancho then complicates things by announcing
their approach on three *cananeas*. You mean *hacaneas* ('hackneys'),
Quixote tells him. What's the difference? says Sancho.[4] When the girls
draw near, Knight and Squire briefly argue over whether they are riding
hacaneas or *borricos* (or *borricas*). Whereupon the narrator, evidently
now in utter confusion himself, proceeds successively to use the words
jumento, *cananea*, *borrica*, *pollina* and *jumenta*. For good measure Sancho
remarks that the peasant girl makes her *cananea* run as fast as a *cebra*
('zebra': p. 111). And there this matter 'of no great importance' (p. 107)
is left to rest.

Although here the question is subordinate and related to the more
important problem of identifying Dulcinea (see Johnson, 1975D), this
is neither the first nor the last, but only the most spectacular in a train of
comic doubts and equivocations over correct equine identification.
Perhaps Don Quixote's own mental transformation of Rocinante (I, 1)
was initially responsible, but I am more inclined to suspect that it
originated outside the book in some joke about confusing asses and
mules. There is one in Alemán's *Guzmán de Alfarache* (II, ii, 5), for
example (though the point there does not lie in the actual confusion:

1967C, p. 647). We may also recall Erasmus' comment: 'A shortsighted man who thinks a mule is an ass is not considered insane . . . '.

Ridiculous though such matters of factual verification are in a work of fiction, they are of no small critical interest. They offer, at least in part, another example of Cervantes's faculty of turning a writer's problems into novelistic material. Natural hesitation over the choice of a word is incorporated into the finished product. Signs of concern with linguistic alternatives appear very early in Part I. The fish Don Quixote has for supper at the first inn he takes to be trout (*trucha*). The narrator says it is a fish known as *abadejo* in Castile, as *bacalao* in Andalusia, and elsewhere as *curadillo* or *truchuela*. Other people in the inn call it by this last name; the narrator calls it successively *bacalao* and *abadejo* (I, 2; i, 86–7).

But it is horses and asses, not fish, which give most occasion for humour of this kind. In Part I, chapter 8, our heroes see coming towards them 'two friars of the Order of St Benedict, riding on two dromedaries' ('caballeros sobre dos dromedarios'). This improbable African note is dispelled the moment the narrator explains that the mules they rode on were as big as dromedaries. It was just a hyperbolical metaphor. Nevertheless, the fact is that the narrator has departed for a moment from his direct and simple (phase one) mode of presentation and imposed, albeit momentarily, on the scene a poetic image more appropriate to Don Quixote's way of seeing things.[5] The argument over the beasts ridden by 'Dulcinea' and her attendants was foreshadowed by the dispute, also running in parallel, in a minor key, over the barber's basin or Mambrino's helmet. Was it a plain pack-saddle (*albarda*) from the owner's grey donkey or the rich trappings (*jaez*) from his dapple grey steed (I, 21 and 44–5)?

Between chapters 9 and 30 of Part II we find the narrator approaching the problem of identifying not just animals, but also persons and things, in the same way as the Knight. With comic caution Quixote addresses the demonic figure as 'Carter, coachman, or devil, or whatever you are' (II, 11); the narrator, hesitating between 'cart or wagon' ('carro o carreta'), offers both in the chapter heading. The sound of Carrasco's armour convinces Don Quixote that he is another knight errant, and the narrator follows suit, calling him the Knight of the Wood (II, 12; ii, 124–5). But with the appearance of Don Diego caution returns. Quixote and Sancho are overtaken by 'a man . . . on a very handsome dapple grey mare, and wearing a coat of fine green cloth . . . ' (II, 16; ii, 149). There is no doubt about the horse this time. But only after two or three pages does he give his own name and status of hidalgo. Meanwhile the narrator has been working through a series of provisional appellations referring to his mount or his dress: *el de la yegua, el caminante, el de lo verde*, to *el del verde gabán*, later consecrated definitively in the title *el Caballero del Verde Gabán*, bestowed on him by Don Quixote, we are told afterwards (ch. 17, p. 168), though we never hear Quixote use it in address. The provisional titles used by the narrator seem to reflect the thought-processes of the two characters who meet him. (We may contrast the introduction of the Canon of Toledo, identified as such by the narrator before anyone else does: I, 47; i, 560.)

Don Quixote's following encounter, with the two student fencers, offers the most elaborate case of gradual identification in the book. Not surprisingly, it has given trouble to textual commentators and been mangled by translators. We begin with the ambivalent and noncommittal statement that 'he encountered two sort of clerics or sort of students and two peasants, riding four asinine beasts' ('encontró con dos como clérigos o como estudiantes y con dos labradores que sobre cuatro bestias asnales venían caballeros': II, 19; ii, 177). 'One of the students' – this is the first refinement, eliminating *clerics* – 'carried, portmanteau-fashion, wrapped in a piece of green bocasine, apparently, a little white cloth and two pairs of grogram hose.' Here the narrator, so cautious until now, in fact exercises his privilege to see inside the bundle. But he continues with the process of gradual identification. One of the students becomes 'the student bachelor, or licentiate, as Don Quixote called him' (p. 180). Then the two students are differentiated as the 'licentiate' and the 'bachelor'. Finally, the latter's name emerges in the dialogue as Corchuelo. Meanwhile the *bestias asnales* have settled down to being *pollinas*.

The whole sequence is a curious example of narrative manipulation. The narrator first proceeds as if he were as ignorant of the students' identities as Don Quixote and Sancho. Then he moves step by step towards identification, using ever more precise appellations, either from his own private store or letting them emerge in conversation. It is as though he were participating in the everyday human mechanics of identifying strangers. But he carefully demonstrates that he has no need whatever to do so, and gives the game away near the start by looking into the bundle.

Passing over a similar passage relating to the page on his way to the wars (II, 24; ii, 226),[6] we come to the last significant example. Just after the calamitous adventure on the River Ebro, Don Quixote saw some people at the far end of a meadow and coming a little closer, he recognized that they were falconers. He approached nearer, and saw among them a gracious lady on a very white palfrey or hackney, adorned with green trappings and a silver saddle. The lady, too, was dressed in green . . . On her left hand she carried a goshawk, which Don Quixote took for a sign that she must be some great lady, to whom all the huntsmen were subject, as was indeed the truth.

(vio gente, y llegándose cerca, conoció que eran cazadores de altanería. Llegóse más, y entre ellos vio una gallarda señora sobre un palafrén o hacanea blanquísima, adornada de guarniciones verdes y con un sillón de plata. Venía la señora asimismo vestida de verde . . . En la mano izquierda traía un azor, señal que dio a entender a don Quijote ser aquélla alguna gran señora, que debía serlo de todos aquellos cazadores, como era la verdad: II, 30; ii, 268.)

The seal of certainty is set on the last inference by that ever reliable phrase in the *Quixote*, 'era la verdad'. The horse is later confirmed as a palfrey, but the Duchess's title, strangely enough, is never discovered. However, not only is reality not belied here by appearances, but also for once it fully measures up to Don Quixote's chivalric expectations.

We have seen the narrator move from a position of relatively commanding omniscience to an ever closer identification with Don Quixote's view of things. But he throws in the occasional reminder of his complete freedom to do as he pleases in such matters. In a general manner he has kept pace with Don Quixote's developing state of mind.

So far we have confined our attention mostly to the first moments of Don Quixote's encounters along the way. Many more and varied examples could be given of momentary departures from the basic, supposedly disinterested narrative line. The shift may be to one which reflects the viewpoint of one of the characters, usually the Knight's; or it may be some other kind of complication. The former, like many of the 'third-phase' examples referred to above, often amounts to a brief anticipation of the so-called 'free indirect style', that genuine invention of the modern novel, rarely if ever found in sustained form before Jane Austen's period. Broadly speaking, it consists of the free passage from the external narrator's point of view to that of a character in the work, without shifting from the verbal third person.[7]

One instance must suffice, and we must dispense with examples of various other narrative complications, interesting though some of them are.[8] All of them have in common with those I am citing a shift of perspective from an objective and impartial (we suppose) narrative line to one more appropriate to a character in the scene described.

Sancho has gone to fetch the Bachelor to tell them about the book which has been published about Don Quixote's exploits. The Knight is left pondering this remarkable news

and he could not persuade himself that there was any such history, for the blood of the enemies he had slain was not yet dry on the blade of his sword, and they would have it that his lofty deeds of chivalry were already in print

(y no se podía persuadir a que tal historia hubiese, pues aún no estaba enjuta en la cuchilla de su espada la sangre de los enemigos que había muerto, y ya querían que anduviesen en estampa sus altas caballerías: II, 3; ii, 58)

Clearly our dependable narrator is not 'stating the facts' here but reflecting Don Quixote's idea of them.

This has been occurring at sporadic moments all through the book, in a simpler form. We recognize it as a parody of chivalric literary language cropping up here and there in the narration. But because Don Quixote sees himself as living a romance of chivalry this terminology also mirrors the Knight's own view of events. The narrator's account of what 'was' is momentarily coloured by what 'seemed' to the hero. He takes his cue from Don Quixote. When the Knight has mentally transformed the trollops at the inn into 'lovely maidens' and 'gracious ladies' he, too, calls them 'maidens' and 'ladies' (I, 3; i, 93). Similarly, when he is put to bed at home his friends, 'catándole las feridas' ('attending to his wounds', in archaic Spanish), cannot find any (ch. 5, p. 108). Dorotea, riding the Priest's mule, 'whipped on her palfrey' (ch. 29, p. 364) and gets called 'the princess' by the narrator (p. 368, for example), just as the innkeeper becomes the 'chatelain'. There are plenty of examples of this kind, especially in Part I. It seems that, as a consequence of Don Quixote himself being the major parodist in the novel, fragments of chivalric literary parody associated with him spill into the third-person narrative. As he searches for chivalric analogies in his everyday life, so does the sympathetic narrator. And so do we. Once, at least, the perspective is fractured by a tremendous irony. After the adventure with the ill-used

Andrés, we read: 'And thus did the valorous Don Quixote repair the injury' (I, 4; i, 98). He has in fact made it much worse, but the narrator's comment mirrors the Knight's inordinate self-satisfaction.

Yet whose view is being reflected when, in the title of Part II, chapter 18, the narrator equivocally announces 'the castle or house of the Knight of the Green Coat'? It is plainly not a castle, but a large house. Don Quixote, who now has no trouble telling inns from castles, is not once reported as saying or supposing that this house is a castle. It would once have been an appropriately parodic term to use in his company; now it is not. The ambivalent 'castle or house' reflects, rather, the cautious attitude of Don Diego and his family watching Don Quixote to assess how mad or sane he is. A little later, the narrator calls Don Diego's wife 'the lady of the castle' (ch. 18, p. 177). This is not even ambivalent, but reflects the attitude of those who think they know Quixote's mind. Can it be that Don Quixote is a jump ahead of his narrator? Be that as it may, 'castle', as used both times, has a potential or hypothetical validity more than a real one.

This odd case seems but a step away from one or two others in which the narrator becomes positively misleading. The puppet master Maese Pedro 'had his left eye and nearly half his cheek covered by a green cloth patch'. This, we are told, is a 'sign that there must have been something wrong [*enfermo*] with all that side of his face' (II, 25; ii, 234). This is unverifiable. What he did have was a slight but distinctive squint – or so the exceptionally attentive reader may recall when he learns that Maese Pedro was actually Ginés de Pasamonte, the convict on the run (see I, 22; i, 270). As such, he had very good reason to keep his face half-covered – as the narrator knows perfectly well, while suggesting something else.

He is even more misleading when the villager with urgent business for the governor interrupts one of Sancho's hard-earned meals in Barataria. Taking his cue from the page who announces the man, the narrator says he 'was of very good presence, and from a thousand leagues off one could see that he was a good man, a good soul' (II, 47; ii, 392). The hyperbole may serve to put us on our guard, but the statement, however true as a comment on his appearance, is entirely misleading inasmuch as his conduct turns out to be that of an arrant scoundrel. The narrator has spoken either as a duper or as one duped himself.[9] But the reason for doing so is not hard to find. Both Sancho and Don Quixote now know better than to accept appearances always at face value. In this passage as in the last it is as if the narrator were giving us a gentle dig in the ribs to be on our guard, too.

Occasionally, something is presented more through the reactions of characters to it than by direct description. But more remarkable than these is a case where two visual perceptions of the same object are recorded and differ significantly from each other. One view is Don Quixote's, to be sure, but though it is not disinterested neither is it insane. This is how he is described as seeing the approach of the wagon bearing the caged lions: 'Lifting his head, Don Quixote saw coming along the road they were travelling a cart covered with royal banners' (*cubierto de banderas reales*: II, 16; ii, 157). Moments later Don Diego de Miranda 'looked all round and saw nothing but a cart coming towards them with two or three small banners on it' (ch. 17, p. 158). The narrator merely says 'the cart with the banners' (p. 159). The previous narrative statements were manifestly coloured by the states of mind of the characters to whom they referred. Each makes a deduction in advance of the cart's arrival. Amusingly, the one made by Don Diego, though rather more probable than Don Quixote's, is not substantially more accurate at all.[10]

(ii) NARRATIVE VERSIONS

When people see the same things differently, small wonder if they tell them differently. There are three versions of Don Quixote's confrontation with the lion. There is the narrator's, whose description of the lion's behaviour is one of the most perfectly visualized pieces of comic writing in the novel (II, 17; ii, 164). It is followed by Don Quixote's, which is almost hilariously objective and succinct. He is addressing the keeper of the animals: 'You opened the lion's cage, I waited for him, he didn't come out, I went on waiting for him, he went on not coming out and he lay down again' (pp. 164–5). When the facts are exciting enough, the Knight has no need to embellish them. Whether he expected the keeper to or not is another question. Anyhow, the keeper does, in the third account referred to. He lays great stress on Don Quixote's bravery and recounts how the lion, 'cowed [*acobardado*] by the sight of Don Quixote, did not want and did not dare [*ni osó*] to come out of the cage' (p. 165). A little interpreting of the facts and history is well on the road to legend.

The book is full of double or even multiple versions of the same event, recounted, referred to or merely inferable. Sancho's realistic but wholly invented account of his embassy to Dulcinea, reworked in gorgeously embroidered comments by Don Quixote (I, 31), is only one of the most obvious. As early as Part I, chapter 5, his dust-up with the Toledan merchants had become a battle with ten ferocious giants. And the interrupted fight with the Basque (I, 8–9) is fragmentarily described by four different narrative 'voices' (Gerli, 1982D). The reporting of events ranges from the brief passing comment to the fully fledged narrative conventionally recognized as a story. One obvious intermediate form is the letter, of which there are half a dozen excellent examples between chapters 36 and 52 of Part II, letters from Quixote, Sancho, Teresa Panza, the Duke and the Duchess. Where 'fact' ends and 'fiction' begins in all these verbalizations of experience would perhaps be as difficult to say as it was to settle the dilemma of the oath and the gallows, posed to test the wit of Governor Sancho (II, 51).

Few novels are more replete with reportage than the *Quixote*, although the novelist spares the reader the repetitiousness of everyday life. We read, for example, that Sancho tells the Duchess all about the transformation of Dulcinea, and of his master's experiences in the Cave (one would like to have heard that version!). The first part of Cardenio's story is actually told several times after the single time it is given to Don Quixote and the reader: twice more by Cardenio ('*almost* with the same words and incidents', it is remarked on one of these occasions: I, 27; i. 332), and possibly a third time by Sancho. In addition it overlaps at several points with the instalment told by Dorotea. Benengeli, too, is not the only one writing things down. A chronicler, apparently the Duke's steward, faithfully recording Sancho's governorship for the Duke and Duchess, is mentioned four times. When the Steward returns to the castle, he gives his masters a spoken version, telling them 'point by point, *almost* all the words and actions spoken and done by Sancho during those days' (II, 56; ii, 461). Those two 'almosts' which I have emphasized imply variations between one version and another. Here they would no doubt be insignificant. Elsewhere, especially when Don Quixote is one of the tellers, questions of interpretation, of truth itself, may be involved.

Cervantes knew he was a great storyteller and openly boasted that his powers of invention exceeded those of many others (*Parnaso*, IV, p. 103). But scarcely less impressive were his powers of suggestion. Like the mind of Don Quixote buzzing with chivalresque fairy-tale, the book about him is alive with story at all stages of realization.

There are stories the reader is told of but which are never recorded. The rescue of Ana Félix's lover from a harem in Barbary must have been a breathtaking exotic adventure, but the account of it by the renegade and Don Gregorio himself is not relayed (II, 65). Other 'stories' exist merely as embryonic possibilities, issuing stillborn from the womb of Gossip – such as the intelligence that the lady whom Don Quixote took for an abducted princess (I, 8) was from Biscay and on the way to Seville to join her husband who was leaving for America with a most honourable commission. This gratuitous information, supplied by the narrator, is just enough to stimulate curiosity. Had her coach rolled into view in the pages of the *Persiles*, where the occasion for another story is rarely missed, the chances are that we should have got it, anguished, piteous and extraordinary. More notable still is the Captive's recollection of meeting a certain Spanish soldier, 'Something Saavedra', whose story, he says, would entertain and amaze them all a good deal more than his own (I, 40; i, 486). And so the most remarkable experience of the author's own life, his years as a soldier and a slave in north Africa, is relegated to the level of a passing remark by one of his novelistic characters.

In Part II hopes of a rewardingly picturesque episode are built up when Quixote, Sancho and the Cousin decide to visit a hermit in the vicinity. Expectations collapse in flatly realistic anticlimax when it turns out that the hermit is not at home (II, 24). Imagine a hermit in a romance of chivalry being out when the hero calls![11] One of the briefest external episodes, barely sufficient to qualify as a *novela corta*, is reduced by Sancho to the nutshell dimensions of a Decameronesque title. He tells the children of Don Diego de la Llana after hearing all about their nocturnal escapade: 'If you had said: "We are So-and-So and went out of our parents' house in this disguise, just for curiosity and no other reason," that would have been the end of the story, without groaning and snivelling and carrying-on' (II, 49; ii, 414).

In a few cases Cervantes contrives to blur the terminal edge of certain stories with the suggestion that more in the lives of the characters remains to be recorded. Thus the Priest and Don Fernando part with the agreement that the Priest shall write and tell Don Fernando what became of Don Quixote, and Don Fernando will keep the Priest informed not only about his own marriage to Dorotea, but also about the baptism of Zoraida, the fate of Don Luis and the return home of Luscinda (I, 47). The final strands of three major episodes in Part I are thus drawn together in the generous hand of Don Fernando.

Since he refers to it, Cervantes must have reflected on the fact that potentially any character's story is as long as his life. When Don Quixote asks the convict Ginés de Pasamonte whether his (picaresque) autobiography is completed, he replies how can it be, when his life is not over yet (I, 22; i, 272)? Ginés's life-story intersects with those of Don Quixote and Sancho, their paths crossing on four separate occasions, each time with some violence. If he is part of their story, they must also be part of his. There is an unusual aura of untold story around this mysterious figure Ginés de Pasamonte, alias Ginesillo de Parapilla, alias Maese Pedro. When he finally disappears, it is to something more like another beginning than an ending:

> and so he rose before the sun, and taking up the remnants of his puppet show, and his monkey, he too went off in search of his adventures
>
> (y así, madrugó antes que el sol, y cogiendo las reliquias de su retablo, y a su mono, se fue también a buscar sus aventuras: II, 27; ii, 249)[12]

At one extreme is the fully developed and rounded *novela* of *El curioso impertinente*; at the other the chance remark. But there is no essential difference between them. The singling out of 'external episode' and main narrative in earlier chapters of this book was just a matter of convenience. Ultimately, the distinguishing of structural components breaks down. As Henry James declared: 'I cannot see what is meant by talking as if there were a part of a novel which is the story and part of it which for mystical reasons is not' (1948E, p. 17). In *Don Quixote* story, anecdote, reportage and spoken remark overflow into the great sea of words. Some episodes trail away almost inconclusively. Potential events come to nothing. Narrators become protagonists and protagonists become audience, round and round (El Saffar, 1968D, p. 173). Part of one character's life-story is part of the life-stories of others. Events told by one person are different when told by another, and yet remain the same. The teller and the tale are part of a bigger tale which includes them both.

Human consciousness ensures that while we live we are constantly re-creating our lives in thoughts and words. In one way or another we are devising narrative most of our waking hours. Once again Don Quixote's self-immersion in story is just an extreme instance of what we all do. By its nature every novel is devoted to the verbalization of experience, but *Don Quixote* shows an unusual awareness of it.[13]

Much in the book depends on the simple pretence that the fiction it purveys is really history. Like many chivalric romances before it, many

mainstream realistic novels after it, like *Robinson Crusoe*, were to take
the same line. Cervantes thus takes the core of his hero's madness – the
belief that a kind of literary fiction is historical fact – and makes it a
principle of his own novel. But with the all-important difference that we
are required to see through the pretence, and admire and enjoy the
illusionism, but not be taken in by it.[14] Entering into the game is not
only a large part of the fun which the book has to offer, it throws more
light on it.

Going along with the pretence of historicity, then, we can discern
three distinct primary versions of Don Quixote's story within the covers
of the novel.[15] *Pace* Henry James perhaps, the novel and the story it
contains are not the same thing here, and if we do not distinguish
between them we quickly bog down in paradox.

The first major version belongs to the Moorish enchanter-chronicler
Cide Hamete Benengeli, supposedly for almost all but the first eight and
a half chapters, the material for which is attributed to other authorial
sources unnamed.[16] The specific idea of Benengeli may have occurred
late to Cervantes, since you would expect him to figure at the start, and
he does not appear until chapter 9. However, Don Quixote is convinced
from the moment he first sets out that some sage will be writing his story
(I, 2). In a sense, he enters the book in response to Don Quixote's need
for him, just as do Dulcinea and Sancho in their different ways. He
achieves little prominence in Part I, being mentioned only four times;
but in the second part Cervantes develops his potential greatly, trans-
forming what might have been an uninspired parody of the chivalric
romances' habit of ascribing to a similar figure the presentation,
translation or narration of their work.[17]

From the 'extra-textual' comments about Cide Hamete we may
deduce that, exemplary historian though he is, his story is not absolutely
reliable. After all, the seventeenth-century Christian reader is reminded,
who would trust a Moor (I, 9, and II, 3)? We are expressly warned
against literally believing the Quixote story in the prologue to Part I and
at the end (ch. 52). Come to that, who could even believe in a narrator
with magical powers? He is the only really incredible figure in the book,
with the possible exception of Don Álvaro Tarfe. It is well to remember
that Cide Hamete is a joke and not solemnly submit this narrator figure
to the rigours of logic-chopping, nor expect complete consistency and
order among the various narrative intermediaries ('translator', 'second
author'). The opening of Part II, chapter 44, is sufficient evidence of
Cervantes's deliberate obfuscation. One should neither ride roughshod

over all the distinctions, nor pick one's way on tiptoe through them, but simply discriminate sensibly between major levels of authorial intervention. Where Benengeli's version of Don Quixote's life-story is concerned, we should, I suggest, take the hints that it is by no means impeccable and at the same time recognize that it is the best one there is.

The second of the three versions is Avellaneda's Part II. This has a place in our considerations only because Cervantes chose to bring it into the fiction of his own sequel – that is to say, into Benengeli's story. It is denounced as false a number of times (chs 59, 62, 70, 72, 74), and that must be its definitive status within the fictional context of the 'true' adventures of Don Quixote and Sancho; but even in that context there is no pretending that it does not exist. False reports may lack all truthful substance, but still have reality. And Avellaneda's, it seems, is not totally without substance. Such is the implication of the enigmatic materialization of one of Avellaneda's characters in Part II, chapter 72. Don Álvaro is apparently introduced for the sole purpose of denying his original creator by authenticating Don Quixote and Sancho as the genuine heroes. So, if the other version is not absolutely dependable, neither is this one absolutely false. At any rate the existence of one of Avellaneda's characters is validated in Benengeli's.

The third version is rather different. It exists only in the mind of Don Quixote, being the account which the Knight believes is being written about him and his adventures. Of course we may be sure that it is selective, flattering and highly coloured. 'Being about a knight errant,' he muses, 'it must perforce be grandiloquent, lofty, distinguished, magnificent and true' (II, 3; ii, 58). It makes a superbly comic ironic contrast with the story Benengeli actually relates. This private version of Don Quixote's is not to be lightly dismissed because it is unrealized fancy. It is significant in two special ways and it has a unique power.

In the first place, this version, naturally, is a potential romance of chivalry: Don Quixote would have it so in every detail. But he sees it as true history because he has never been able to tell the difference between true history and idealized romance. The two genres are brought into open confrontation (only they are called history and poetry respectively) in the memorable dialogue between the Knight, the Squire and the Bachelor at the beginning of Part II (ch. 3). Since the historicity of Don Quixote's life is just a literary pretence, however, the real confrontation for the reader is between romance and realistic fiction, not romance and history. These theoretical considerations are not a side-issue, but integral to the structure of the work. The argument in Part II, chapter 3, shows that Cervantes was well aware of them, even if he did not know our terminology.

In the second place, this imaginary version of his life-story which Don Quixote carries in his head is a major determinant of his actions. It is almost entirely a mental reality, but one with material consequences. If he did not see himself as a knight errant in a story-book, how recognizable would he be as Don Quixote? Consequently, any historical account of his life – Benengeli's and even Avellaneda's spurious one – depends upon it. (Indeed, so perhaps does Benengeli's very existence.) It is hard to overrate the importance of the third version.

These games with fiction call to mind those of twentieth-century writers, from Pirandello to Nabokov and Unamuno to Borges. Cervantes, however, was tapping a vein which not for the first time had run up close to the surface in literary history. We glimpse it as early as some of the ancient Greek romances, and see it again more consistently in some of the prose fiction and drama of the seventeenth century. The basic condition for its emergence seems to be a strongly developed consciousness in writers of the artificial nature of the end-product of their efforts to 'imitate nature' (or 'capture reality', as we might say). It was equally strong in the visual arts of the sixteenth and seventeenth centuries. Cervantes may be numbered among those who have realized that the more completely a character is represented by art, in other words the more 'real' he is made to seem to be – that is, the more *realistic* the representation – the more complete is the *illusion*.[18]

We have seen in this chapter the seeds of some other vital developments in the modern novel: the occasional fusion of narrator's viewpoint with that of a character, the beginnings of an unreliable narrator, an interplay between the actual and potential. We have noticed how Cervantes shows some concern over referential exactness, even while laughing at its misuse – a concern which novelists have habitually shown at least from Defoe onwards.

As a representation of a certain human experience *Don Quixote* is unusually complete. It is complicated with sporadic little uncertainties, mostly trivial, mostly having to do with interpretation, with identification. The effect is to bring us, as readers, closer to Don Quixote, who is in the end not so different from the rest of us. Little uncertainties customarily cloud our day-to-day apprehension of what things are and of what happens – though we generally put them out of our mind at once – both because we have insufficient data and because of differences of perspective. This deficiency and these differences are incorporated into the structure and fabric of *Don Quixote*.

The novelistic fiction is an imitation of historical fact, but by blurring the facts here and there Cervantes does not detract from the realism – he adds to it. In much the same way, the great pictures by Leonardo with their *sfumato* outlines, and the great mind-teasing paintings by Velasquez, are more true to life than those academic paintings of the nineteenth century with their cut-and-dried statement and needle-sharp realism[19] The fiction which aims to resemble fact looks truer when shadowed with uncertainties and cross-lit by conflicting opinions. It is something like a transcendent realism. And Cervantes includes in his book the observers with the observed, and the judges with the judged, which, in the end, includes the last observer, the last judge: the reader.

NOTES: CHAPTER 13

1   See Leo Spitzer's seminal essay on linguistic perspectivism in *Don Quixote* (1948D), pp. 41–85.

2   I have traced the succession of these phases elsewhere: (1973[2]D), pp. 65–71. Also see Predmore (1967D), pp. 30–4; Mancing (1972D); Johnson (1975D); Torrente Ballester (1975D), pp. 107 ff.

3   It could be misleading to refer to Cide Hamete Benengeli in person in this context, so I have retained the anonymous term.

4   This was a common confusion, noted as an example of the comic in language by López Pinciano, *Philosophia antigua poetica* ([1596] 1953C), III, 59.

5   There is an early hint of metaphorical complication when Don Quixote sights the first inn: 'it was as if he saw a star guiding him, not to the portals, but to the very fortress [*alcázares*] of his redemption' (I, 2; i, 82).

6   There is here another passing speculation on the contents of the bundle of clothing he carries. Similar bundles figure in *Rinconete y Cortadillo* (*Novelas ejemplares*, i, 192–3, and also the Porras version) and *La gitanilla* (Novelas ejemplares, i, 123), perhaps bearing the seed of the little joke in *Don Quixote*, Part II.

7   See López Blanquet (1968E); Verdín Díaz (1970E); Rosenblat (1971D), p. 32. Also, in relation to the stylistic levels in *Don Quixote*, Meyer (1968E), pp. 59 ff.

8   There are at least a dozen passages, nearly all in Part II, where there is a shift from indirect to direct speech, or more rarely from direct to indirect, in mid-speech. These probably unintentional transitions are halfway to the free indirect style: e.g. II, 22; ii, 203. See Rosenblat (1971D), pp. 332–7.

9   A multiple irony is possible, I suppose. Assuming the incident is another trumped-up case designed to put Sancho to the test, we might infer that the man was a thoroughly honest fellow, after all, acting the part of a rogue. But the statement still remains misleading in relation to his behaviour. There is another instance in II, 38; ii, 329.

10 Fielding's *Tom Jones* gives clear signs of its ancestry in an instance like the following, which amalgamates items from several passages in *Don Quixote*: 'On a sudden they heard the music of a drum that seemed at no great distance. This sound presently alarmed the fears of Partridge and he cried out, "Lord have mercy on us all: they are certainly a coming!"' His fears that these are the rebel troops ('perhaps fifty thousand') are enhanced when they see 'something painted flying in the air', which he

takes to be the colours of the enemy. But, as Tom Jones correctly divines, these things are the advance-guard advertisement of the travelling puppet-show (XII, 5; 1963E, p. 507).

11   The main point of the incident is almost certainly satirical. Sancho looks forward to drinking there, and they find a female 'subhermit' on the premises.

12   On Don Quixote and Ginés de Pasamonte, see Weiger (1978D).

13   See Barbara Hardy's excellent study (1975E). It pays appropriate attention to *Don Quixote*.

14   As Michel Butor shrewdly observed about fairy-tales: 'And most of all, to begin with, there is the pleasure of knowing that all this isn't true, the pleasure of not being taken in by fiction' (1968E, p. 213). And Ernst Kris: 'The mechanism of denial can operate; a firm belief in the "reality of play" can coexist with the certainty that it is play only. Here lie the roots of aesthetic illusion' (1952E, p. 42).

15   For a fuller account, see Riley (1973[1]D.

16   A good deal has been written about Benengeli and the narrators in *Don Quixote*. See: e.g. Gerhardt (1955D); Riley (1962D), pp. 205 ff.; Haley (1965D); Allen (1969D[1]), Vol. 1, ch. 1, and (1979D), Vol. 2, ch. 1; Forcione (1970D), pp. 156 ff.; El Saffar (1975D); Percas de Ponseti (1975D), Vol. 1, pp. 88 ff., 115 ff.; Tate (1977D); Flores (1982[1]D).

17   There actually was a Morisco, one Ramón Ramírez, a public storyteller, who memorized the gist of romances of chivalry and improvised them. He was persecuted by the Inquisition in the 1590s, and was alleged *inter alia* to have ridden on a magic flying horse. See Harvey (1974E.)

18   For a good survey of the range and ramifications of the subject in *Don Quixote*, see Alter (1975E), ch. 1.

19   'The amount of information packed into the picture may hinder the illusion as frequently as it helps it. The reason lies precisely in the limitations of the medium that may occasionally obtrude themselves and contradict the impression the painter wanted to conjure up. No wonder, therefore, that the greatest protagonist of naturalistic illusion in painting, Leonardo da Vinci, is also the inventor of the deliberately blurred image, the *sfumato*, or veiled form, that cuts down the information on the canvas and thereby stimulates the mechanism of projection' (Gombrich, 1960E, p. 221).

CHAPTER 14

Inner and Outer Worlds

'Universal' as it is, *Don Quixote* naturally belongs to its own age, and not only inasmuch as it makes fun of the romances of chivalry. While I have tried in this book to keep in mind the historical literary context in which *Don Quixote* is situated, I have not tried to fix its position amid the intellectual currents of the time – not that anyone has yet succeeded in doing that to the general satisfaction of scholars.[1] However, there are two passages in the novel which between them so clearly illustrate two related developments of major importance in the intellectual history of the age – an importance which in the second case has by no means faded with time – that they deserve mention. They both have to do with myth, authority and experience.

The first one is a matter of epistemology. Probably the greatest development in the methodology of intellectual inquiry *circa* 1600 was the gradual shift from reliance on authority as the ultimate source of true knowledge to observation, experiment and induction – the empirical method on which the new science and philosophy of Kepler, Bacon, Galileo and Descartes were based.[2] One could indeed take Experience versus Authority as a general theme for study throughout the *Quixote*, but a passage in Part II, chapter 1, concentrates the issue nicely. The topic is mythical. Don Quixote with the Priest and the Barber is discussing giants:

'On this matter of giants,' replied Don Quixote, 'there are different opinions as to whether or not they have existed in the world. But Holy Scripture, which cannot depart one inch from the truth, demonstrates that they existed by telling us the story of that great Philistine Goliath, who was seven and a half cubits tall, which is a singular height. Moreover, in the isle of Sicily shin bones and shoulder blades have been discovered, of a size that shows that their owners were giants as big as great towers; geometry proves this is true beyond a doubt.

(– En esto de gigantes – respondió don Quijote – hay diferentes opiniones, si los ha habido o no en el mundo; pero la Santa Escritura, que no puede faltar un átomo en la verdad, nos muestra que los hubo, contándonos la historia de aquel filisteazo de Golías, que tenía siete codos y medio de altura, que es una desmesurada grandeza. También en la isla de Sicilia se han hallado canillas y espaldas tan grandes, que su grandeza manifiesta que fueron gigantes sus dueños, y tan grandes como grandes torres; que la geometría saca esta verdad de duda: II, 1; ii, 50.)[3]

So giants have existed (*a*) because the ultimate accepted authority, the revealed truth of the Bible, says so; and (*b*) because they have been empirically proved to exist by process of scientific induction. Each method is used in support of the other here to prove the validity of the opinion. The passage vividly illustrates the curious co-existence in this period of two approaches to knowledge which to modern eyes look almost incompatible. Given the speaker and the subject of discussion, it is of course quite possible that Cervantes was making fun of their liaison here; but it is by no means certain that he was even conscious of any incongruity.

The second instance concerns myth and experience as well as authority and experience. When Don Quixote first announced his intention of exploring the wonders of the Cave of Montesinos, he gave as an additional reason his intention of seeking there the origin and source of the nearby Lakes of Ruidera and the River Guadiana which runs partly underground (see II, 18; ii, 176, and II, 22; ii, 205). Now, this is a straightforward matter of exploration: empirical investigation, that is. But when he later recounts the dream of his experience in the Cave he gives the answer to the problem of where these waters rise in very different terms. Montesinos has told him that the lakes had once been the duenna Ruidera and her two daughters and seven nieces, and the River Guadiana the squire of Durandarte. They had grieved so much for the death of Durandarte that Merlin metamorphosed them into lakes and a river. One can tell how sad Guadiana must be, Montesinos explains, because he plunges underground at intervals, and furthermore the fish in the river are of very poor quality (ch. 23, p. 216). Don Quixote appears to be quite satisfied. A simple matter of geographical or geological inquiry is metamorphosed into pure myth (and a delightful piece of myth-making it is) on the authority of Montesinos, a fictitious hero of the balladry of Carolingian lore.

The information is accepted without question by the Scholar Cousin, who is symbolically connected with this confusion of empirical fact and poetic myth. His profession is that of 'humanist' (ch. 22, p. 205). He is composing a *Metamorfoseos, o Ovidio español* and a *Suplemento a Virgilio Polidoro*, dealing with the origins and invention of things (p. 206). Apart from the fact that Cervantes is here satirizing compendiums of curious information like Polydore Vergil's and, in Spain, those of Pedro Mexía and Antonio de Torquemada, the symbolic relevance of his books to the Knight's cave adventure is obvious. The Cousin displays a certain kind of Renaissance erudition, heavily dependent on the word of authorities.[4] His method is to accumulate as many references as possible to authenticate facts ('facts' like who was the first man on earth to have a cold). He accepts Durandarte on the word of Don Quixote as giving evidence of the antiquity of playing-cards (ch. 24, p. 224). One of the works he is engaged on is Ovidian mythology, poetic fable; the other purports to be fact. The important thing about the Cousin is that he is incapable of discriminating between them. Not for nothing is he, on the one hand, the cousin of the 'scientific' fencing expert (ch. 19) and, on the other, 'very fond of reading books of chivalry' (p. 205). Spiritually you could call him a cousin of Don Quixote's, whose madness precisely consists in his inability to distinguish between historico-empirical fact and chivalric romance, which is grounded in poetic myth. It will also be remembered that the entire account of the events in the Cave rests on the authority of Don Quixote, which the narrator Benengeli himself casts doubt upon.

But that is not the only striking connection between the provinces of myth and actuality in the Cave episode. Unlike the Cousin and the Knight, Cervantes carefully distinguishes between the dream world described by Quixote within the Cave and the everyday world outside, where he tells his story. The interior as described by Don Quixote has recognizable otherworld features, both of Hades and the Earthly Paradise, which proclaim its mythic origins. But the Cave of Montesinos is not a Cervantine invention: it exists in La Mancha, and Cervantes's references to its environs are reasonably exact.[5] He introduces an unusual amount of physical measurement in describing the preliminaries to Don Quixote's descent, the descent itself, then the ascent and aftermath. References to time: 'two in the afternoon', 'about four in the afternoon', 'about half an hour', 'little more than an hour' (pp. 208, 210, 211, 219); and space: 'not . . . more than two leagues', 'a hundred fathoms', 'a little more than eighty fathoms', 'ten fathoms' (pp. 207, 209, 210). This is the reliable, measurable, physical world. But after

Don Quixote 'awakes' in the otherworld, and applies the old test of pinching himself, with misleading results, it is clear that these basic empirical criteria no longer work in a credible fashion. Dulcinea's attendant cuts a caper two *varas* (five and a half feet) high in the air (p. 222); the Knight thinks he has been below for three days and nights, whereas the narrator and Sancho make it around half an hour and an hour respectively. The weights and measures of the terrestrial world become meaningless in the other one.

The incongruous effects in Don Quixote's dreamworld (noted in Chapter 12 above) are seen upon examination to consist largely (not wholly) of superfluous factual precision, details of physical measurement and intrusions of alien terrestrial time (the two-pound heart preserved in brine, the type of knife used to extract it, the size of the rosary beads, the sums of money, Belerma being past the menopause, and other things). Not only is their matter-of-factness infallibly comic in this context, in terms of Don Quixote's state of mind they signal the encroaching of a prosaic sense of everyday reality on his personal fantasy. The wonderful inner world of the Cave is being infiltrated by elements of external actuality. Cervantes presents the two worlds here as contiguous – even interpenetrating – but separate domains. We are not allowed to immerse ourselves for long in Don Quixote's mythic otherworld. There is little chance of our being carried away by his strange tale, because Sancho's interruptions three times bring us sharply back to this world, the last one effectively putting an end to the story. The otherworld of the Cave of course belongs to romance (here burlesqued and decorated with figures from balladry, and with audible echoes of epic,[6] just as the everyday world on the surface where most of the rest of *Quixote* takes place is the terrain of the realistic novel.

It is very doubtful whether at any earlier period of history this distinction could have been made as decisively as Cervantes makes it.[7] There was a conscious and growing sense of fundamental difference between poetic myth and historico-empirical actuality. The polarizing of Poetry and History in the literary theory debates, the cleavage between medieval romance and modern realistic novel, and ultimately between religious belief and science were all different aspects of the same prodigiously consequential event.

It would be quite wrong, however, simply to identify Cervantes with progressive modernity. Although it is easy to read *Don Quixote* as a tremendous attack on the poetic myth underlying romance, its author is not so easily pinned down. He spoofs overpunctilious factual exactitude with obvious relish. With perceptible insistence his characters use the phrase 'tocar' or 'tocar con la mano' ('touch with one's hand') in a variety of circumstances, often inappropriate, where appearances can hardly be believed.[8] His joking is not all one-sided. The point here is that the truths of myth and of science are of different kinds. Marvellous metamorphoses have nothing to do with the rising of rivers, just as weights and measures have nothing to do with the death of heroes or the devotion of lovers. It is a question of not confusing them. A tendency still to confuse them and a growing readiness to criticize such confusion were characteristic of the age of Cervantes.

Since that time it is hardly surprising that modern sympathies should have swung towards Don Quixote. The new world view has come almost to blot out the old one. Twentieth-century voices which say it better than I can have been raised against the damage done. Jung:

As scientific understanding has grown, so our world has become dehumanized. Man feels himself isolated in the cosmos, because he is no longer involved in nature and has lost his emotional 'unconscious identity' with natural phenomena . . . No voices now speak to man from stones, plants, and animals, nor does he speak to them believing they can hear. His contact with nature has gone, and with it has gone the profound emotional energy that this symbolic connection supplied. (1978E, p. 85).

R. D. Laing:

As a whole generation of men, we are so estranged from the inner world that there are many arguing that it does not exist; and that even if it does exist, it does not matter. Even if it has some significance, it is not the hard stuff of science, if it is not, then let's make it hard. Let it be measured and counted . . . For without the inner the outer loses its meaning and without the outer the inner loses its substance. (1975E, p. 46)

Joseph Campbell:

The lines of communication between the conscious and the unconscious zones of the human psyche have all been cut, and we have been split in two. The hero-deed to be wrought is not today what it

was in the century of Galileo. Where then there was darkness, now
there is light; but also, where light was, there now is darkness . . .
man himself is now the crucial mystery. (1973E, pp. 388, 390)

Reintegration of the inner and the outer is what is needed, each of them
says. And so have others. In one of those imaginative speculations which
Cervantes's novel has so often provoked from its readers, one might
describe Don Quixote as an early modern man who, in the dawning
scientific age, presciently subject to unconscious pressures, overreacts
with a backwards leap away from the advancing tide of history, into
madness. Be that as it may, Cervantes performs another act of reintegration in his novel.

He puts poetic myth, which underlies romance, back where it came
from: the human mind and psyche. Don Quixote did not really descend
into a wonderful world inside the Cave of Montesinos; he fell asleep
down a hole in the ground. The world of the Cave was real and alive
inside him. His subsequent uncertainty about the nature of this experience stems from his halting movement towards awareness of the true
interiority of his chivalric ideals, a condition not fully achieved until his
deathbed return to sanity. There he renounces the romances of chivalry
for the excesses and absurdities to which he was driven by his attempt to
live one literally. To conclude from this that the author of *Don Quixote*
rejects the values embodied in romance is to ignore a good half of his
whole prose-fiction production, including the *Persiles*, which he wrote
last of all and which no one in his right mind could mistake for a mimetic
representation of 'real life'.

When Don Quixote declares to the Canon of Toledo that since (thanks
to the romances of chivalry) he took up knight errantry he has become
'brave, polite, liberal, well-bred, generous, courteous, bold, gentle,
patient and long-suffering' (I, 50; i, 586) we are amused at the
presumption, but we can hardly deny the worthiness of the conviction.
When he demands of Sancho whether, as a knight errant, he is obliged to
recognize and distinguish between different sounds and know which
ones come from fulling mills and which do not, like any peasant born
and bred among such things, we know he is ridiculously wrong (I, 20; i,
249). The *ejemplo*, the message, of *Don Quixote* surely is what most
readers have always taken it to be: that personal visions must be
accommodated to the external facts of living. To do otherwise is to live
quixotically. Don Quixote tries to live meaningfully according to a
providential plan, which informs most of medieval and Renaissance

romance. Cervantes's novel says that such a plan is not to be found externalized in the world around, but exists within him.[9] That indeed is where the great dramas are enacted, as the nineteenth-century novelists realized.

Anselmo, the *curioso impertinente*, tried to impose on his flesh-and-blood wife the obligation of living the ideal of chastity, with tragic consequences. Don Quixote tried to live the ideal of fictional knight errantry, with ridiculous results. To restate the *ejemplo*: ideals are not for living literally, but for living by.

And how many people are in danger of such quixotries today? Precious few, no doubt.

But what would a Don Quixote at the other extreme be like? Anti-idealistic, sinister, a pessimistic believer in force – and yet a Don Quixote?

The thought occurred to Thomas Mann (1969D, p. 64), and he wrote it down in his travel diary on 20 May 1934, the year Hitler assumed supreme power. Invert the major premiss of Cervantes's novel and many of the essentials would be unchanged.

NOTES: CHAPTER 14

1   Among the more important studies on Cervantes's 'thought' in the intellectual context of his age are: Bonilla (1905D), Toffanin (1920D), Castro (1966D, 1967[1]D, 1972D), Hazard (1931D), Bataillon (1950D), Parker (1948D), Vilanova (1949D), Vilar (1956D), Wardropper (1965D), Forcione (1970D and, though in relation to the *Novelas ejemplares*, 1982D), Avalle-Arce (1975D), Morón Arroyo (1976D), Maravall (1976D), Ife (1982D), Garrote Pérez (1982D).

2   For Francisco Suárez the three sources of knowledge were still sacred and human authority and reason. José de Acosta in his *Historia natural y moral de las Indias* (1590) said, not at all untypically of the age: 'I cannot bring myself to oppose Aristotle except in things that are very certain' (O. H. Green, 1963–6E, Vol. 3, pp. 329–30). At the same time, as Hiram Haydn notes, the word 'experience' was nearly as popular in the sixteenth century as the word 'reason' in the eighteenth (1960E, p. 190; and see the rest of ch. 4).

3   A similar conclusion reached by 'good geometry' is found in Torquemada's book of curiosities ([1570] 1943C), p. 54.

4   The cult of authority is notably attacked by the sceptic Francisco Sánchez in *Quod nihil scitur* (1581), Spanish translation *Que nada se sabe* (Buenos Aires, 1944C), pp. 134 ff.

5   It is now thought to be the shaft of an ancient Phoenician mine. The Cave is referred to and the region described in contemporary works like the *Relaciones topográficas* (1572). See Astrana Marín (1948–58B), Vol. 7, pp. 359 ff.; 'Azorín' (1964D), pp. 83 ff.

6   See Percas de Ponseti (1975D), Vol. 2, pp. 449 ff.; Dunn (1972D).

7   'Perhaps no other single characteristic of the Counter-Renaissance has so extensive an elaboration in the sixteenth- and early seventeenth-century literature as the pragmatic

emphasis of its empiricists upon the discrepancy between the ideal and the actual. And in this observation is to be found one key to the importance of this movement to the disintegration of the medieval world-view' (Haydn, 1960E, p. 227). The sentences are clumsy, but the meaning is plain enough.

8   At least nine times in Part II, probably more: ch. 1, p. 46; ch. 9, p. 100; ch. 11, p. 117; ch. 14, p. 136; ch. 23, p. 220; ch. 36, p. 325; ch. 50, p. 420; ch. 52, p. 438; ch. 72, p. 579.

9   'The message of all romance is *de te fabula*: the story is about you' (Frye, 1976E, p. 186). Not 'all around you'.

CHAPTER 15

The Fortunes of *Don Quixote*

There has been a great deal of writing on Cervantes, *Don Quixote* and posterity, as the more than two hundred relevant entries in Murillo's very select bibliography clearly indicate, though only a small proportion of them rival in bulk a work like J. J. A. Bertrand's *Cervantès et le Romantisme allemand* (Paris, 1914). This profusion reflects both the great variety of interpretations and the seminal role of the *Quixote* in the development of modern prose fiction. Lukács saw *Don Quixote* as 'the first great novel of world literature' (1971E, p. 103) and the key link in the narrative chain from ancient epic to the modern *Bildungsroman*. Lionel Trilling (1961E, p. 209) said:

> In any genre, it may happen that the first great example contains the whole potentiality of the genre. It has been said that all philosophy is a footnote to Plato. It can be said that all prose fiction is a variation on the theme of *Don Quixote*.

In the circumstances, perhaps it will be accepted that my remarks on the publishing history, critical history and literary influence of *Don Quixote* should be very brief and basic.[1]

After 1617 the publication of Spanish editions was irregular. There is no known edition between that year and 1637; ten between 1637 and 1674; then only one until 1704, the century when *Don Quixote* came into its own. Outside Spain its fame spread quickly after its first appearance. The Irishman Thomas Shelton evidently made his translation in 1607, using the Brussels Spanish edition of the same year. It came out in 1612, without the name of Cervantes on the title page. Though not distinguished for its accuracy, the flavour of its contemporary Shakespearian English makes it still one of the most enjoyable to read. Part II followed in 1620. In France the *Curioso impertinente* appeared in a translation by Nicholas Baudouin in 1608. Oudin's complete Part I came out in 1614 and Rosset's Part II in 1618. Franciosini's Italian translation of the two parts appeared in 1622 and 1625; a German one in 1648, and a Dutch in 1657, the Dutch being the first of many *Quixotes* with illustrations.[2]

Interest in the work gathered way in France late in the seventeenth century, when there was a new translation, and thirty-six known editions appeared in the course of the eighteenth. In England, too, it had now become a classic, the most celebrated translations of the age being those of Motteux (1700–3), Jarvis (1742, the first with annotations) and Smollett (1755, a reworking of Jarvis). Spain had been rather slow on the uptake but now took her cue from England and produced important biographies. Don Gregorio Mayáns was commissioned by Lord Carteret to write the first, for the Spanish edition published in London in 1738, after being published on its own in Madrid the previous year. In 1780 the Royal Spanish Academy brought out an important Spanish edition with biographical and documentary material by Vicente de los Ríos. The first edition with a commentary, the work of the Rev. John Bowle, was published in Salisbury, in Spanish, the following year. There were more biographical contributions by M. J. Quintana and J. A. Pellicer in two notable end-of-century editions, but it was Fernández de Navarrete who in 1819 laid the foundation for every modern Life of Cervantes.

Translations now existed in Danish, Russian, Polish and Portuguese. By the end of the nineteenth century the *Quixote* could be read in many more languages, from Bulgarian to Hindustani and Japanese. By 1958, according to Astrana Marin, it had been translated in whole or in part into sixty-eight languages. Cervantes's little joke about its being used for the teaching of Spanish in China has not proved too wide of the mark. New Spanish editions have proliferated since the early nineteenth century. The most important are those of Diego Clemencín (1833–9A), C. Cortejón (1905–13); R. Schevill and A. Bonilla (1928–41), F. Rodríguez Marín (1947–9A), M. de Riquer (1962A) and L. Murillo (1978A).[3] For the same period Murillo lists eleven principal French translations, eight each in English, Russian, German and Italian. The most used contemporary English versions have been those of the American Samuel Putnam (1949A), J. M. Cohen (Penguin, 1950A) and W. Starkie (1964). It has to be said that they leave a good deal to be desired as regards accuracy and stylistic modulation. Occasionally the delightful linguistic equivocations of Cervantes have even been 'corrected' by the translator who has missed the point or the joke; none of them is blameless in this respect (see Allen, 1979D). A new version of Ormsby's 1885 translation by Jones and Douglas (1981A) appears to be an improvement in all respects, more accurate than Cohen and more readable than Putnam.

The first 'public' reactions to *Don Quixote*, Part I, are incorporated in the novel itself (II, 2–4). Of course it is impossible to tell just how far they really reflected other people's opinions, although they sound plausible enough. It is at any rate worth noting that Cervantes has here anticipated several reactions to his hero, which, with due allowance for the speaker and the context, are notable for their variety of response:

> 'As regards your worship's valour, courtliness, deeds and enterprise,' Sancho went on, 'there are different opinions. Some say: "Mad, but amusing"; others, "Brave, but unfortunate"; others, "Courteous, but presumptuous".'

> (– En lo que toca – prosiguió Sancho – a la valentía, cortesía, hazañas y asumpto de vuestra merced, hay diferentes opiniones: unos dicen: "Loco, pero gracioso"; otros, "Valiente, pero desgraciado"; otros, "Cortés, pero impertinente": II, 2; ii, 56)

The most striking feature of the corpus of *Don Quixote* criticism as a whole is its diversity.

Cervantes's contemporaries do not seem to have taken the novel very seriously. The relatively few recorded critical comments suggest that it was largely seen as the comic scourge of the books of chivalry the author proclaimed it to be, no more. The criticisms of Charles Sorel (1633) seem rather exceptional. Being mainly for alleged lapses of verisimilitude, they suggest a more serious approach, albeit from one who, as an imitator, was not a disinterested party (Morón Arroyo, 1976D, pp. 316–19).

In the first half of the eighteenth century *Don Quixote* came to be admired particularly for its irony and satire. Cervantes was ranked with Lucian and Rabelais, the 'grave and serious air' of his irony being considered peculiarly effective. The book was seen as a mock-epic in prose, and a burlesque, the Knight as a caricature of a hero. The words *quijotada* and *quijotesco* came into use as derogatory terms in Spanish.

A long-lived legend was given expression by Père Rapin when he said in 1675 that Cervantes's book was 'une satire très fine de sa nation: parce que toute la noblesse d'Espagne, qu'il rend ridicule par cet ouvrage, s'était entêtée de chevalerie' (1970E, p. 126). The idea persisted outside

Spain – through Walpole, Byron, Barbey d'Aurevilly – that Cervantes
had killed Spanish chivalry by mockery, as though the practice of it had
not in fact died long before. Rapin's assertion that Cervantes was
secretly getting at the Duke of Lerma and his court is perhaps the
beginning, too, of the long tradition of esoteric interpretations of *Don
Quixote* as concealing some recondite sense, usually crypto-sectarian.
José Cadalso in one of his *Cartas marruecas* (1789) was convinced that it
contained a great mystery: 'the literal meaning is one thing and the true
one is something very different'.[4] These readings flourished in the later
nineteenth century, and they have continued to appear from time to
time since. A *Don Quichotte, prophète d'Israel* came out in 1966. Critics
who discern ideologically radical, 'anti-establishment' sentiments in
Cervantes are apt to find themselves pushed in this direction.

Although the prevailing view of *Don Quixote* before the later
eighteenth century was as a burlesque and satirical work, its supposed
target began to shift from chivalric romance to the more diffuse areas of
Enthusiasm and Sensibility. However, a pre-Romantic view seems to
be forming in Johnson's remark that 'very few readers, amidst their
mirth or their pity, can deny that they have admitted visions of the
same kind' – though in ways less extreme than Don Quixote and
Sancho (1750, in Close, 1978[2]D, p. 12). With the acquisition of new
information about Cervantes's own heroic career, *Don Quixote* began to
be seen as a defence of chivalry by the gallant and long-suffering
author, and the Knight as the idealist misunderstood and knocked
about by the vulgar everyday world (see Burton, 1968D).[5] The tendency to identify the hero with his creator seems to begin here. It still
persists in popular dramatic adaptations, and is especially conducive to
the sentimentality which sticks to such treatments.

The revolution came with the German Romantics first. Don Quixote
was soon the tragic hero of the saddest of books, where formerly he had
been the most ridiculous hero of the most comical. For the Schlegels,
Schelling, Tieck and Richter, Cervantes became the philosopher-poet.
Hegel and Schopenhauer, among others, saw the perennial dilemmas of
metaphysics in the persons of Quixote and Sancho. And Cervantes was
the great Romantic ironist.

How the Romantic view came to shape and dominate modern criticism of *Don Quixote* is the subject of A. J. Close's study (1978[2]D),
much the best, if avowedly partisan, account of the critical history of
the work. Whoever would unravel the woolly strands of later nineteenth-century criticism is referred to it. Unamuno's very personal

approach to the novel represents in certain respects an extreme Romantic viewpoint.

Cervantes criticism has rarely been a predominantly Spanish activity, and while this internationalism is a tribute to Spain's greatest prosewriter, there are still national or linguistically defined parochialisms in some degree.

Its diversity is undiminished in this century. We have been given a Cervantes *reazionario* and champion of Counter-Reformation orthodoxy, a crypto-Judaizing Cervantes and a Cervantes *fondateur de la libre pensée*, a Leftist Cervantes (*izquierdista*) and a 1970s campus radical. He has been presented as a polymath and untutored (*ingenio lego*). We have had Don Quixote as an ascetic, as a Christian gentleman, a saint (this from W. H. Auden) and a hubristic fool. These examples are extreme, of course, but they explain and up to a point justify attempts to distribute Cervantine critics in schools or movements. Hence the 'hard' and 'soft' critics discerned by Mandel (1957–8D) – those who see Don Quixote as the butt of Cervantes's satire and essentially a fool, and those who find him an object of sympathy, essentially heroic, in the extreme view a Christ-figure. Hence, too, the Symbolical, Perspectivist and Existentialist groups identified by Close. But such terms blur distinctions between individual critical approaches, which may be as important as what is held in common, and they tend to carry an emotional charge. In this they are unlike generic descriptions applied to creative works and all too like political labels attached to people ('wets' and 'dries', 'doves' and 'hawks'). 'Perspectivist' even seems to be in danger of being regarded as a term of abuse! So I shall simply identify in the briefest manner some of the modern writings which are generally agreed to have advanced understanding of *Don Quixote* with occasional reference to follow-up works.

Ortega y Gasset's *Meditaciones del Quijote* ([1914] 1957D), imbued with his own philosophical ideas, is perhaps the most seminal work of the century, full of insights to be developed later by others. It influenced Américo Castro's own monumentally influential *Pensamiento de Cervantes* ([1925] 1972D). This identified key ideas in Cervantes, systematized and situated them in the tradition of Renaissance thought. While Castro's later work on Cervantes took him into the polemical arena of his theory of Spanish history, Bataillon ([1937] 1950D) clarified the Erasmian connection. This line has been reopened recently by Forcione (1982D, 1984D). Hatzfeld's stylistic study ([1927] 1966D) was based on ideas of period styles borrowed from art history, as was Casalduero's sensitive analysis of theme and structure (1949D), related to New Criticism. Madariaga's 'psychological' study ([1926] 1947D) does not live up to that adjective, but is, as Close says, in the tradition of Unamuno; it remains an influential work more often followed than acknowledged.

One strand of Leo Spitzer's work (1948D), by definition perspectivist, led the way to contemporary investigations into the self-reflexive and related aspects of *Don Quixote* by Gerhardt (1955D), Levin ([1957] 1969D), Haley (1965D) and others, and into areas where the techniques of post-realist fiction were seen to have Quixotic antecedents. The Italians Toffanin (1920D) and De Lollis (1924D) prepared the ground for the study of Cervantes's literary aesthetic in the Golden Age context by Castro and later Riley (1962D) and Forcione (1970D). Riquer's work on the Spanish chivalric romances led to redefinitions of its relationship with the chivalresque, culminating (to date) in Williamson's synthesis with novelistic history (1984D). Márquez Villanueva (1973D) has thrown valuable new light on proto-novelistic forebears of *Don Quixote*.

Russell (1969D) and Close (1978[2]D), reacting against the excesses of solemnity, sentimentality and anachronism in much modern criticism, have had a generally salutary effect on Anglo-American critics, some of whom, however, appear to have been struck into awkward postures. Maravall (1976D) has provided most of the framework of contemporary history and ideology. French scholars in the wake of Bakhtin, notably Redondo (1978D) and Joly (1982E), have broken new ground in the study of traditional folkloric elements and affiliations. Stagg's reconstruction of the composition of Part I (1959D) has proved seminal; the textual investigations of Flores (1975D) indispensable; and Rosenblat's linguistic study (1971D), so far, definitive. Levin (1963E, [1970] 1973D) and Girard (1966E) have made the most original studies of *Don Quixote*'s relations with the classic novels of modern realism. Emanating from outside the Hispanist world, the voices of Trilling, Frye and Booth, Lukács, Foucault and Bakhtin may be clearly heard. Structuralism has borne fruit in a few essays like Segre's (1974D).

Don Quixote's key position in the history of the genre makes the extent of its influence, direct and indirect, on later prose fiction incalculable. It appears, however, to have been slight before the later seventeenth century, although obvious in Salas Barbadillo's *Caballero puntual* (1614) and perceptible in Sorel's *Berger extravagant* (1627), the author's protestations notwithstanding. But nothing like the reaction to *Guzmán de*

Alfarache occurred. Adaptations and reminiscences were at first more abundant in the theatre, Spanish and English.

In the eighteenth century Cervantes's influence was first felt most strongly on the novel in England, despite the wide diffusion of *Don Quixote* in France. From the early nineteenth century onwards it was felt in all the major European literatures where the novel thrived. There must be very few major prose-writers with whom some Cervantine connection has not been noticed by someone: Defoe, Lesage, Fielding, Smollett, Sterne, Breckenridge, Goethe, Scott, Stendhal, Balzac, Dickens, Flaubert, Galdós, Dostoevsky, Turgenev, Melville, Twain, Manzoni, Carroll, Alas, Daudet, Unamuno, even Proust – and others I have missed out. Harry Levin has traced with brilliant succinctness some of the principal ways in which they are indebted. And there are the recorded testimonies: Sir Walter Scott declaring that Cervantes was the storyteller who inspired him to become a writer, and having Lockhart read Cervantes's dying words to him on his own deathbed. Flaubert finding again his 'origins' in the book he claimed (one forgives the hyperbole) to have known by heart in infancy. Faulkener declaring that he read the *Quixote* every year the way some folks do the Bible.

Many works (not all of them novels, to be sure) advertised their relationship to the originator in their titles, *Don Quixote Redivivus*, *The Female Quixote*, *Don Quixote the Second*, the *Philosophical Quixote*, the *Political Quixote*, the *Spiritual Quixote*, and others, down to the latest of them, Graham Greene's *Monsignor Quixote* (1982). There have been a *Don Quixote in England*, a *Don Quichotte français*, a *Deutscher Don Quijote* and a *Don Quixote USA*, and such works as Fielding's *Joseph Andrews*, 'written in the manner of Cervantes'.

Then there is the more diffuse category of works, including some of the greatest modern novels, whose romantic heroes and heroines, idealists, crusaders or self-deluded misfits, from Dostoevsky's Prince Mishkin, through Stendhal's Julien Sorel to Flaubert's Emma Bovary and Galdós's Isabel Rufete, find themselves at odds with the world. Clearly, a great many variations on the theme were possible. The difference between what one is or appears to be and what one thinks one is or would like to be – one can hardly imagine the classic realist novel without this theme. This does not presuppose direct indebtedness to Cervantes every time, but he anticipated it (see Girard, 1966E and Welsh, 1981E).

Many novelists have used what Harry Levin has called the 'Quixotic principle'. Cervantes discovered, Levin says, how 'by attacking literary illusions he could capture the illusion of reality. He could attain realism by challenging the conventions that gave literature its frequent air of unreality' (1963E, p. 47). The fictional genre attacked, of course, is romance, or inclines strongly to it. The critical stance adopted by the writer assumes a shared attitude with the reader. 'Can't you see', he insinuates, 'how much truer the world in my book is than the world in theirs?' Cervantes did not exactly invent the procedure; something like it is found in Chaucer, but nobody had exploited it more thoroughly. Scarron, Fielding, Jane Austen, Galdós and Flaubert were among those who followed suit.

The whole apparatus of allegedly found documents, translated source materials, substitute authors and what-have-you was certainly not invented by Cervantes, either, but its use in modern fiction from Cervantes to Cela and Nabokov again owes not a little to him.

Lastly – to pursue no further trails in the vast and vaguely defined field of Cervantine influence – there are the fleeting reminiscences one meets, or thinks one does. When Huckleberry Finn hides the butter in his cap and it starts melting, and Aunt Sally, white as a sheet, exclaims, 'He's got the brain-fever as shore as you're born, and they're oozing out!' (ch. 40), how can one fail to recall Don Quixote with the helmetful of curds thinking he has cerebral seepage (II, 17)?

Surprisingly, at first sight, the *Quixote* has shown itself to be relevant not only to the great realist novels of the last century, but also to many modernist and post-modernist works of our own. To Kafka, to Joyce, to Nabokov, to Borges, to writers of *nouveaux romans* and Latin American fantasists. A principal reason for this is the prominence that Cervantes gives to the idea of his novel as a literary artefact, the way he shows that the carefully built-up effect of historicity is pretence, that an event is a choice of words. The autonomous existences of Don Quixote and Sancho are seen to be illusion. The book is only a book.

The preoccupation with the fictionality of fiction is of course very twentieth-century, It is also an easy step from this awareness of artistic illusion to the conclusion that human existence, so fraught with doubts, snares and confusions, is itself illusory. Arrest the action in the ducal castle, switch to Don Quixote's point of view and you would be virtually in the ambience of many contemporary works of fiction: in Kafka's castle, a dubious entity in a *nivola* of Unamuno, lost in Borges's labyrinth of existence, trapped amid mirror-reflections of the mocking grins of madmen in a novel by Nabokov, caught somewhere between life and literature with Butor, an identity submerged in an almost anonymous centre of consciousness around whom other people appear as mere illusions, modalities or dependencies of the self, as Nathalie Sarraute put it.

To get here, however, to take the step from the seventeenth-century belief that Life's a Dream to the twentieth century's nightmare view of it, you have to throw out the spiritual certainties and moral convictions held by the great majority of writers of the age, and certainly by Cervantes. You must throw out his comic sense, too. To pretend that the *Quixote* opens the door on some existentialist void of doubt and absurdity is anachronistic nonsense. But if we sense its presence behind the door it is because *Don Quixote* 'contains the whole potentiality of the genre'.

NOTES: CHAPTER 15

1   A useful breakdown of the numerous studies may be found in Murillo (1978B), pp. 65–96.

2   A single picture had appeared in the English edition of 1618, and another one in the German edition of 1648.

3   A rigorously edited up-to-date *Obras completas* is badly needed. A move towards this end was made at the first Congreso Internacional sobre Cervantes, held in Madrid in 1978, but the project did not get off the ground. Since then there has been some inconclusive debate in America over editorial norms for *Don Quixote* (see *Cervantes*, Vol. 2, 1982B, 69 ff., 181 ff.; Vol. 3, 1983B, 3 ff.).

4   Cited in Montesinos (1953D), p. 508 n. See also Close (1978[2]D), pp. 98 ff. By some sort of sympathetic magnetism *Quixote* criticism seems to have attracted an unusually large lunatic fringe – persons attempting to prove that the book was really written by El Greco or the like.

5   'Fielding was the first writer in England to make Don Quixote a noble symbol, and it took him some time to develop that' (Tave, 1960E, p. 155; see pp. 151 – 63 for a good short account of the changing view of Don Quixote in eighteenth-century England).

BIBLIOGRAPHY

(A) TEXTS OF *DON QUIXOTE* AND OTHER WORKS BY CERVANTES

Don Quixote

Facsimile edition of *El ingenioso hidalgo Don Quijote de la Mancha* (Madrid: Juan de la Cuesta, 1605) and *Segunda Parte* (Madrid: Juan de la Cuesta, 1615) by the Hispanic Society of America, 2 vols (New York, 1905).

El ingenioso hidalgo Don Quijote de la Mancha . . . , comentado por Diego Clemencín, 6 vols (Madrid: E. Aguado, 1833–9).

El ingenioso hidalgo Don Quijote de la Mancha, nueva edición crítica . . . por Francisco Rodríguez Marín, 10 vols (Madrid: Ediciones Atlas, 1947–9).

Don Quijote de la Mancha, seguido del 'Quijote' de Avellaneda, ed. Martin de Riquer (Barcelona: Planeta, 1962).

El ingenioso hidalgo Don Quijote de la Mancha, ed. Luis A. Murillo, 3 vols (Madrid: Castalia, 1978).

The Ingenious Gentleman Don Quixote de la Mancha, trans. Samuel Putnam (New York: Modern Library, 1949).

The Adventures of Don Quixote, trans. J. M. Cohen (Harmondsworth: Penguin, 1950).

Don Quixote. The Ormsby Translation Revised. Backgrounds and Sources, Criticism, ed. Joseph R. Jones and Kenneth Douglas (New York: Norton, 1981).

Other Works

Comedias y entremeses, ed. R. Schevill and A. Bonilla, 6 vols (Madrid: B. Rodríguez/Gráficas Reunidas, 1915–22).

La Galatea, ed. J. B. Avalle-Arce, 2 vols, Clásicos Castellanos (Madrid: Espasa-Calpe, 1961).

Los trabajos de Persiles y Sigismunda, ed. J. B. Avalle-Arce (Madrid: Castalia, 1969).

Novelas ejemplares, ed. H. Sieber, 2nd edn, 2 vols (Madrid: Cátedra, 1980).

Obras completas, ed. R. Schevill and A. Bonilla, 18 vols (Madrid: B. Rodríguez/ Gráficas Reunidas, 1914–41).

Obras completas, ed. A. Valbuena Prat (Madrid: Aguilar, 1942).

Viaje del Parnaso, ed. Vicente Gaos (Madrid: Castalia, 1973).

Viaje del Parnaso, ed. F. Rodríguez Marín (Madrid: Bermejo, 1935).

(B) BIBLIOGRAPHY, BIOGRAPHY, REFERENCE

Ríus, Leopoldo, *Bibliografía de las obras de Miguel de Cervantes Saavedra*, 3 vols (Madrid, 1895–1904); facsimile edn, 3 vols (New York: Burt Franklin, 1970).

Simón Díaz, José, *Bibliografía de la literatura hispánica*, Vol. 8 (*Siglos*

XVI–XVII, Cervantes–Coquela) (Madrid: Consejo Superior de Investigaciones Científicas, 1970).

Drake, Dana B., *Don Quixote (1894–1970): A Selective, Annotated Bibliography*, Vol. 1 (Chapel Hill, NC: University of North Carolina Press, 1974); Vol. 2 (Miami, Fla: Universal, 1978); Vol. 3 (New York: Garland, 1980).

Murillo, Luis A., *Don Quijote de la Mancha: Bibliografía fundamental*; Vol. 3 of his edition of the novel (1978; see section A above).

Astrana Marín, Luis, *Vida ejemplar y heroica de Miguel de Cervantes Saavedra*, 7 vols (Madrid: Reus, 1948–58).

Cabezas, Juan Antonio, *Cervantes: del mito al hombre* (Madrid: Biblioteca Nueva, 1967).

Byron, William, *Cervantes: A Biography* (London: Cassell, 1979).

McKendrick, Melveena, *Cervantes* (Boston, Mass.; Little, Brown, 1980).

Anales cervantinos (1951–). Consejo Superior de Investigaciones Científicas, Instituto Miguel de Cervantes. Published yearly.

Cervantes (1981–). Bulletin of the Cervantes Society of America. Published twice yearly.

Fernández Gómez, Carlos, *Vocabulario de Cervantes* (Madrid: Real Academia Española, 1962).

Ruiz-Fornells, E., *Las concordancias de 'El ingenioso hidalgo Don Quijote de la Mancha'* Vols 1–2 (A–C), (Madrid: Cultura Hispánica, 1976–80); in progress.

(C) CONTEMPORARY AND EARLIER WORKS

Alemán, Mateo (1967), *Guzmán de Alfarache*, in F. Rico (ed.), *La novela picaresca española*, (Barcelona: Planeta), pp. 83–914.

Ariosto, L. (1963), *Orlando furioso*, ed. L. Caretti (Milan: R. Ricciardi).

Aristotle (1945), *On the Art of Poetry*, trans. Ingram Bywater (Oxford: Clarendon Press).

Avellaneda, Alonso Fernández de (1972), *El ingenioso hidalgo Don Quijote de la Mancha*, ed. M. de Riquer, 3 vols (Madrid: Espasa-Calpe).

Covarrubias, Sebastián de (1943), *Tesoro de la lengua castellana o española*, ed. M. de Riquer (Barcelona: S. A. Horta).

The Death of King Arthur (1978), trans. James Cable (Harmondsworth: Penguin).

Entremés de los romances (1874), attrib. Cervantes, in Adolfo de Castro (ed.), *Varias obras inéditas de Cervantes* (Madrid: A. de Carlos), pp. 129–74. Free translation into English by J. R. Jones in the revised Ormsby translation of *Don Quixote* (1981; see section A above), pp. 841–8.

Erasmus, D. (1964), *The Praise of Folly*, in *The Essential Erasmus*, trans. J. P. Dolan (New York: Mentor-Omega Books), pp. 94–173.

Fernández, Jerónimo (1547), *El libro primero del valeroso e inuencible principe don Belianís de Grecia*, Parts I and II (Burgos: Martín Munoz); Parts III–IV (Burgos: Pedro de Santillana, 1579).

Gil Polo, Gaspar (1953), primera parte de la *Diana enamorada*, ed. R. Ferreres (Madrid: Espasa-Calpe).

González, Gregorio (1973), *El guitón Honofre*, ed. Hazel Généreux Carrasco (Chapel Hill, NC: University of North Carolina Press).

Heliodorus (1954), *Historia etiópica de los amores de Teágenes y Cariclea*, trans. F. de Mena, ed. F. López Estrada (Madrid: Aldus, Artes Gráficas).

Historia del caballero de Dios que auia por nombre Cifar (1954), in F. Buendía (ed.), *Libros de caballerías españoles* (Madrid: Aguilar), pp. 43–294.

Lazarillo de Tormes (1967), in F. Rico (ed.), *La novela picaresca española* (Barcelona: Planeta), pp. 3–80.

López de Úbeda, F. (1977), *La pícara Justina*, ed. A. Rey Hazas, 2 vols (Madrid: Editora Nacional).

López Pinciano, A. ['El Pinciano'] (1953), *Philosophia antigua poetica*, ed. A. Carballo Picazo (Madrid: Consejo Superior de Investigaciones Científicas).

Lucas Hidalgo, Gaspar (1950), *Diálogos de apacible entretenimiento*, Biblioteca de Autores Españoles XXXVI (Madrid: Atlas).

Martí, Juan (pseud. 'Mateo Luján de Sayavedra') (1946), *Segunda parte de la vida del pícaro Guzmán de Alfarache*, in A. Valbuena Prat (ed.), *La novela picaresca española* (Madrid: Aguilar), pp. 579–702.

Martorell, Johannot (1979), *Tirant lo Blanc*, ed. M. de Riquer (Barcelona: Clàssics Catalans Ariel).

Mercader, Gaspar (1971), *El Prado de Valencia*, ed. H. Mérimée (Toulouse, 1907; New York/London: Johnson Reprint).

Montemayor, Jorge de (1946), *Los siete libros de la Diana*, ed. F. López Estrada (Madrid: Espasa-Calpe).

Núñez de Reinoso, A. (1846), *Historia de los amores de Clareo y Florisea*, Biblioteca de Autores Españoles III (Madrid: Rivadeneyra).

Ortúñez de Calahorra, Diego (1975), *Espejo de príncipes y caballeros*, ed. D. Eisenberg, 6 vols (Madrid: Espasa-Calpe).

Pérez de Herrera, Cristóbal (1975), *Discursos del amparo de los legítimos pobres*, ed. M. Cavillac (Madrid: Espasa-Calpe).

The Quest of the Holy Grail (1977), trans. P. M. Matarasso (Harmondsworth: Penguin).

Quevedo, F. de (1965), *La vida del buscón llamado don Pablos*, ed. F. Lázaro Carreter (Salamanca: Acta Salmanticensia).

Ripa, Cesare (1618), *Nova Iconologia* (Padua).

Rodríguez de Montalvo, Garci (1959–69), *Amadís de Gaula*, ed. E. B. Place, 4 vols (Madrid: Consejo Superior de Investigaciones Científicas); *Amadis of Gaul*, trans. E. B. Place and H. C. Behm, 2 vols (Lexington, Ky: University of Kentucky Press, 1974).

Rojas, Agustín de (1972), *El viaje entretenido*, ed. J. P. Ressot (Madrid: Castalia).

Rojas, Fernando de (1969), *La Celestina*, ed. D. S. Severin (Madrid: Alianza).

Sánchez, Francisco (1944), *Que nada se sabe* [*Quod nihil scitur*, 1581] (Buenos Aires: Nova).

Sidney, Sir Philip (1904), *An Apologie for Poetry*, in G. G. Smith (ed.), *Elizabethan Critical Essays*, 2 vols (Oxford: Clarendon Press), Vol. 1, pp. 148–207.

Silva, Juan de (1602), *Historia famosa del principe don Policisne de Boecia* (Valladolid: J. Iñiguez de Lequerica, herederos).

Torquemada, Antonio de (1943), *Jardín de flores curiosas*, ed. A. González de Amezúa (Madrid: Sociedad de Bibliófilos Españoles).

Vega, Lope de (1973), *El peregrino en su patria*, ed. J. B. Avalle-Arce (Madrid: Castalia).

Vega, Lope de (1975), *Arcadia*, ed. E. S. Morby (Madrid: Castalia).

Vives, Juan Luis (1947–8), 'Del socorro de los pobres', in *Obras completas*, trans. L. Riber, 2 vols (Madrid: Aguilar), Vol. 2, pp. 1355–1411.

(D) STUDIES OF *DON QUIXOTE* AND CERVANTES

Alfaro, G. (1971), 'Cervantes y la novela picaresca', *Anales cervantinos*, vol. 10, pp. 23–31.

Allen, J. J. (1969), *Don Quixote: Hero or Fool?* (Gainesville, Fla: University of Florida Press).

Allen, J. J. (1979[1]), *Don Quixote: Hero or Fool?*, Part 2 (Gainesville, Fla: University of Florida Press).

Allen, J. J. (1979[2]), 'Traduttori traditori: *Don Quixote* in English', *Crítica Hispánica*, vol. 1, pp. 1–13.

Alonso, Dámaso (1962), 'Sancho-Quijote, Sancho-Sancho', in *Del Siglo de Oro a este siglo de siglas* (Madrid: Gredos), pp. 9–19.

Andrist, D. D. (1983), 'Male versus female friendship in *Don Quijote*', *Cervantes*, vol. 3, pp. 149–59.

Atlee, A. F. M. (1976), 'Concepto y ser metafórico de Dulcinea', *Anales cervantinos*, vol. 15, pp. 223–36.

Atlee, A. F. M. (1982), 'En torno a una frase del *Quijote: el Caballero de la Triste Figura*', *Anales cervantinos*, vol. 20, pp. 49–57.

Auerbach, Erich (1969), 'The enchanted Dulcinea', in Lowry Nelson, Jr (ed.), *Cervantes: A Collection of Critical Essays* (Englewood Cliffs, NJ: Prentice-Hall), pp. 98–122.

Avalle-Arce, J. B. (1975), *Nuevos deslindes cervantinos* (Barcelona: Ariel).

Avalle-Arce, J. B. (1976), *Don Quijote como forma de vida* (Madrid: Castalia).

Avalle-Arce, J. B., and Riley, E. C. (eds) (1973), *Suma cervantina* (London: Támesis).

Aylward, E. T. (1982), *Cervantes: Pioneer and Plagiarist* (London: Támesis).

'Azorín' [J. Martínez Ruiz] (1964), *La ruta de Don Quixote* (Buenos Aires: Losada).

Bandera, C. (1975), *Mimesis conflictiva: Ficción literaria y violencia en Cervantes y Calderón* (Madrid: Gredos).

Barrick, Mac E. (1976), 'The form and function of folktales in *Don Quijote*', *Journal of Medieval and Renaissance Studies*, vol. 6, pp. 101–38.

Barto, P. S. (1923), 'Cervantes' subterranean Grail Paradise', *PMLA*, vol. 38, pp. 401–11.

Bataillon, Marcel (1950), 'El erasmismo de Cervantes', in *Erasmo y España*, trans. A. Alatorre, 2 vols (Mexico City: Fondo de Cultura Económica), Vol. 2, pp. 400–27.

Bataillon, Marcel (1973), 'Relaciones literaras', in J. B. Avalle-Arce and E. C. Riley (eds), *Suma cervantina* (London: Támesis), pp. 215–32.

Bell, Michael (1968), 'The structure of *Don Quixote*', *Essays in Criticism*, vol. 18, pp. 241–57.

Bell, Michael (1982), 'Sancho's governorship and the "vanitas" theme in *Don Quixote*, Part II', *Modern Language Review*, vol. 77, pp. 325–38.

Blanco Aguinaga, C. (1957), 'Cervantes y la picaresca: notas sobre dos tipos de realismo', *Nueva Revista de Filología Hispánica*, vol. 11, pp. 313–42.

Bonilla, Adolfo (1905), *Don Quijote y el pensamiento español* (Madrid: Bernardo Rodríguez).

Brenan, Gerald (1969), 'Cervantes', in Lowry Nelson, Jr (ed.), *Cervantes: A Collection of Critical Essays* (Englewood Cliffs, NJ: Prentice-Hall), pp. 13–33.

Burton, A. P. (1968), 'Cervantes the man seen through English eyes in the seventeenth and eighteenth centuries', *Bulletin of Hispanic Studies*, vol. 45, pp. 1–15.

Canavaggio, Jean (1977), *Cervantès dramaturge* (Presses Universitaires de France).

Canavaggio, Jean (1981[1]), 'La dimensión autobiográfica del *Viaje del Parnaso*', *Cervantes*, vol. 1, pp. 29–41.

Canavaggio, Jean (1981[2]), 'Le "vrai" visage d'Agi Morato', *les Langues néo-latines*, *Hommage à Luis Urrutia*, tirés à part, no. 239, pp. 23–38.

Casalduero, Joaquín (1943), *Sentido y forma de las 'Novelas ejemplares'* (Buenos Aires: Sudamericana).

Casalduero, Joaquín (1947), *Sentido y forma de 'Los Trabajos de Persiles y Sigismunda'* (Buenos Aires: Sudamericana).

Casalduero, Joaquín (1949), *Sentido y forma del 'Quijote'* (Madrid: Insula).

Castro, Américo (1962), prólogo to second edition of *Don Quijote de la Mancha* (Mexico City: Porrua).

Castro, Américo (1966), *Cervantes y los casticismos españoles* (Madrid/Barcelona: Alfaguara).

Castro, Américo (1967[1]), *Hacia Cervantes*, 3rd edn revised (Madrid: Taurus).

Castro, Américo (1967[2]), 'Los prólogos al *Quijote*', in *Hacia Cervantes*, 3rd edn revised (Madrid: Taurus), pp. 262–301.

Castro, Américo (1971), 'Cómo veo ahora el *Quijote*', introduction to edition of *Don Quijote*, 2 vols (Madrid: Novelas y Cuentos), Vol. 1, pp. 1–102.

Castro, Américo (1972), *El pensamiento de Cervantes*, 2nd edn amplified by the author and J. Rodríguez-Puértolas (Barcelona/Madrid: Noguer).

Cernuda, Luis (1964), 'Cervantes poeta', in *Poesía y Literatura*, Vol. 2 (Barcelona: Seix Barral), pp. 43–57.

Chevalier, Maxime (1983), '*El cautivo*, entre cuento y novela', paper given at VIII Congreso de la Asociación Internacional de Hispanistas (Providence, RI).

Close, Anthony (1972), '*Don Quixote* and the "intentionalist fallacy"', *British Journal of Aesthetics*, vol. 12, pp. 19–39.

Close, Anthony (1973[1]), '*Don Quixote*'s love for Dulcinea: a study of Cervantine irony', *Bulletin of Hispanic Studies*, vol. 50, pp. 237–55.

Close, Anthony (1973[2]), 'Sancho Panza: wise fool', *Modern Language Review*, vol. 68, pp. 344–57.

Close, Anthony (1978[1]), '*Don Quixote*'s sophistry and wisdom', *Bulletin of Hispanic Studies*, vol. 55, pp. 103–14.

Close, Anthony (1978[2]), *The Romantic Approach to 'Don Quixote'* (Cambridge: Cambridge University Press).

Close, Anthony (1981), 'Characterization and dialogue in Cervantes's "comedias en prosa"', *Modern Language Review*, vol. 76, pp. 338–56.

De Chasca, Edmund (1964), 'Algunos aspectos del ritmo y del movimiento narrativo del *Quijote*', *Revista de filología española*, vol. 47, pp. 287–307.

Deutsch, Helene (1965), 'Don Quixote and Don Quixotism', in *Neuroses and Character Types: Clinical Psychoanalytical Studies* (New York: International University Presses), pp. 218–25.

Dudley, Edward (1972), 'Don Quijote as magus: the rhetoric of interpolation', *Bulletin of Hispanic Studies*, vol. 49, pp. 355–68.

Dunn, Peter N. (1972), 'Two classical myths in *Don Quijote*', *Renaissance and Reformation*, vol. 9, pp. 2–10.

Dunn, Peter N. (1973), 'La cueva de Montesinos por fuera y por dentro: estructura épica, fisonomía', *Modern Language Notes*, vol. 88, pp. 190–202.

Dunn, Peter N. (1982), 'Cervantes de/reconstructs the picaresque', *Cervantes*, vol. 2, pp. 109–31.

Durán, Manuel (1960), *La ambigüedad en el Quijote* (Xalapa: Universidad Veracruzana).

Durán, Manuel (1973), 'El *Quijote* de Avellaneda', in J. B. Avalle-Arce and E. C. Riley (eds), *Suma cervantina* (London: Támesis), pp. 357–76.

Eisenberg, D. (1973), '*Don Quijote* and the romances of chivalry: the need for a re-examination', *Hispanic Review*, vol. 41, pp. 511–23.

El Saffar, Ruth (1968), 'The function of the fictional narrator in *Don Quijote*', *Modern Language Notes*, vol. 83, pp. 164–77.

El Saffar, Ruth (1974), *Novel to Romance* (Baltimore, Md: Johns Hopkins University Press).

El Saffar, Ruth (1975), *Distance and Control in 'Don Quixote': A Study in Narrative Technique* (Chapel Hill, NC: University of North Carolina).

Entwistle, W. J. (1940), *Cervantes* (Oxford: Clarendon Press).

Ferreras, J. I. (1982), *La estructura paródica del 'Quijote'* (Madrid: Taurus).

Flores, A., and Bernadete, J. (1969), *Cervantes across the Centuries* (New York: Gordian Press).

Flores, Robert (1975), *The Compositors of the First and Second Madrid Editions of 'Don Quixote' Part I* (London: Modern Humanities Research Association).

Flores, Robert (1980[1]), 'El caso del epígrafe desaparecido: capítulo 43 de la edición príncipe de la Primera Parte del *Quijote*', *Nueva Revista de Filología Hispánica*, vol. 28, pp. 352–60.

Flores, Robert (1980[2]), 'The loss and recovery of Don Quixote's ass in *Don Quixote*, Part I', *Modern Language Review*, vol. 75, pp. 301–10.

Flores, Robert (1981), 'The compositors of the first edition of *Don Quixote*, Part II', *Journal of Hispanic Philology*, vol. 6, pp. 3–44.

Flores, Robert (1982[1]), 'The role of Cide Hamete in *Don Quixote*', *Bulletin of Hispanic Studies*, vol. 59, pp. 3–14.

Flores, Robert (1982[2]), *Sancho Panza through Three Hundred Seventy-Five Years of Continuations, Imitations and Criticism, 1605–1980* (Newark, Del.: Juan de la Cuesta).

Forcione, Alban K. (1970), *Cervantes, Aristotle and the 'Persiles'* (Princeton, NJ: Princeton University Press).

Forcione, Alban K. (1972), *Cervantes' Christian Romance: A Study of 'Persiles y Sigismunda'* (Princeton, NJ: Princeton University Press).

Forcione, Alban K. (1982), *Cervantes and the Humanist Vision: A Study of Four 'Exemplary Novels'* (Princeton, NJ: Princeton University Press).

Forcione, Alban K. (1984), *Cervantes and the Mystery of Lawlessness* (Princeton, NJ: Princeton University Press).

Gaos, Vicente (1959), 'El *Quijote*: aproximaciones', in *Temas y problemas de la literatura española* (Madrid: Guadarrama), pp. 95–118.

García Chichester, Ana (1983), 'Don Quijote y Sancho en el Toboso: superstición y simbolismo', *Cervantes*, vol. 3, pp. 121–33.

Garrote Pérez, F. (1982), 'Algunas cuestiones cervantinas: una vía clarificadora de su pensamiento', *Anales cervantinos*, vol. 20, pp. 59–92.

Gerhardt, Mia (1955), *'Don Quijote': la vie et les livres* (Amsterdam: Noord-Hollandsche Uitgevers Maatchappij).

Gerli, E. M. (1982), 'Estilo, perspectiva y realidad: *Don Quijote*, I, 8–9', *Thesaurus, Boletín del Instituto Caro y Cuervo*, vol. 37, pp. 1–8.

Gilman, Stephen (1951), *Cervantes y Avellaneda: Estudio de una imitación*, trans. M. Frenk Alatorre (Mexico City: Colegio de México).

González de Amezúa, A. (1956), *Cervantes creador de la novela corta*, 2 vols (Madrid: Consejo Superior de Investigaciones Científicas).

Green, Otis H. (1970), 'El Ingenioso Hidalgo', in *The Literary Mind of Medieval and Renaissance Spain* (Lexington, Ky: University Press of Kentucky), pp. 171–84.

Guilbeau, J. J. (1962), 'Some folk-motifs in *Don Quixote*', in *Studies in Comparative Literature* (Baton Rouge, La: Louisiana State University Press), pp. 69–83, 287–91.

Haley, George (1965), 'The narrator in *Don Quijote*: Maese Pedro's puppet show', *Modern Language Notes*, vol. 80, pp. 145–65.

Halka, Chester S. (1981), *'Don Quijote* in the light of Huarte's *Examen de ingenios*: a re-examination', *Anales cervantinos*, vol. 19, pp. 3–13.

Hart, T., and Rendall, S. (1978), 'Rhetoric and persuasion in Marcela's address to the shepherds', *Hispanic Review*, vol. 46, pp. 287–98.

Hatzfeld, Helmut (1966), *El 'Quijote' como obra de arte del lenguaje* (Madrid: Consejo Superior de Investigaciones Científicas).

Hazard, Paul (1931), *Don Quichotte de Cervantes* (Paris: Melotée).

Herrero, Javier (1976–7), 'The beheading of the Giant: an obscene metaphor in *Don Quijote*', *Revista Hispánica Moderna*, vol. 39, pp. 141–9.

Herrero, Javier (1981[1]), 'Dulcinea as goat', paper given to the Association of Hispanists of Great Britain and Ireland (Oxford).

Herrero, Javier (1981[2]), 'Sierra Morena as labyrinth: from wildness to Christian knighthood', *Forum for Modern Language Studies*, vol. 17, pp. 55–67.

Hughes, Gethin (1977), 'The Cave of Montesinos: Don Quixote's interpretation and Dulcinea's enchantment', *Bulletin of Hispanic Studies*, vol. 54, pp. 106–13.

Ife, B. W. (1982), 'Cervantes and the credibility crisis in Spanish Golden-Age fiction', *Renaissance and Modern Studies*, vol. 26, pp. 52–74.

Ihrie, Maureen (1982), *Skepticism in Cervantes* (London: Támesis).

Immerwahr, Raymond (1958), 'Structural symmetry in the episodic narratives of *Don Quijote*, Part One', *Comparative Literature*, vol. 10, pp. 121–35.

Iventosch, H. (1974), 'Cervantes and Courtly Love: the Grisóstomo–Marcela episode of *Don Quixote*', *PMLA*, vol. 89, pp. 64–76.

Johnson, Carroll B. (1975), 'A second look at Dulcinea's ass', *Hispanic Review*, vol. 43, pp. 191–8.

Johnson, Carroll B. (1982), 'Organic unity in unlikely places: *Don Quijote* I, 39–41', *Cervantes*, vol. 2, pp. 133–54.

Joly, Monique (1977), 'Sémiologie du vêtement et interprétation de texte', *Revista canadiense de estudios hispánicos*, vol. 2, pp. 54–64.

Joly, Monique (1983), 'Para una reinterpretación de *La ilustre fregona*: ensayo de tipología cervantina', in *Aureum Saeculum Hispanum: Festschrift für Hans Flasche zum 70 Geburtstag* (Wiesbaden: F. Steiner), pp. 103–16.

Joly, Monique (1984), 'Le discours métaparémique dans *Don Quichotte*', in F. Suard and C. Buridant (eds), *Richesse du proverbe*, Vol. 2 (Lille: Université de Lille), pp. 245–60.

Kong, Deborah (1980), 'Don Quijote, Melancholy Knight', in 'A study of the medical theory of the humours and its application to selected Spanish literature of the Golden Age', unpublished PhD dissertation, University of Edinburgh.

Levin, Harry (1969), 'The example of Cervantes', in Lowry Nelson, Jr (ed.), *Cervantes: A Collection of Critical Essays* (Englewood Cliffs, NJ: Prentice-Hall), pp. 34–48.

Levin, Harry (1973), 'The Quixotic principle: Cervantes and other novelists', in M. W. Bloomfield (ed.), *The Interpretation of Narrative* (Cambridge, Mass.: Harvard University Press, 1970); trans. as 'Cervantes, el quijotismo y la posteridad', in J. B. Avalle-Arce and E. C. Riley (eds), *Suma cervantina* (London: Támesis), pp. 277–96.

Lollis, C. de (1924), *Cervantes reazionario* (Rome: Treves).

McGaha, M. D. (ed.) (1980), *Cervantes and the Renaissance* (Easton, Pa: Juan de la Cuesta).

Madariaga, Salvador de (1961), *Guía del lector del 'Quijote'* (Buenos Aires: Sudamericana, 1947); trans. as *Don Quixote: An Introductory Essay in Psychology* (London: Oxford University Press).

Mancing, Howard (1972), 'Dulcinea's ass: a note on *Don Quixote*, Part II, chapter 10', *Hispanic Review*, vol. 40, pp. 73–7.

Mancing, Howard (1982), *The Chivalric World of 'Don Quixote': Style, Structure and Narrative Technique* (Columbia, Mo.: University of Missouri Press).

Mandel, Oscar (1957–8), 'The function of the norm in *Don Quixote*', *Modern Philogy*, vol. 55, pp. 154–63.

Mann, Thomas (1969), 'Voyage with Don Quijote', in Lowry Nelson, Jr (ed.), *Cervantes: A Collection of Critical Essays* (Englewood Cliffs, NJ: Prentice-Hall), pp. 49–72.

Maravall, J. A. (1976), *Utopía y contrautopía en el 'Quijote'* (Santiago de Compostela: Pico Sacro).

Márquez Villanueva, F. (1973), *Fuentes literarias cervantinas* (Madrid: Gredos).

Márquez Villanueva, F. (1975), *Personajes y temas del 'Quijote'* (Madrid: Taurus).

Márquez Villanueva, F. (1980), 'La locura emblemática en la segunda parte del

Quijote', in M. D. McGaha (ed.), *Cervantes and the Renaissance* (Easton, Pa: Juan de la Cuesta), pp. 87–112.

Martínez Bonati, F. (1977), 'Cervantes y las regiones de la imaginación', *Dispositio*, vol. 2, pp. 27–53.

Menéndez Pidal, R. (1948), *Cervantes y el ideal caballeresco* (Madrid: Patronato del IV Centenario del Nacimiento de Cervantes).

Menéndez Pidal, R. (1964), 'Un aspecto en la elaboración del *Quijote*', in *De Cervantes y Lope de Vega* (Madrid: Espasa-Calpe), pp. 9–60.

Meregalli, F. (1971), 'Profilo storico della critica cervantina nel settecento', in *Rappresentazione artista e rappresentazione scientifica nel 'Secolo dei Lumi'* (Florence: Sansoni), pp. 187–210.

Molho, Maurice (1976), *Cervantes: Raíces folklóricas* (Madrid: Gredos).

Montesinos, J. F. (1953), 'Cervantes anti-novelista', *Nueva Revista de Filología hispánica*, vol. 7, pp. 449–514.

Morón Arroyo, C. (1976), *Nuevas meditaciones del Quijote* (Madrid: Gredos).

Murillo, Luis (1975), *The Golden Dial: Temporal Configuration in 'Don Quijote'* (Oxford: Dolphin).

Murillo, Luis (1983), 'Cervantes y el *Entremés de los romances*', paper given at VIII Congreso de la Asociación Internacional de Hispanistas (Providence, RI).

Navarro González, A. (1964), *El Quijote español del siglo XVI* (Madrid: Rialp).

Nelson, Lowry, Jr (ed.) (1969), *Cervantes: A Collection of Critical Essays* (Englewood Cliffs, NJ: Prentice-Hall).

Neuschäfer, Hans-Jörg (1963), *Der Sinn der Parodie im Don Quijote* (Heidelberg: C. Winter).

Oliver Asín, J. (1947–8), 'La hija de Agi Morato en la obra de Cervantes', *Boletín de la Real Academia Española*, vol. 27, pp. 245–333.

Ortega y Gasset, José (1957), *Meditaciones del Quijote*, ed. J. Marías (Madrid: Revista de Occidente).

Osterc, Ludovik (1963), *El pensamiento social y político del 'Quijote'* (Mexico City: Andrea).

Parker, A. A. (1948), 'El concepto de la verdad en el *Quijote*', *Revista de Filología española*, vol. 32, pp. 287–305.

Parker, A. A. (1956), 'Fielding and the structure of *Don Quijote*', *Bulletin of Hispanic Studies*, vol. 33, pp. 1–16.

Percas de Ponseti, Helena (1975), *Cervantes y su concepto del arte*, 2 vols (Madrid: Gredos).

Pope, Randolph D. (1979), 'El Caballero del Verde Gabán y su encuentro con Don Quijote', *Hispanic Review*, vol. 47, pp. 207–18.

Pope, Randolph D. (1983), 'Especulaciones sobre el ajedrez, Sansón Carrasco y Don Quijote', *Anales cervantinos*, vol. 20, pp. 29–47.

Predmore, Richard L. (1967), *The World of Don Quixote* (Cambridge, Mass.: Harvard University Press).

Redondo, Agustín (1978), 'Tradición carnavalesca y creación literaria del personaje de Sancho Panza al episodio de la ínsula Barataria en el *Quijote*', *Bulletin hispanique*, vol. 80, pp. 39–70.

Redondo, Agustín (1980), 'El personaje de don Quijote: tradiciones folklórico-literarias, contexto histórico y elaboración cervantina', *Nueva Revista de Filología Hispánica*, vol. 29, pp. 36–59.

Redondo, Agustín (1981), 'El proceso iniciático en el episodio de la Cueva de Montesinos del *Quijote*', *Iberoromania*, vol. 13, pp. 47–61.

Riley, E. C. (1962), *Cervantes's Theory of the Novel* (Oxford: Clarendon Press).

Riley, E. C. (1973[1]), 'Three versions of Don Quixote', *Modern Language Review*, vol. 68, pp. 807–19.

Riley, E. C. (1973[2]), 'Teoría literaria', in J. B. Avalle-Arce and E. C. Riley (eds), *Suma cervantina* (London: Támesis), pp. 293–322.

Riley, E. C. (1976), 'Cervantes and the cynics (*El licenciado Vidriera* and *El coloquio de los perros*)', *Bulletin of Hispanic Studies*, vol. 53, pp. 189–99.

Riley, E. C. (1979), 'Symbolism in *Don Quixote*, Part II, chapter 73', *Journal of Hispanic Philology*, vol. 3, pp. 161–74.

Riley, E. C. (1981), 'Cervantes: a question of genre', in *Mediaeval and Renaissance Studies on Spain and Portugal in Honour of P. E. Russell* (Oxford: Society for the Study of Mediaeval Languages and Literature), pp. 69–85.

Riley, E. C. (1982), 'Metamorphosis, myth and dream in the Cave of Montesinos', in *Essays on Narrative Fiction in the Iberian Peninsula in Honour of Frank Pierce* (Oxford: Dolphin), pp. 105–19.

Riquer, M. de (1961), 'La technique parodique du roman médiéval dans le *Quichotte*', *Colloque de Strasbourg*, 23–5 avril 1959 (Paris: Presses Universitaires de France), pp. 55–69.

Riquer, M. de (1967), *Aproximación al 'Quijote'* (Barcelona: Teide).

Riquer, M. de (1973), 'Cervantes y la caballeresca', in J. B. Avalle-Arce and E. C. Riley (eds), *Suma cervantina* (London: Támesis), pp. 273–92.

Rivers, E. L. (1960), 'On the prefatory pages of *Don Quixote*, Part II', *Modern Language Notes*, vol. 75, pp. 214–21.

Rivers, E. L. (1973), '*Viaje del Parnaso* y poesías sueltas', in J. B. Avalle-Arce and E. C. Riley (eds), *Suma cervantina* (London: Támesis), pp. 119–46.

Robert, Marthe (1977), *The Old and the New: From Don Quixote to Kafka* (Berkeley, Calif.: University of California Press).

Rodríguez-Luis, J. (1965–6), 'Dulcinea a través de los dos *Quijotes*', *Nueva Revista de Filología Hispánica*, vol. 18, pp. 378–416.

Rosales, Luis (1960), *Cervantes y la libertad*, 2 vols (Madrid: Gráficas Valera).

Rosenblat, Ángel (1971), *La lengua del 'Quijote'* (Madrid: Gredos).

Russell, P. E. (1969), '*Don Quixote* as a funny book', *Hispanic Review*, vol. 64, pp. 312–26.

Sánchez, Alberto (1961–2), 'El Caballero del Verde Gabán', *Anales cervantinos*, vol. 9, pp. 169–201.

Schevill, R. (1966), *Cervantes* (New York: Ungar).

Segre, Cesare (1974), 'Costruzioni rettilinee e costruzioni a spirale nel *Don Chisciotte*', in *Le Strutture e il Tempo* (Turin: G. Einaudi), pp. 183–219.

Sobejano, Gonzalo (1975), 'El *Coloquio de los perros* en la picaresca y otros apuntes', *Hispanic Review*, vol. 43, pp. 25–41.

Sobejano, Gonzalo (1978), 'Sobre tipología y ordenación de las *Novelas ejemplares*', *Hispanic Review*, vol. 46, pp. 65–75.

Socrate, Mario (1974), *Prologhi al 'Don Chisciotte'* (Venice/Padua: Marsilio Editori).

Spitzer, Leo (1948), 'Linguistic perspectivism in the *Don Quijote*', in *Linguistics and Literary History* (Princeton, NJ: Princeton University Press), pp. 41–85.

Spitzer, Leo (1969), 'On the significance of *Don Quijote*', in Lowry Nelson, Jr (ed.), *Cervantes: A Collection of Critical Essays* (Englewood Cliffs, NJ: Prentice-Hall), pp. 82–97.

Stagg, Geoffrey (1959), 'Revision in *Don Quijote*, Part I', in *Hispanic Studies in Honour of Ignacio González Llubera* (Oxford: Dolphin), pp. 347–66.

Stagg, Geoffrey (1964), 'Sobre el plan primitivo del *Quijote*', *Actas del Primer Congreso Internacional de Hispanistas* (Oxford: Dolphin), pp. 463–71.

Stegmann, Tilbert D. (1971), *Cervantes' Musterroman 'Persiles': Epentheorie und Romanpraxis um 1600* (Hamburg: Hartmut Ludke).

Tate, R. B. (1977), 'Who wrote *Don Quixote?*', *Vida Hispánica*, vol. 25, pp. 6–12.

Toffanin, G. (1920), 'Il Cervantes', in *La fine dell' umanesimo* (Turin: Bocca), pp. 211–21.

Togeby, Knud (1957), *La composition du roman 'Don Quijote'* (Copenhagen: Munksgaard).

Torrente Ballester, G. (1975), *El 'Quijote' como juego* (Madrid: Guadarrama).

Ullman, Pierre (1961–2), 'The burlesque poems which frame the *Quijote*', *Anales cervantinos*, vol. 9, pp. 213–27.

Unamuno, M. de (1967), *The Life of Don Quixote and Sancho, Our Lord Don Quixote*, trans. A. Kerrigan (Princeton, NJ: Princeton University Press).

Urbina, Eduardo (1982), 'Sancho Panza a nueva luz: ¿tipo folklórico o personaje literario?', *Anales cervantinos*, vol. 20, pp. 93–101.

Van Doren, Mark (1958), *Don Quixote's Profession* (New York: Columbia University Press).

Vilanova, A. (1949), *Erasmo y Cervantes* (Barcelona: Consejo Superior de Investigaciones Científicas).

Vilar, Pierre (1956), 'Le temps du *Quichotte*', *Europe*, vol. 34, pp. 3–16.

Wardropper, Bruce W. (1965), '*Don Quixote*: story or history?', *Modern Philology*, vol. 63, pp. 1–11.

Weiger, J. G. (1978), 'La superchería está descubierta: Don Quijote y Ginés de Pasamonte', *Philological Quarterly*, vol. 57, pp. 173–9.

Weinrich, H., (1956), *Das Ingenium Don Quijotes* (Münster/Westfallen: Aschendorff).

Williamson, Edwin (1982), 'Romance and realism in the interpolated stories of the *Quixote*', *Cervantes*, vol. 2, pp. 43–67.

Williamson, Edwin (1984), *The Halfway House of Fiction: 'Don Quixote' and Arthurian Romance* (Oxford: Clarendon Press).

Willis, R. S. (1953), *The Phantom Chapters of the 'Quijote'* (New York: Hispanic Institute).

Zimic, Stanislav (1972), 'El "engaño a los ojos" en las *Bodas de Camacho*', *Hispania*, vol. 55, pp. 881–6.

Zimic, Stanislav (1974–5), '*Leucipe y Clitofonte y Clareo y Florisea* en el *Persiles* de Cervantes', *Anales cervantinos*, vol. 13–14, pp. 37–58.

(E) RELATED STUDIES AND OTHER WORKS

Alter, Robert (1975), *Partial Magic: The Novel as a Self-Conscious Genre* (Berkeley, Calif.: University of California Press).

Babb, Lawrence (1951), *The Elizabethan Malady: A Study of Melancholia in*

English Literature from 1580 to 1642 (East Lansing, Mich.: Michigan State College Press).

Bakhtin, Mikhail (1968), *Rabelais and His World*, trans. H. Iswolsky (Cambridge, Mass.: MIT Press).

Bataillon, Marcel (1969), *Pícaros y picaresca* (Madrid: Taurus).

Beer, Gillian (1970), *The Romance* (London: Methuen).

Bjornson, Richard (1977), *The Picaresque Hero in European Fiction* (Madison, Wis.: University of Wisconsin Press).

Blecua, Alberto (1971–2), 'Libros de caballerías, latín macarrónico y novela picaresca: la adaptación castellana del *Baldus* (Sevilla, 1542), *Boletín de la Real Academia de Buenas Letras de Barcelona*, vol. 35, pp. 147–239.

Bradbury, G. (1981), 'Irregular sexuality in the *Comedia*', *Modern Language Review*, vol. 76, pp. 566–80.

Butor, Michel (1968), *Inventory: Essays by Michel Butor*, ed. and trans. R. Howard and others (New York: Simon & Schuster).

Campbell, Joseph (1973), *The Hero with a Thousand Faces* (Princeton, NJ: Princeton University Press).

Cavillac, M. (1983), *Gueux et marchands dans le 'Guzmán de Alfarache'* (Bordeaux: Institut d'Etudes Ibériques et Ibéro-américaines de l'Université de Bordeaux).

Chandler, F. W. (1961), *Romances of Roguery* (New York: Burt Franklin Bibliography and Reference Series 31).

Chapman, Robin (1980), *The Duchess's Diary* (London: Boudica Books).

Chevalier, Maxime (1966), *L'Arioste en Espagne (1530–1650)* (Bordeaux: Institut d'Etudes Ibériques at Ibéro-américaines de l'Université de Bordeaux).

Chevalier, Maxime (1968), *Sur le public du roman de chevalerie* (Talence: Université de Bordeaux).

Chevalier, Maxime (1976), *Lectura y lectores en la España de los siglos XVI y XVII* (Madrid: Turner).

Clements, R. J., and Gibaldi, G. (1977), *Anatomy of the Novella: European Tale Collections from Boccaccio and Chaucer to Cervantes* (New York: New York University Press).

Colie, Rosalie L. (1966), *Paradoxia Epidemica: The Renaissance Tradition of Paradox* (Princeton, NJ: Princeton University Press).

Colie, Rosalie L. (1973), *The Resources of Kind: Genre-Theory in the Renaissance* (Berkeley, Calif.: University of California Press).

Cozad, Mary L. (1981), 'Experiential conflict and rational motivation in the *Diana enamorada*: an anticipation of the modern novel', *Journal of Hispanic Philology*, vol. 5, pp. 199–214.

Cros, Edmond (1971), *Mateo Alemán: Introducción a su vida y a su obra* (Madrid: Anaya).

Cruickshank, D. W. (1978), 'Literature and the book trade in Golden-Age Spain', *Modern Language Review*, vol. 73, pp. 799–824.

Deyermond, A. D. (1975), 'The lost genre of medieval Spanish literature', *Hispanic Review*, vol. 43, pp. 231–59.

Dickens, Charles (n.d.), *Nicholas Nickleby* (London/Glasgow: Collins).

Dickens, Charles (n.d.), *The Posthumous Papers of the Pickwick Club* (London: Nelson).

Domínguez Ortiz, A. (1971), *The Golden Age of Spain, 1516–1659*, trans. J. Casey (London: Weidenfeld & Nicolson).

Dubrow, Heather (1982), *Genre* (London: Methuen).

Dunn, Peter N. (1979), *The Spanish Picaresque Novel* (Boston, Mass.: Twayne).

Dunn, Peter N. (1982), 'Problems of a model for the picaresque and the case of Quevedo's *Buscón*', *Bulletin of Hispanic Studies*, vol. 59, pp. 95–105.

Eco, Umberto (1966), 'James Bond: une combinatoire narrative', *Communications*, vol. 8, pp. 77–93.

Eisenberg, Daniel (1979), 'Does the picaresque exist?', *Kentucky Romance Quarterly*, vol. 26, pp. 201–19.

Eisenberg, Daniel (1982), *Romances of Chivalry in the Spanish Golden Age* (Newark, Del.: Juan de la Cuesta).

Elliott, J. H. (1963), *Imperial Spain, 1469–1716* (London: Edward Arnold).

Fielding, Henry (1963), *The History of Tom Jones* (London/Glasgow: Collins).

Fitzmaurice-Kelly, J. (1926), *A New History of Spanish Literature* (London: Oxford University Press).

Foucault, M. (1970), *The Order of Things* (New York: Pantheon Books).

Fowler, Alastair (1982), *The Kinds of Literature* (Oxford: Clarendon Press).

Frenk, Margit (1982), '"Lectores y oidores": la difusión de la literatura en el Siglo de Oro', *Actas del séptimo Congreso de la Asociación Internacional de Hispanistas* ([Venice, 1980]; Rome: Bulzoni), vol. 1, pp. 101–23.

Freud, Sigmund (1953), *The Interpretation of Dreams*, the Standard Edition of the Complete Psychological Works, Vol. 4 (London: Hogarth Press).

Frye, Northrop (1957), *The Anatomy of Criticism* (Princeton, NJ: Princeton University Press).

Frye, Northrop (1976), *The Secular Scripture* (Cambridge, Mass./London: Harvard University Press).

Gale, Stephen H. (1973), 'Cervantes' influence on Dickens, with comparative emphasis on *Don Quijote* and *Pickwick Papers*', *Anales cervantinos*, vol. 12, pp. 135–56.

Gebhart, Emile (1911), *De Panurge à Sancho Panza* (Paris: Bloud).

Girard, René (1966), *Deceit, Desire and the Novel*, trans. Y. Freccero (Baltimore, Md/London: Johns Hopkins University Press).

Gombrich, E. H. (1960), *Art and Illusion* (New York: Pantheon Books).

Green, Otis H. (1963–6), *Spain and the Western Tradition*, 4 vols (Madison, Wis.: University of Wisconsin Press).

Greene, Graham (1971), *Travels with My Aunt* (New York: Bantam Books).

Greene, Graham (1980), *Ways of Escape* (London: Bodley Head).

Guillén, Claudio (1971), *Literature as System* (Princeton, NJ: Princeton University Press).

Hardy, Barbara (1975), *Tellers and Listeners (The Narrative Imagination)* (London: Athlone Press).

Harvey, L. P. (1974), 'Oral composition and the performance of novels of chivalry in Spain', *Forum for Modern Language Studies*, vol. 10, pp. 270–86.

Haydn, Hiram (1960), *The Counter-Renaissance* (New York: Grove Press).

Herrero, Javier (1979), 'Renaissance poverty and Lazarillo's family: the birth of the picaresque genre', *PMLA*, vol. 94, pp. 876–86.

Huizinga, Johan (1970), *Homo ludens* (London: Paladin).

Hume, Kathryn (1974), 'Romance: a perdurable pattern', *College English*, vol. 36, pp. 129–46.

James, Henry (1948), 'The art of fiction', in *The Art of Fiction and Other Essays* (New York: Oxford University Press), pp. 3–23.

Joly, Monique (1976), 'D'Alberto Naseli, di Ganasse, au comte de Benavente: deux notes cervantines', *Bulletin hispanique*, vol. 78, pp. 240–53.

Joly, Monique (1982), *La Bourle et son interprétation (Espagne, XVIe–XVIIe siècles)* (Lille: Atelier National Réproduction de Thèses, Université de Lille, III).

Jung, C. G. (1978), *Man and His Symbols* (London: Picador).

Kris, Ernst (1952), *Psychoanalytic Explorations in Art* (New York: International Presses).

Kristeller, P. O. (1965), *Renaissance Thought II: Papers on Humanism and the Arts* (New York: Harper).

Laing, R. D. (1975), *The Politics of Experience* (Harmondsworth: Penguin).

Laurenti, J. F. (1971), *Los prólogos en las novelas picarescas españolas* (Madrid: Castalia).

Lázaro Carreter, F. (1972), 'Para una revisión del concepto "novela picaresca"', in *Lazarillo de Tormes en la picaresca* (Barcelona: Ariel), pp. 193–229.

Leonard, Irving (1949), *Books of the Brave* (Cambridge, Mass.: Harvard University Press).

Levin, Harry (1963), *The Gates of Horn: A Study of Five French Realists* (New York: Oxford University Press).

Lewis, C. S. (1965), *The Allegory of Love* (New York: Oxford University Press).

López Blanquet, M. (1968), *El estilo indirecto libre en español* (Montevideo: Talleres Don Bosco).

Lukács, Georg (1971). *The Theory of the Novel* (Cambridge, Mass.: MIT Press).

McCarthy, Mary (1962), 'Characters in fiction', in *On the Contrary* (London: Heinemann), pp. 271–92.

Marinelli, P. V. (1978), *Pastoral* (London: Methuen).

Márquez Villanueva, F. (1983), 'La identidad de Perlícaro', in *Homenaje a José Manuel Blecua* (Madrid: Gredos), pp. 423–32.

Martin, Graham D. (1975), *Language, Truth and Poetry* (Edinburgh: University of Edinburgh Press).

Martin, June Hall (1972), *Love's Fools: Aucassin, Troilus, Calisto and the Parody of the Courtly Lover* (London: Támesis).

Menéndez y Pelayo, M. (1946), *Orígenes de la novela*, 3 vols (Buenos Aires: Espasa-Calpe).

Meyer, Herman (1968), *The Poetics of Quotation in the European Novel*, trans. T. and Y. Ziolkowski (Princeton, NJ: Princeton University Press).

Moll, J. (1979), 'Problemas bibliográficos del libro del Siglo de Oro', Boletín de la Real Academia Española, vol. 59, pp. 49–107.

Muir, Kenneth (1960), *Shakespeare as Collaborator* (London: Methuen).

Nelson, William (1973), *Fact or Fiction: The Dilemma of the Renaissance Storyteller* (Cambridge, Mass.: Harvard University Press).

O'Connor, John J. (1970), *'Amadis de Gaule' and Its Influence on Elizabethan Literature* (New Brunswick, NJ: Rutgers University Press).

Oreglia, Giacomo (1968), *The Commedia dell'Arte*, trans. L. F. Edwards (London: Methuen).

Orwell, George (1950), *1984* (London: Secker & Warburg).
Osuna, Rafael (1972), *La Arcadia de Lope de Vega* (Madrid: Anejo del Boletín de la Real Academia Española).
Pabst, Walter (1972), *La novela corta en la teoría y en la creación literaria*, trans. R. de la Vega (Madrid: Gredos).
Parker, A. A. (1967), *Literature and the Delinquent* (Edinburgh: Edinburgh University Press).
Porqueras Mayo, Alberto (ed.) (1965), *El prólogo en el Renacimiento español* (Madrid: Consejo Superior de Investigaciones Científicas).
Porqueras Mayo, Alberto (ed.) (1968), *El prólogo en el manierismo y barroco españoles* (Madrid: Consejo Superior de Investigaciones Científicas).
Pritchett, V. S. (1965), 'Quixote's translators', in *The Working Novelist* (London: Chatto & Windus), pp. 166–71.
Randall, Dale B. J. (1963), *The Golden Tapestry: A Critical Survey of Non-Chivalric Spanish Fiction in English Translation (1543–1647)* (Durham, NC: Duke University Press).
Rapin, René (1970), *Les Réflexions sur la poétique de ce temps*, ed. E. T. Dubois (Geneva: Librairie Droz).
Reed, Walter L. (1981), *An Exemplary History of the Novel: The Quixotic versus the Picaresque* (Chicago, Ill./London: University of Chicago Press).
Rey Hazas, A. (1982), 'Poética comprometida de la novela picaresca', *Nuevo hispanismo*, vol. 1, pp. 55–76.
Rico, Francisco (1973), *La novela picaresca y el punto de vista* (Barcelona: Seix Barral).
Riquer, Martín de (1967), *Caballeros andantes españoles* (Madrid: Espasa-Calpe, Austral).
Rodríguez-Moñino, A. (1968), *Construcción crítica y realidad histórica en la poesía española de los siglos XVI y XVII* (Madrid: Castalia).
Ruskin, John (1855), *Lectures on Architecture and Painting Delivered at Edinburgh, November 1853* (London: Smith, Elder).
Russell, P. E. (1982), 'The last of the Spanish chivalric romances', in *Essays on Narrative Fiction in the Iberian Peninsula in Honour of Frank Pierce* (Oxford: Dolphin), pp. 141–52.
Scholes, R., and Kellogg, R. (1975), *The Nature of Narrative* (London/Oxford/New York: Oxford University Press).
Severin, Dorothy S. (1982), 'Is *La Celestina* the first modern novel?', *Revista de estudios hispánicos*, vol. 16, pp. 205–9.
Shergold, N. D. (1967), *A History of the Spanish Stage from Medieval Times until the End of the Seventeenth Century* (Oxford: Clarendon Press).
Solé-Leris, A. (1980), *The Spanish Pastoral Novel* (Boston, Mass.: Twayne).
Stevens, John (1973), *Medieval Romance* (London: Hutchinson).
Storr, Anthony (1972), *The Dynamics of Creation* (London: Secker & Warburg).
Storr, Anthony (1981), *The Integrity of the Personality* (Harmondsworth: Penguin).
Tave, Stuart M. (1960), *The Amiable Humorist* (Chicago, Ill.: University of Chicago Press).
Terry, Arthur (1982), 'Character and role in *Tirant lo Blanc*', in *Essays on Nar-

rative Fiction in the Iberian Peninsula in Honour of Frank Pierce (Oxford: Dolphin), pp. 177–95.

Trilling, Lionel (1961), 'Manners, morals and the novel', in *The Liberal Imagination* (London: Mercury Books), pp. 205–22.

Trilling, Lionel (1972), *Sincerity and Authenticity* (London: Oxford University Press).

Verdín Díaz, G. (1970), *Introducción al estilo indirecto libre en español* (Madrid: Consejo Superior de Investigaciones Científicas).

Vilar, Jean (1973), *Literatura y economía: la figura satírica del arbitrista en el Siglo de Oro*, trans. from French (Madrid: Revista de Occidente).

Weinberg, Bernard (1961), *A History of Literary Criticism in the Italian Renaissance*, 2 vols (Chicago, Ill.: Chicago University Press).

Welsh, Alexander (1981), *Reflections on the Hero as Quixote* (Princeton, NJ: Princeton University Press).

Whinnom, Keith (1980), 'The problem of the "best-seller" in Spanish Golden-Age literature', *Bulletin of Hispanic Studies*, vol. 57, pp. 189–98.

Whinnom, Keith (1982), 'The *Historia de Duobus Amantibus* of Aeneas Sylvius Piccolomini (Pope Pius II) and the development of Spanish Golden-Age fiction', in *Essays on Narrative Fiction in the Iberian Peninsula in Honour of Frank Pierce* (Oxford: Dolphin), pp. 243–55.

Wicks, Ulrich (1974), 'The nature of picaresque narrative: a modal approach', *PMLA*, vol. 89, pp. 240–9.

Wicks, Ulrich (1978), 'The romance of the picaresque', *Genre*, vol. 11, pp. 29–44.

Yates, Alan (1980), 'Tirant lo Blanc: the ambiguous hero', in *Hispanic Studies in Honour of Frank Pierce* (Sheffield: Department of Hispanic Studies), pp. 181–98.

INDEX